The Last Miner

THE LAST MINER

A Memoir of Alta's Final Mining Explorations

Dick Fluehe

with Dan Schilling

The University of Utah Press
Salt Lake City

The Defiance House Man colophon is a registered trademark of the University of Utah Press. It is based on a four-foot-tall Ancient Puebloan pictograph (late PIII) near Glen Canyon, Utah.

LIBRARY OF CONGRESS CATALOGING-IN-PUBLICATION DATA

Names: Fluehe, Dick, author. | Schilling, Dan, writer of foreword, editor.

Title: The last miner : a memoir of Alta's final mining explorations / Dick Fluehe with Dan Schilling.

Description: Salt Lake City : The University of Utah Press, [2025] |

Identifiers: LCCN 2024046678 | ISBN 9781647692148 (paperback) | ISBN 9781647692155 (ebook)

Subjects: LCSH: Silver mines and mining--Utah--Alta--History--20th century. | Silver miners--Utah--Alta--Social conditions--20th century.

Classification: LCC HD9537.U63 A4845 2025 | DDC 331.7/622342309792--dc23/eng/20250114

LC record available at https://lccn.loc.gov/2024046678

Errata and further information on this and other titles available at UofUpress.com

Dedicated to a breed of men no longer in existence.
The old-time hardrock stiff.

CONTENTS

PUBLISHER'S NOTE

The University of Utah Press acknowledges that this text contains language considered offensive or outdated by today's standards and we recognize that in many cases these words and references are upsetting or problematic. The language reflects a very specific historical context; we have chosen to retain it to preserve the integrity and authenticity of the author's experience.

FOREWORD

I HAD THE good fortune to make Dick Fluehe's acquaintance a few short years ago through our mutual friend Keith Hansen, who at the time ran the Salt Lake County Service Area 3 water district. This is the entity that oversees all the water that flows from Little Cottonwood Canyon into the greater Salt Lake Valley and comprises some 20 percent of its water supply. Much of that water starts its journey from within the more than 100 miles of mines in the canyon and Keith knows many of their secrets. But he'd tell you his 40 years of subterranean knowledge pales in comparison to Dick's and I agree. Dick's firsthand knowledge is positively encyclopedic.

An example: The three of us looking at mine schematics (picture a spaghetti bowl of multicolored and interconnected lines) in the Service 3 office near Snowbird. Keith asks, "Is that section still reachable?" Dick, without missing a beat, "Well not from that level. You'd have to come around from the other side, then drop down to that level, but you'd need to be crazier than shithouse rats to do that because right here"—he points—"has come in [caved]. But this 300-foot shaft here"—points again to a nearby shaft—"still has the pipe that the last elevator operator left behind on a shelf by the winch, but I'm probably the last guy who's ever going to see those. His name was . . ." and off he'd go into a lengthy tale about how *that guy* ran a bordello or possibly a moonshine business in Elko.

In many ways, Dick is the last miner. He denies this of course, claiming that most-honorable title belongs only to those who committed themselves to facing the perils and gambles that come from a lifetime of chasing subterranean precious metals, and his was but a fleeting glimpse. I disagree. His is a spirit that is the very essence of those men he admired so and therefore places him securely among their ranks. Dick missed being a real miner by probably 20 years or so and therefore possibly a richer life—but then again possibly not, because those in the mines often did not fare well in the end.

At the time Dick undertook his explorations and dabbled in mine labor, the workings of upper Little Cottonwood Canyon in Alta were in some cases already nearly 100 years old. They were dangerous places and unpredictable in an instantaneously fatal sort of way. Some are now unreachable let alone passable. Such is history. But that also reveals the importance of this book. To understand these people and their efforts to reach precious metals is to better understand the human desire to achieve difficult goals and our spirit of adventure.

These stories and Dick's experiences are not so far in the past that we're not directly connected via living memory. Thanks to Dick. Yet as you'll read, it's simultaneously an entire world apart from the contemporary one of convenience and instant gratification we know today. I don't believe you'll find anything quite like it elsewhere.

This book is neither scientific nor comprehensive but a firsthand account of one man's fascination with, and good fortune to journey into, a rarely plumbed world. To share this journey with someone as fascinating and entertaining as Dick is tantamount to the mining version of a float down the Mississippi River with Mark Twain as your guide. Certainly, that has been my experience. I'm pleased that in the course of my time as a captivated listener and then book editor that I should be so fortunate as to come to call Dick friend. It is very good fortune indeed and we continue to meet regularly for lunch in Little Cottonwood, along with Keith, to tell each other lies and generally bullshit away a couple of hours. I've never not learned something during our sessions.

A coauthor/editor's job is to make order and improve readability. But I've done precious little of either here for two reasons. First, Dick's a natural storyteller and well organized, like any good miner. Second, his voice is that of the generation he represents and his tales should be read as an oral history from that era, with all the accompanying linguistic and grammatical idiosyncrasies such a time and place encompass. So turn the page and strap in; you're in for an adventure.

CAST OF CHARACTERS

PEOPLE

Swinger, a.k.a. John Thomas Campbell—Swinger was one of Dick's best lifelong friends. An old-time "tramp miner," he came to be Dick's guide to the inner workings of mines and the introduction to the many characters and flavors involved in the Alta mining community.

Slick, a.k.a. Whitney Charles Hansen—He was Dick's initial contact who would result in his participation in this unique period that would mark the end of major mining activity underground in the Little Cottonwood mining district. Hansen was for the most part a hardworking individual and responsible—until he was not. He had a serious problem with alcohol. When he would start down that road, he became the village idiot.

The Bull, a.k.a. Albert J. Wondershek—He was the superintendent of the Wasatch Drain Tunnel / Cardiff Mining and Milling drive to reach the lower workings of the Cardiff Mine in the Big Cottonwood mining district. The "Bull" title fit the individual, a man both respected and on occasion feared. The stories of him are legion.

The General Mess of Crap—This was Dick's 1941 GMC pickup, purchased from a wrecking yard and cobbled together with a variety of scrap components from other junked trucks that existed in the wrecking yard. Dick never owned this thing; it owned him.

Dan Jacobson—Dan was a hardrock miner born in Alta in 1919 and would, before he passed, accumulate 50 years underground in the Alta district. When he and Dick became acquainted, Dan was the shifter (supervisor) running the night shift in the Wasatch Drain Tunnel. Swinger, who referred to Dan as a "real miner," introduced Dick and Dan to each other.

Mack and Mark Jacobson—They were Dan's younger brothers. Mark was the older of the two, and they both started at a very young age learning the mining game. The two were seasoned miners when Dick met them. Both were the key to Dick being able to find the Jewel Stope, an almost legendary place. Having been there a number of times, they did not minimize the risks involved, likely embellishing them to properly strike fear into Dick. To little avail.

Almond Joy, a.k.a. Gus Almon—Swinger renamed Gus "Almond Joy" immediately after he met him. Gus could well have been the only Black miner that ever worked in the district. Gus had worked for the Bull during his superintendence of two large mines in Butte, Montana. Gus could do any type of work expected of a miner and worked both underground and on the surface at the Wasatch Drain Tunnel. He was extremely loyal to the Bull, and the Bull to him.

Alimony Bill—Swinger of course bestowed the name Alimony on him. Dick never knew his real name and did not spend a lot of time around him and did not know him well. Alimony and Tokyo Joe worked as partners in the Col-Rex and had done the same in other mines, several under the control of Slick (Hansen).

Tokyo Joe—Dick surmised that the "Joe" part of his name was probably real. Swinger was of course responsible for the "Tokyo" prefix. For some reason, Tokyo Joe considered it a sport to aggravate Alimony whenever the opportunity came up, but both, even with that business going on, worked well together.

Matt Martinson—Matt according to one source had a degree in engineering. The Bull hired him because of his ability as a surveyor and his drafting skills. Matt drafted the company maps that required regular updating. He also on occasion filled in for the Bull when the Bull was absent and there were those who said he made a good miniature Bull.

Robin Hood, a.k.a. Virgil Johnson—Virgil during his employment at the mine worked as an outside man on the night shift. Once again, Swinger was the one responsible for the nickname business. Dick and Virgil became good friends and, after Virgil went back home to Kanorado, Kansas, they stayed in contact by letter for some time but eventually lost contact.

Sweet Pea, a.k.a. Vernon Barr—Sweet Pea worked in the mine office taking care of various administrative chores. Sweet Pea's desk was just a few feet from where the Bull had his, though the Bull had the best chair. Sweet Pea's critical function was as the Bull's driver, as the Bull's eyesight would no longer let him operate a motor vehicle. This being a daily requirement was employment security for Sweet Pea.

Francis M. Jolley—Dick met this old miner at the Flagstaff Mine. He was occupying a dilapidated old cabin that he had recently made habitable and had an active exploration underway in the old mine. He had first come into the old camp as a young man in the late 1890s. They would run across each other several more times, enjoying good conversations, with Jolley doing most of the talking.

MINES

Wasatch Drain Tunnel—This long tunnel, its purpose being just what its name implies, came into being out of necessity. The Columbus-Consolidated encountered heavy water flows as the workings extended downward. The existing pumps located on the lowest level, the 400 level, could no longer handle the incoming water. Pumps of higher capacity were available, but the expense was not economically feasible.

Columbus-Rexall, a.k.a. Col-Rex—The Columbus-Rexall began its life as the Columbus-Extension in April of 1906. Tony Jacobson was the driving force behind this project that would require a tunnel a mile long to reach the objective he had in mind. The actual Columbus-Extension Tunnel began in the Enterprise drift of the Howland Tunnel some 350 feet from its portal. At the end of that mile-long tunnel, it would come in at depth beneath old producers that had been very productive indeed. Two of them, the Toledo and the Rexall Silver mining companies, had great influence on the decision to drive the long tunnel. June of 1916 seen the merger of The Columbus-Extension and Rexall Silver companies. Thus, the name Columbus-Rexall came into being.

The Columbus-Rexall connected to the Cardiff Mine in 1920, initially by a winze intersecting the 800 level 70 feet below. An inclined shaft also connects the two mines running from the 600 level downward to the Sulfide (Jewel) Stope. In the west drift area of the Columbus-Rexall, a 35-foot raise from the Frederick Tunnel connects the two mines. In this area is found the main access to, and the outlet for, the ore produced in the West Toledo. The story of the Columbus-Rexall Mine would fill hundreds of pages. That is for another time.

Columbus-Consolidated, a.k.a. Col-Con—Tony Jacobson, his brother A. O. Jacobson, and three other men formed the Columbus-Consolidated Mining Company in April 1902. At the close of 1902, three other men had joined the company as sources of development money with contacts that also could provide funding.

The first shipment of concentrates from the mill shipped to the smelter in mid-November. Development work came to a halt on the 400 level at the end of May 1908. It was then the miners opened up a watercourse, known as a bug hole, to lower the water. Low metal prices, limited shipments, time lost due to flooding, and equipment failures inflicted a tremendous burden on finances. By the end of 1912, they gave up the battle with nature, pulled the pumps, and shut down the mill. In February 1913, the Wasatch Mines Company was incorporated and the Columbus-Consolidated Mining Company ceased to exist.

Howland Tunnel—William Howland, early in 1872, filed a tunnel claim along with 14 other men. The result of that was the incorporation of the Howland Tunnel Company. The intention was to drive a tunnel 6,000 feet in a northeast direction, a goal never attained. The tunnel would over the coming decades involve many ownership changes along with name changes suiting the individual operators.

The tunnel served as the portal for the Columbus-Rexall workings and served as the main working tunnel for the Columbus-Consolidated Mine in its production period. Today the tunnel carries its original name, the Howland Tunnel.

Frederick Tunnel—The tunnel of many names. First located as a tunnel site in October 1870 under the name Bismarck, it's located in the same area where the Frederick and Crown Prince claims sit higher on the mountain. The original locators sold their interest to an out-of-state organization, and the tunnel location was renamed the Pittsburgh. By that time, the Frederick and Crown Prince had opened three shafts, all producing ore. Their location in an extremely rugged area and at high altitude presented a number of problems. After many discussions and one long shut down of all work, the owners decided to drive a tunnel to come in at depth beneath the high workings. When the work started, the tunnel became the Allegheny.

In the spring of 1880, when the tunnel had reached 1,500 feet, a major reorganization took place and the project in its entirety became the Frederick and Crown Prince Mining and Tunnel Company. The tunnel at that point became the Frederick Tunnel. The last decade of the 19th century brought about the doldrums, and mining came to an almost complete halt. By 1896, only one man remained at the mine, Fritz Rettich. He served as watchman and did a variety of maintenance work. The company at length owed him for two years' work. Fritz sued them for the money owed but they could not pay him. The court ordered the property in its entirety sold at public auction. Fritz, being the highest bidder, bought the property and everything connected to it. Eventually he deeded all of it to his son Hugo who organized a new company called the Hellgate Mining Company. With that final change, the Frederick Tunnel became the Hellgate Tunnel, as it is known today.

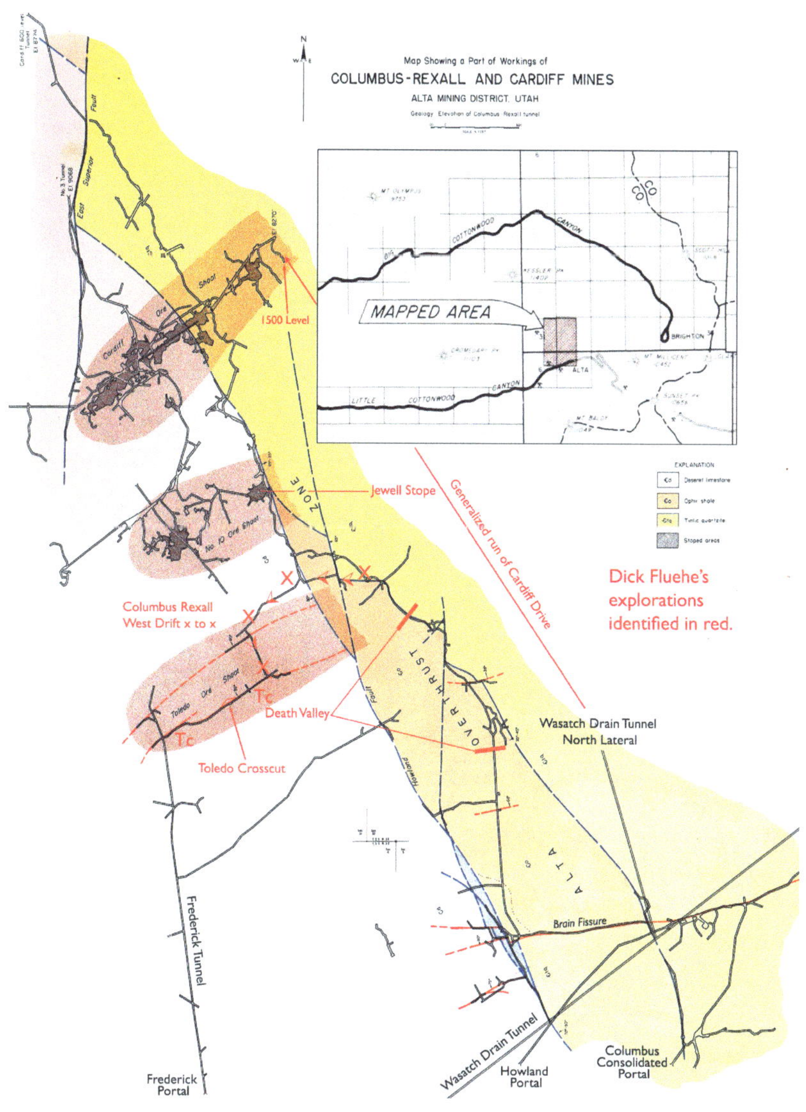

Subterranean map showing Dick's explorations. From Western States Map Co.

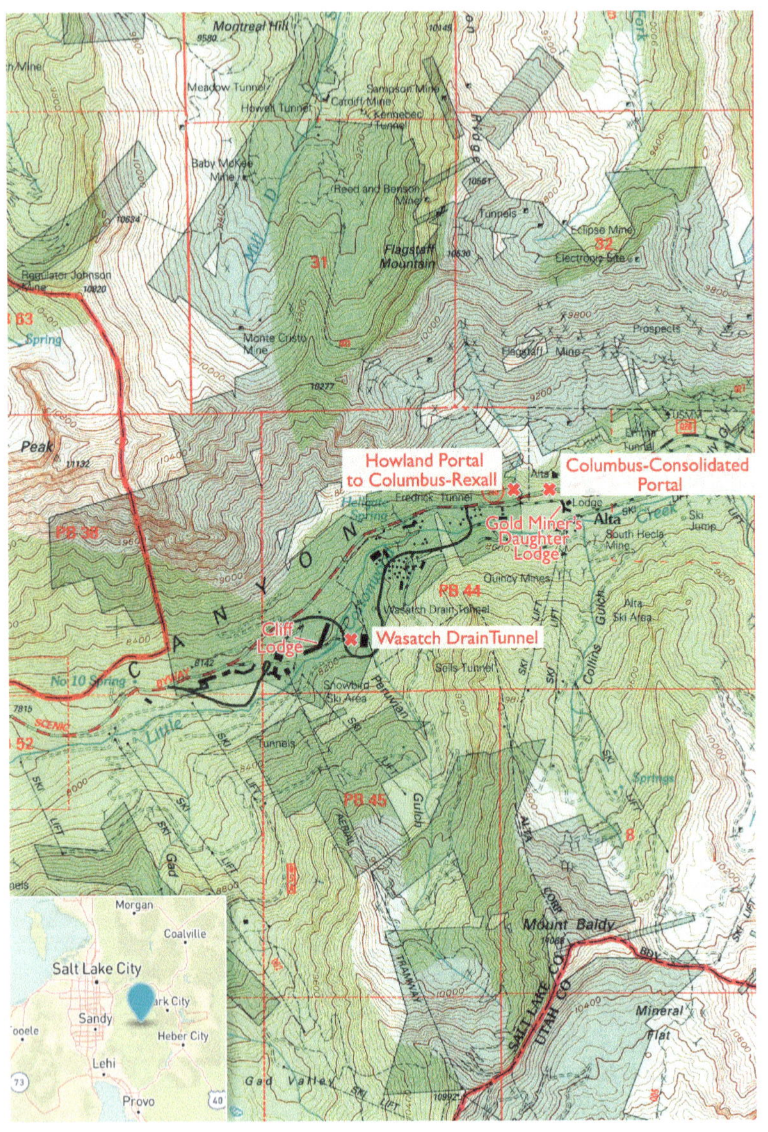

Surface map showing portals and contemporary landmarks. From United States Geological Survey map, Dromedary Peak Quadrangle.

INTRODUCTION

THE COTTONWOOD MINING districts located in Salt Lake County, Utah, comprise Big Cottonwood and Little Cottonwood Canyons, divided by a ridgeline of high steep mountains that trend west to east. A vast underground world exists in this combined area, and few, very few, have any idea how extensive this now inaccessible region is, and even fewer have seen any part of it. Over the long history of the two mining districts, there have been, in a number of places, connections made to tie the two districts together. Due to the great depths of these connections, there is not now and never were any surface indications that would reveal their existence. There are numerous professional papers and various company reports, now mostly unattainable, that contain information on the subject. That kind of overall detailing has no place in this story, as the stories here are limited to one particular complex in Alta, inside Little Cottonwood Canyon, involving five separate mining operations.

In 1955, a group of men came together to promote the extension of the Wasatch Drain Tunnel's north lateral to come in below the deepest workings of the Cardiff Mine on the Big Cottonwood side of the divide. It would require a drive of well over 4,500 feet from the mine's existing working face.* When the new tunnel arrived at its intended position below the Cardiff, a series of drill holes, known as long holes, were extended upward. The drilled holes would make the connection between the Wasatch Drain Tunnel and the flooded 1500 level of the Cardiff Mine. This phase of the job would allow the water to drain in a controlled manner from the extensive flooded workings that extended from the Cardiff's 800 station down to the 1500. The connection of the Wasatch Drain Tunnel to the Cardiff

* The end of the drift, crosscut, or tunnel, generally where the miners work. The term *heading* means the same thing and is often used in place of *working face*.

Mine was the last great exploration effort undertaken in the Cottonwood mining districts, and it plays a major part in this story.

Three additional extensive properties are also very prominent in this tale. The Columbus-Rexall, the Columbus-Consolidated, and the Howland Tunnel. The Columbus-Rexall and the Howland Tunnel share a common portal.* The Columbus-Consolidated, in the beginning, had its own portal 1,100 feet to the east and 32 feet lower in elevation than the Howland. However, when the mine reached its high production days, it used the Howland Tunnel as its main working tunnel. The Columbus-Consolidated, like most mines in the two districts, had very serious and expensive problems with water as the workings extended downward. The difficulties encountered in the Columbus-Consolidated are what precipitated the driving of the Wasatch Drain Tunnel. The drain tunnel was portaled a mile west of the other three mines and connected with, originally, only the Columbus-Consolidated by a raise to the 400 level in 1920. The Wasatch Drain Tunnel portal elevation is 8,120 feet above sea level and the elevation of the Howland Tunnel lies at 8,450 feet above sea level. Residing in that 320-foot block of ground lies a world that is interesting, unique, and above all, in places, so extremely dangerous that only a fool would venture into it. As is usually the case, some fools did. The writer of this tale is probably the last living individual to have seen any part of that underground world.

Today no access exists to any part of the workings that are part of this story. As for me, I feel a great personal loss and sadness that these mines are no longer, in any way, accessible to anyone. I realize that people living currently, with few exceptions, are completely ignorant of the dangers related to these old, abandoned mines. They are of a different era. Through natural processes of nature and organizations involved in mine-reclamation work, large numbers of old mines all over the nation are now inaccessible. For those living in present times, this is, unquestionably, a good thing.

This would be a good place to issue a forewarning before going

* The entrance of a tunnel or adit into the side of a hill or a mountain.

on with this story. Not knowing who might end up reading this, and I am sure not many will, those easily offended by what on occasion is known as "colorful" language will find an abundance throughout. Many of the expressions and the language in general used by the characters involved in this story are, well, rather salty. Most of these men, all of them old-school hardrock miners, had a language of their own, which at times, most times, involved a lot of profanity and a broad range of vulgarities seldom heard in civil settings. To say they were somewhat colorful in expressing themselves would qualify as a gross understatement. Though there will be a degree of sanitization, there was a lot of pepper in their speech, and I intend to let most of it stand.

The conversations that will appear in the following narrative are not verbatim, as many years have now passed since they took place. All dialogue as written, however, will accurately represent the language and manner of speaking that was unique to the individuals involved. Most of those men had a habit of corrupting certain words to mean something entirely different from their normal meaning, and they did that on purpose. Many of the expressions were unique to the miner of old and the period in which he existed. Because of this, there are a number of footnotes of their words or expressions and a glossary for easy reference.

It took only a short period after I became acquainted with one of the main characters in this story to realize that I was witnessing the end of an era. I was fortunate in the fact that he knew it too and did not hesitate to confirm its imminent demise. I paid attention to the advice he repeatedly offered with a great deal of reluctance, wishing things could be different. Had it been 1927 rather than 1957 (the year I made his acquaintance), I would have become a miner, a hardrock* stiff, and likely, a tramp miner, such as my friend had been most of his life.

* Hardrock, used as one word by miners, is a term to indicate a fellow miner. Hard rock, when separated, is used to denote the hardness of the rock encountered in mining operations.

Because of a convergence of unique circumstances, the late summer of 1957 opened up opportunities that had not existed prior to that time. Before then, risky exploration of underground mine workings in both Big and Little Cottonwood had been undertaken. These explorations took place with little knowledge concerning the multitude of risks associated with those activities. In mid-August of 1957, the author, through luck and design, commenced his education in the old Columbus-Rexall Mine. It was not a full-time job because the author's full-time employment paid enough to survive on and required shift work.

From August on through the day before Christmas, December 1957, I learned the basics under the tutelage of an experienced hardrock miner, well known in the mining game as Swinger, who features heavily throughout these pages. I make no claim as to being a miner myself because I know what a *real* miner is. I learned much from this fellow, and it would pay off over the years in the form of underground explorations made much safer. For the time spent in that old mine, I received no monetary compensation and feel that the experience gained more than paid for those efforts in full measure. Another benefit was that being a familiar presence on the ground afforded unquestioned access to accessible workings in the Columbus-Rexall and the Columbus-Consolidated mines for my own explorations.

During the week between Christmas and the New Year, Swinger left the Columbus-Rexall to move down to the Wasatch Drain Tunnel, where he had been working before going up canyon to the Columbus-Rexall. This opened up a bonanza opportunity that would allow firsthand observation of the last great underground exploration effort in the Cottonwood districts. An enduring friendship came of that, involving a man named Dan Jacobson. Through Dan, Swinger, and the mine's superintendent, Albert "Bull" Wondershek, the author enjoyed extraordinary access to the Wasatch Drain Tunnel that lasted until 1960.

The lower workings of the Columbus-Consolidated, consisting of three levels below the main, were in the late '50s and early '60s very limited as to accessibility due to caving ground, deep water, and bad air caused by the concentration of carbon dioxide and the abundance of sulfide deposits in most areas. There were three points of access to the Wasatch Drain Tunnel from the Columbus-Consolidated, Howland, and the Columbus-Rexall workings. One was a vertical shaft from the Howland and the other an inclined shaft from the Columbus-Consolidated. The vertical shaft was not even remotely passable. To descend the incline would likely be a fatal undertaking. The third point was a raise* driven upward from the old number-five stope† on the 400 level of the Columbus-Consolidated. This raise accessed the Columbus-Rexall main level.

From the Wasatch Drain Tunnel, additional raises would furnish access to the 400 level and to the number-five stope. Here again were found the same impediments encountered when attempting to penetrate the lower workings from above. Caving ground, water, broken timber, and bad air limited exploration of the old Columbus-Consolidated lower levels. The author, during the span of years that this story takes place, had the opportunity to access a very limited part of those lower workings and somewhat more of the upper levels. Several hazardous ventures made at different times attempting to find a complete passage between the Wasatch Drain Tunnel, the Columbus-Consolidated, Howland, and the Columbus-Rexall main levels failed, as such a hazardous enterprise would have been a nonsurvivable tunnel system.

The following pages tell the story of my adventures during a five-year period running from 1955 through 1960. This is not a formal report nor is it written as such and only concerns the five mines previously mentioned. Therefore, from memories and a chaotic collection of scribbled notes, this is what I experienced. In referring to the year 1955, the reason that it is set as a start date is because it was in the late summer of that year that I first noticed

* A vertical or inclined passageway driven between levels. The average raise rises upward on about an 80-degree angle.

† A cavernous area opened up by the extraction of an ore body.

the construction of new buildings and other work taking place at a location about a mile west of Alta.

At that time, I had no idea what was going on or the reason for it. The only thing that had any familiarity was a sign nailed to a big pine tree that stated that the property belonged to Cardiff Mining and Milling Company. Below that sign was an even bigger one saying, "No Trespassing." On the gate used to block the road, another large sign said, "No Admittance." The Cardiff Mine in the South Fork of Big Cottonwood Canyon was no stranger to me as I had been there a number of times (starting when I was 13 years old). I was 17 by this time and in my junior year of high school and engaged in excessive truancy. This was a habitual activity and, I will admit, not a good one, but it worked very well for me.

When the year 1957 came about, all manner of things had changed. At that time at the tender age of 18, I had been married for four months. In late summer, I was somewhat voluntarily unemployed, deciding I did not want to continue as an apprentice painter any longer, having started that messy profession. Out of necessity, the financial type, I started working for Phillips Petroleum Company as a service station attendant. Something I hated more than high school, if such a thing were even possible. It involved shift work that I liked even less than the job. However, that shift work schedule did open a door because it gave me daytime hours to wander the Cottonwood mining districts. An opportunity that otherwise I never would have had.

1

Who the Hell Are You?

THE HIGHWAY UP Little Cottonwood Canyon, in the late 1950s, followed the narrow-gauge railroad grade that it was built upon. Today, the highway in the most part still does. A few hundred yards west of the Peruvian Lodge, the highway departed the railroad grade and followed the line of the old mule tram that had been the predecessor of both the railroad and the highway. At this point, west of the Peruvian Lodge, the road's grade increases. Driven into a buttress of limestone near its crest was a length of pipe. Hanging from that pipe was a small sign that was showing its age.

"Welcome to Alta" were the words on that old, now faded sign, whose background at one time may have been white. Immediately past the sign, the road leveled, and the Peruvian Lodge was on the right, sitting at a lower elevation than the road. Right in front of me, on the right at roadside, stood a collection of attached wooden structures that later that day I would find out was part of the Columbus-Rexall Mine. A short spur of a road led to the buildings, and parked on it was a Chevrolet flatbed truck. It was the first vehicle that I had seen at the mine in my trips to Alta.

I went on up the road beyond that mine and parked close to an open mine portal that had the usual "No Trespassing" sign nailed to the cap timber* of the portal set.† Another sign in its proximity identified it as the famous Emma Mine. It should be noted that at this point in time, I had absolutely no knowledge of any mining terms.

* The horizontal timber at the top of a timber set (see photo insert).

† The timber structure at the entrance of a tunnel or adit into the side of a hill or a mountain.

I would not have known a portal set from a leg* or post,† let alone a cap timber. Also, at the time, I did not know I was standing at the portal of the Bay City Tunnel that had been connected with the original Emma Mine high on the mountain above many years ago.

What I did know was that I intended to hike up Grizzly Gulch, which I had identified, to have a look around at some interesting mines that lay farther up the branch canyon. I went up the bottom along the creek bed, which was dry in August. It was hard going, and I soon figured there had to be a road up to those workings. I found it after a steep climb out of the bottom, which made the walk a lot easier, and soon arrived in a small basin that contained many mines and good-sized waste rock dumps. I spent a lot of time poking around that basin and did not go very high on the slopes above. Many dumps were scattered everyplace on those slopes. One day up there would not begin to furnish enough time to look at everything that was in sight.

It was early afternoon when I started down out of Grizzly Gulch. As I made my way down the road, I could not get that Chevrolet flatbed out of my mind. I knew for sure I would have to make a stop and try to find out what was going on at that old mine. I picked up my pace, as I would soon run out of time to get out of Little Cottonwood Canyon and get to work on time. What happened next would end up making me considerably late for work and get me in trouble with my wife.

Reaching the car, I headed on down to the parked Chevrolet at the old mine. I pulled in behind it and to the side, so it was not completely blocked. I got out of my car and headed for a door in the side of what I came to know as the snowshed. With that simple walk, I took my first steps into what I considered a dream world. This so-called dream world was not something that others would consider ideal, but it fit me perfectly. Eventually, however, it would create a few problems on the home front. More than a few at times.

There was no scarcity of the usual "No Trespassing," "Keep Out,"

* The vertical timbers of a timber set that support the cap (see photo insert).

† An alternate name for a leg. A leg and a post are the same thing.

and "Danger" signs that had been nailed up at many places outside on the old wooden walls. All that wood was showing the ravages of the long years they had stood. This made the whole layout even more intriguing, and following my usual pattern of ignoring signs, I walked through the doorway of the snowshed. I found myself standing between a set of rails after my eyes adjusted from the bright sunshine outside. This place seemed to be full of all manner of assorted junk.

There was a little light coming from the east side of the partially roofed-over area that I was standing in. Standing on rails that run south toward the ore bins were several one-ton mine cars. I was standing to the side of a switch,* from which another set of rails extended in a southeastern direction through another snowshed. The rails extended on out of the snowshed into the sunshine to the end of the dump. While I was engaged in this assessment of my immediate surroundings, I became aware of the sound of hammer blows and a hissing that drew my attention to another location. That which I found there proved interesting.

I walked toward a man busily engaged in what he was doing, his attention focused on the work at hand. This fellow was hammering on something laid out on an anvil that I could not see. His nearly bald head shined just a little less than the flame of the acetylene torch he had going. He was very absorbed in the job at hand, and the hissing of the torch covered my approaching footfalls. I most definitely did not do it right when I yelled out in a loud voice, "Howdy!"

He jumped like a jack-in-the-box. The hammer was in an upswing, and he nearly dropped it on his head, and he turned fast staring in my direction.

"GODDAMN!" he bellowed. "You scared the supreme shit out of me! WHO THE HELL ARE YOU?"

That was how I became acquainted with Whitney C. Hansen, and it was a poor way to meet someone for the first time. It required some conversation, and shortly we had everything smoothed out

* A device that allows a train to change from one set of tracks to another. There are many different configurations.

satisfactorily. He was still holding on to the hammer with one hand, and in the other, he still had what appeared to me as a pair of oversized ice tongs. I had not seen a pair of ice tongs for years by that time, not since sometime in the 1940s. He laid the hammer down, finally, and the ice tongs, and shut off the acetylene torch, and then started in on me. I more or less was expecting what was going to come out of this fellow next.

He started out by mentioning that some sonofabitch must have stolen all his "No Trespassing" signs along with the goddamn "Danger" signs because I should have seen them. I knew that to him I looked like one that would fit the profile of a young vandal, and he made no bones about that. In his opinion, most young people only existed to bust up anything that they could get their hands on unless they considered it worth stealing or taking a shit in. In that assessment, he most definitely had a point. Vandalism has always been around, it seems, but it really began to flourish in the 1950s for some reason, and nothing was safe from destruction. This held true in the mining districts everywhere, and unless watched around the clock nothing was safe. Alta was no exception.

When he stopped talking and I had an opening, I told him that I was 100 percent in agreement with him and that I had no use whatsoever for assholes who did those kind of things. At that point, I added that my idea of a cure for that type of stuff was to declare an open season on those types. If I had my way, I went on, they should be shot or otherwise disposed of permanently, and that no penalties should be leveled for such actions that got the job done. He looked somewhat funny for a second or two, then grinned and nodded his head. The chill that had surrounded us in the beginning disappeared. I told him that my interests ran to mines and mining, and with that, we shook hands and exchanged names.

The next thing that Whitney came up with was an unexpected question. What he wanted to know then was if I was a miner and rustling for a job. That was the last thing on my mind at the time, and I told him I was no miner and never worked in a mine. I went on to tell him that I had been underground many times exploring old workings in the Cottonwood districts. He just shook his head at that and made no comment. I went on to tell him that I wished I knew more about the business and how to do the job when it came to the actual physical work involved. I explained that I had a vague idea of some of it thanks to an old miner who I had met years before in the South Fork (Cardiff) of Big Cottonwood Canyon. We talked for a few minutes more, and then he told me what he had been up to when I "scared the supreme shit" out of him.

He called the tool he had been working on "timber tongs," and he had been reworking the tips to better their ability to bite into a "stick"[*] of timber. I was to learn during that part of the conversation that a "stick" of timber encompassed a very wide variety of sizes. Anything from a 2-by-4 up through a 12-by-12, the latter being more than a man wanted to carry when over eight feet in length. That and other variations is what comprised a "stick" of timber. As Whitney put it, the tongs were useful when "sucking" a timber up a raise using a tugger[†] at the top. Well, I was stuck on trying to figure out what a raise was and had no idea what a tugger was either. All this I would learn as I, over time, came to understand the language of the miner and became able to figure out what they were saying.

We stood there in one place for a while just talking back and forth and getting to know one another better. Finally, tired of standing in one place, Whitney took me on what he called the nickel tour, saying the two-bit tour we would have to pull off some other time. We walked to the ore bins,[‡] then came back and walked outside to the end of the dump[§] where the cars loaded with waste rock were

* Miners' slang for any type or dimension of timber or lumber.

† A winch operated by compressed air. The method of mounting depends on the location and usually utilizes heavy timber as the base.

‡ A structure that holds ore until the accumulation is sufficient to transfer to a truck or railroad car for transport to a smelter or other type of refining facility. Sizes vary greatly depending on the ore-producing capacity of the mine.

§ The waste rock brought out of underground workings. It is a slang term, short for *waste rock dump*. It is often confused by the layperson with *tailing*, which is waste rock that has been processed for ore.

unloaded. From there we walked back to the portal of the tunnel after passing underneath the highway through a bridge with walls of stone and a concrete cap. A good stream of water was coming out of that mine and running through a ditch off to the side of the rails. Thick iron-stained mud was in abundance on the railbed and off to the sides of the rails.

Standing there just back from the portal, which was supported by heavy timbering, was when Whitney told me the name of that old mine. He identified it as the Columbus-Rexall Mine and he explained that he had secured a lease on a section that he hoped would pay off with some decent ore. He added also that he was just getting started on the project and needed a good miner to help make the thing work. By then it was obvious that I was not a candidate for that job. Whitney said he had several men in mind, but at the time, they were working elsewhere and tied up by their regular jobs.

I had lost track of the time of day by then, and a sudden realization hit me that I was not going to get down out of Alta in time to be at work when I was supposed to be there. A part of me really did not care all that much, as I had no love for that service station job. I left the Columbus-Rexall that afternoon with a good solid invitation to return any time I wanted. When finally I got home, I had the concept of time of day noisily explained to me. The bulk of the lecture involved how late I was going to be getting to work. This would be just one of many episodes involving unfavorable marital critiques concerning what I would become involved with over the coming years in Alta.

2

Swinging Door

ON A MORNING about a week after I met Whitney Hansen, I was once again on my way to Alta. It was a weekday, the same old drill of taking my wife to work was still in place, and that meant that I would have to pick her up after work. Her shift was over at 6:00 p.m., and I figured I would be down in ample time to take care of that chore. I did not have a shift that day at the much-despised service station, so that would be an easy task to accomplish.

Approaching the Columbus-Rexall, I noticed a Chevrolet sedan parked where Whitney's truck had been the week before. I figured it was not Hansen, so I went on up the road. I parked on the Bay City Tunnel dump and set out from there on my hike for that day. I worked my way up the mountain straight above the Bay City portal and ended up at the foot of a big dump. In time, I learned that dump belonged to the Illinois Tunnel, whose workings were quite extensive. From that location, I started up an old road that was to the left of the gulch where the Illinois dump was located. I followed the road upward and in a westerly direction, the road passing over two more large dumps, arriving shortly at the foot of a very large waste rock dump.

When I climbed to the top of the dump, I found an array of old machinery and other rusted and unidentifiable junk scattered all around the area, and that intrigued me to no end. Loose unconsolidated material and rocks from the steep slope above had partially blocked the mine portal. A small cabin, more accurately described as a shack, stood back from and just to the right of the mine's portal. Opening the door took some effort, as it had only one intact hinge, and scraped against the rough wooden floor. The interior was dim and some old shelves that had fallen from the walls were on the floor. One other item in that shack, however, really stood out. Standing near the east wall of that dilapidated old place was a still-intact stove. The fact that a stove remained anywhere in that area, still in one piece, was one of the world's wonders.

That old stove had not ended its duty days because sometime in the summer of the following year, 1958, the old shack underwent a transformation. The renovation obviously required considerable material and labor to become habitable. The work accomplished, the old place found itself with an occupant who I was fortunate to become acquainted with in the late summer of 1958. As remembered now, he simply introduced himself as Jolley, the only name he ever gave up. Many years later, from another source, I was to learn his full name was Francis Marion Jolley. He was a genuine old-time hardrock stiff and was 75 years old when I met him in the late summer of 1958.

It was sometime after noon when, driven by curiosity, I arrived at the Columbus-Rexall Mine. I parked alongside the Chevrolet sedan that had been in evidence earlier in the day. Having already ignored the signage once before, it was no problem to pull off that same stunt once again. I got out of the car and walked through the door of the snowshed. I stepped over the tracks and looked around. This day, there were no sounds of hammering or the hissing of an acetylene torch, so I just stood in place and let my gaze wander. There was no one in sight and no sound of voices, just the noisy silence that filled old structures. Back across the tracks and to my left was what I suspected might be living quarters of some sort, with a door closing off access. I recalled seeing this before but paid little attention to it, as Whitney Hansen and I were working to straighten out a bad beginning.

I was about to find out that my assessment of what might lie beyond that door was indeed a form of living quarters and that there was an occupant. Something was coming from the mine's portal area beyond the stone-walled highway bridge. There was rumbling, clanking, and other assorted racket. The cause of this disturbance appeared after passing beneath that old concrete-capped stone-walled bridge that carried the highway over its top. The first thing that came into view was a mine locomotive, a designation seldom used by the miner. To those men, this piece of equipment is a trammer,* and it operates on battery power I was soon to learn. It slowed to a stop directly in front of me, the three loaded cars behind it banging into one another as the operator glanced back at them.

The man sitting on the machine drew my complete attention immediately. He could not be termed a small fellow by any means; the work gear he was wearing seemed to emphasize his bulk. The outfit he had on consisted of a heavy coat and bulky pants, which were in actuality of the same design as bib overalls and were made of heavyweight neoprene. There appeared to be no dry spot anywhere on that black outfit and no shortage of smears consisting of mud stained red by its iron content. He wore a hard hat, which I soon learned was commonly termed *hard-boiled hat*, with a carbide lamp hooked to the bracket on its front. The hat was as wet as everything else was and exhibited some of the same mud smears that decorated everything else. He caught sight of me as he swung his rubber-booted feet off the trammer and stood up.

He looked at me for a second or two as his eyes adjusted to the light behind me, then spit a stream of tobacco juice onto the ground at his feet. His face was round and pleasant. With the spit completed, he immediately broke out in a friendly grin. He nodded his head toward me and in a loud voice said, "Hullo, kid! How's she hummin', chum?"

I liked that big fellow instantly, and the years that were to follow improved the bond that developed that day between us. I introduced myself and moved to shake his hand. He pulled off his heavy rubber glove, let it drop to the ground, and we shook hands. There was plenty of strength in that big paw of his. With that, he told me to

* Also known as a motor, it is the locomotive used to pull the train of cars into and out of the underground workings. Batteries most often power them.

call him Swinger. I told him that I had been there at the mine the week before and met a fellow who told me his name was Whitney. I went on to tell him that Whitney had told me that it was OK with him if I came around now and again. I suppose that Swinger took the last part of what I said more or less like a question and wasted no time in telling me that it was OK with him too. He went on to tell me that Slick (who would turn out to be Whitney Hansen) had mentioned that some kid had showed up and they had talked for quite a while. He said Slick told him that this kid seemed interested in the mining game, and he figured I was that kid.

Apparently, Whitney had told Swinger not to worry about letting me have a free run around the project, and that included the underground workings. If it included going underground for the start of any of that kind of business, Slick apparently wanted Swinger to keep a close eye on me. That opened a door for me that a few years down the road would have required all kinds of paperwork involving release of liability and such. In those days, the situation was much different, because at that time, no one gave much thought to being sued over things as minor as, say, wet feet and a minor bump on the head or a turned ankle. It seems that the main concern that Whitney had expressed to Swinger was to make sure I did not gob myself in the hole.

Swinger was silent for a short span before he commenced talking again, as he knew that I must have a lot of questions, and he decided to shortcut that business and get to it.

"Well." He paused for a few seconds. "Okay, well, Whitney Hansen would be Slick, as that is what I call him. That is shortened up some from 'Slick Sheet Hansen,' the stretched-out version that most guys like to use on him. Because I flunked kindergarten, kid, I need to use and hear small words, so I don't short out trying to figure out what in hell big, long words mean. Tell you what, why don't we talk more about this in the shack. It is time to put the feedbag on anyhow. I have to tell you kid, it ain't goin' to be nothin' fancy. I can chloride out a cheese sandwich or two and a big pot of coffee. How would that set you up?"

I answered in the affirmative. *How could it be any better?* I said silently to myself. This situation was getting better by the minute. Swinger removed and hung up his work suit on a couple of spikes driven into the wall next to the door. He hung his hat on another spike, the lamp's flame now extinguished. On spikes next to his hung another set of black neoprene work gear, composed of bib-type bottoms and a coat, decorated with iron stains. That gear belonged to Slick, Swinger announced.

3

The Shack

IT IS WORTH recalling here as accurately as I can remember the layout of the shack at that time. *Shack* was Swinger's term for the place, but it was not a shack in any sense of that word, although it could not be termed a palace either. The original construction of the buildings took place about 1910.

The so-called shack was a single-room affair whose interior dimensions would have been roughly 15 by 16 feet, as best recalled now. To the left side of the entrance doorway was a closet, the door of the shack just barely clearing it upon opening. Other than the closet, the room was entirely open. Between the closet and the west wall of the room was a six-pane window that overlooked the Alta Peruvian Lodge. This window was at about the same elevation as the lodge's roof. This vista would furnish considerable amusement to all who had the opportunity to be in the shack at the right time with a pair of binoculars. Centered on the west wall was another window, and just right of it was a big old wood/coal-fired stove. That old stove was the only source of heat for warming the room and cooking. That stove was from the old days and may have been a Monarch, but I cannot recall that with any certainty.

The inside walls and the ceiling were wood. The floor was, of course, thick wood planking, as no flexing was apparent when walking on it. The old place was tight all around, indicating good care during its lifetime of use. A big wooden box next to the stove contained kindling wood and lumps of stove-sized coal. Sitting on one of the stovetop's four lids was a big, enameled coffeepot. There was a stout table with four chairs in position around it. They were wood and were "old-timers," rough and serviceable. The place had electrical power wired in the old-time way, all of it on the outside of the walls and held off the walls and ceiling using white porcelain cylindrical insulators, something of a collector's item nowadays. A single lightbulb, screwed into a socket hanging from the ceiling, furnished the lighting for the room.

A big double bed was located with its headboard against the east wall. The bedding was not all rumpled up and carelessly strewn about; it looked like a hotel's room service had just finished up with it. The floor was clean and was obviously well acquainted with the broom standing in the corner by the stove. Another noticeable thing was the cleanliness of all the glass panes of the windows. The window glass had to be many years old, and it must have been a challenge to put it in its present condition. There was a small old-time refrigerator between the foot of the bed and the stove on the north wall. Sitting on a big wooden box on the right side of the bed was a small water barrel with a spigot. The whole place was clean and felt comfortable, and it was very apparent that Swinger was fussy when it came to his living quarters.

Swinger grabbed the coffeepot off the stovetop, lifted one of the stove lids off with the other hand, and peered into the firebox. "Still got some hot coals in her, kid," he said as he thrust the coffeepot toward me. "Take her outside and flip the grounds and whatever else may be livin' in there on top of the muck* in one of the cars. Don't be concerned if all the grounds don't dump—hell, we will run those through again along with the new stuff. I do it like that all the time. When you get back in here, go over to the water barrel and load her with water and we will have coffee damn quick."

It did not take long, as he put it, "to get the coffee built," and that coffee was very good. Swinger made that coffee like most old-timers liked to do it—the old-fashioned way. He let the water in the pot come to a boil, set it off to the side on a cooler part of the stovetop, then spooned in a large amount of coffee, and he was not stingy with

* The waste rock broken up by blasting that has very little or no value as ore.

it. When the grounds settled to the bottom of the pot, it was ready. The simple cheese sandwiches really hit the spot, and the environment, and the company, had much to do with that.

We must have spent an hour and a half over those sandwiches and coffee. Swinger asked me what I did for work. I explained I was working in a service station and went on to tell him that I'd decided I did not want to be a painter either and quit the business with just six months left to complete my apprenticeship. He just shook his head at this and then asked me what got me interested in mining. I told him I had no good answer to that question other than it had been with me since I was about eight years old. He looked at me gravely and did not smile before he remarked back, "You want to look out for it kid, but I think it is already too late. Mining is a disease, chum, one of the worst you can gather up. It will never let you alone, it gets in your blood, and you can't get it loose. Now I would guess that you, from what you have let on and Slick mentioned, have been underground a few times. Have you ever worked at any job in a mine?"

I had to tell him that I never had but would do anything to learn something about it. I went on to explain that if they would let me go underground and work that I would not require any pay. I told him what was important to me was getting the experience. He just stared at me and shook his head, then broke out into what would become a now familiar one-of-a-kind grin and said, "Well, kid, you are too far gone to be saved, I have to say. If you are willing to do what you say, then it has got you good, so let's play with this thing for now. To start, I guess we better get off our dead asses and I will open school by having you dump those muck cars.* Now this is going to be without putting them over the dump. The worst thing about a car or a train over the dump is the part about getting them back up again. Ah, hell, it is kind of fun watching them fly though, but in the end it ain't worth it."

* A seldom-used term describing the transport cars used to transport muck or ore from the underground workings to the outside.

When he made that last remark about fun, he was looking out the window like he was somewhere else, and he was kind of chuckling as he said it. With that, we departed the shack and headed out to, as Swinger put it, get me "some educated."

4

Show-and-Tell Time

SWINGER CLIMBED ABOARD the trammer and moved the train back, clearing the switch, shut it down, and commenced issuing orders. The first thing he had me do was put a wedge under a wheel of each car and said to "bang 'em in tight" so they could not roll forward. I unhooked the chain of the lead car from the hook at the rear of the trammer, and Swinger moved the trammer past the switch down toward the ore bins. When he once again shut down the trammer, he walked back to the switch and motioned me over. He instructed me on how to change the switch over to the outside track that ran to the end of the dump, a simple operation done in less than a minute's time.

We stood there at the switch just long enough for Swinger to check that I had done the job to his satisfaction, then he said, "Well kid, let's take us a little stroll out in the sunshine and I will tell you how it works out there."

We stood there in the afternoon sun at the end of the dump, which fell away at our feet, the bottom of it on the edge of the Peruvian Lodge parking lot. The rails extended about 10 feet beyond the dump's end, supported by two posts for each rail. The posts were cross-braced effectively, tying the two sets of rails together in the correct gauge.* Swinger said they were on a very slight downhill grade, as were the rails coming out onto the dump. At the end of the track, secured in place over the tops and around both rails, was

* The inside distance between the rail track heads determines the gauge of the railroad system. Example: *The typical gauge of a Cottonwoods district rail system is 18 inches.*

a chain. I had just started to inquire about that item when Swinger gave forth: "Well, about that chain out there kid, that is sort of an insurance policy. Now the grade* is some downhill comin' out of the snowshed to make trammin' the cars easier. A man can hold them back without much trouble as long as he don't let 'em pick up much speed. It ain't unknown to have one get away once in a while but that don't usually end up so good. So, that is what the chain is all about. To stop a runaway. Sometimes it don't. It is bad enough to get the car back up and they are usually busted up good. It would get really interesting if, say, the car ended up on the roof of some ski queer's whoopee. That goddamn chain needs to be on the rails at all times."

Swinger announced it was about time to get the three cars dumped, and we headed back to where they were wedged in place on the tracks. I was thinking on the way that this was going to prove interesting because what I knew about those cars, how they worked, and what it took to unload them would not fill a thimble. Swinger commenced giving me what he called "the rundown" on the upcoming operation, and when he finished that show-and-tell, I knew most of what I needed to know.

The cars in use at the mine were at least 40 years old and possibly older. There was not anywhere on them that was not covered with rust, but they were still solid and capable of carrying the loads placed in them. This type of car, the most common in the district mines, had a capacity of one ton and was often referred to as a "one tonner." It also had other names depending on the circumstance at the time, all extremely colorful if not outrageously profane, some of sermon-length duration. On that day, I had no idea that during my time in the mine, that I would become an accomplished preacher of many of those colorful sermons.

Swinger had me unhook the chains between the cars and kick

* The slope of a tunnel. These always trend upward from the tunnel entrance to facilitate drainage. Example: *The Columbus-Rexall Tunnel's angle upward is 1.89 percent.*

the wedge out from under the wheel of the lead car. "Okay kid," Swinger started, "now toss the wedge on top of the muck, as you're goin' to have use for it. Then get it rollin' and don't forget to hold on to her as she is goin' to go easy. Now, being I am a magnodious [magnanimous] bastard I shall just walk along, play with my Cope [Copenhagen tobacco], 'cause I don't want to hog your fun."

It took little effort to get the car rolling and considerably more effort to control the roll as we headed out to the end of the dump. Once there, Swinger told me exactly where to stop the car and kick the wedge under one wheel to hold it in place.

When the car was securely in place, I was not sure what was to come next, but that did not last long. Swinger pointed to a long lever on the rear of the car that was inside a guide bracket. The lever was over to the left, and Swinger told me to raise the drop latch that held it in that position and move the lever as far to the right as it would go.

That simple move unlocked the dump gate at the front of the car, allowed the body of the car to swivel so it could be dumped to the left, right, or straight ahead, and also enabled the tilting of the body for dumping.

With the car in position, Swinger told me to dump it straight ahead and do the same with the next two. The tilting of the car took a little effort but was easier than I thought it would be. The load slipped out of it and fell away down the face of the dump, and I could see how the dump would eventually fill in and bring the top of it up to the tracks. When the three cars were empty, there was little noticeable evidence of any filling in. It would take an immense amount to fill in the gap underneath those extended rails.

The miners called moving cars "hand tramming" when a man moved them around as I was doing. I would have a good run of that business before the train would be ready for the next day's trip into the mine. While tramming those cars around, I noticed more switches and tracks, tracks I could make no sense of, as they just seemed to run all over and go nowhere. Before we put the train back together, Swinger told me we needed to turn the trammer so its front with the light led the train into the mine. That of course required reversing the way it was sitting on the tracks now. That is when I found out what all the switches and seemingly randomly scattered tracks were about. Using a track arrangement known as a wye* is how that reversal of direction is accomplished.

"What you are looking at kid, is the most stubby-legged goddamn wye that was ever put together. If you go six inches too far on the sonofabitch's tail, you're off the rails. Got to tie a chain on the ends of those damn tracks," Swinger said with a shake of his head.

The three empty cars were together on the track headed for the ore bins, their wheels wedged. I had hooked the cars together with their chains as instructed. By the time I finished that chore, Swinger had the trammer off the wye and back on the main track, and I connected the cars. Swinger pulled the train ahead and stopped next to a charging station located just to the right of the opening. This occurred every day at the end of shift so the trammer was ready for the next day's work. Swinger looked the train over and pronounced it ready to go for the next day.

He consulted his watch, then said, "Well, chum, she ain't late and again it ain't none too early neither so we'll call her deep enough for this day."

When he said that, I figured I had better have a look at my watch. Damn! Hell, I thought, it couldn't possibly be that late, the watch must be running fast or something. I told Swinger that I better be heading down the hill and the reason for it. Even with no problems going down the canyon (never a sure bet), I would be, at least, a half hour late, maybe more, for my work shift. I hated to see that afternoon end. There were so many questions. So many things to be seen and to do, and they could not happen soon enough for me.

* A triangular arrangement of three rail lines with a switch at each corner connecting to each incoming line. This allows the reversal of the direction of travel of a trammer or a full train. The tail of the wye is usually where a siding, also called a tail track, is located.

The mining bug had taken another bite, and it was a big one too. Why was I not doing real work like mining? It just had to beat the hell out of filling some old biddy's Cadillac full of "Flite-Fuel" while her old man squinted and whined about a streak on the windshield. How I hated that service station job!

When I headed down the canyon that day, my mind was so crowded it was a wonder that I paid enough attention to the road to stay out of trouble. Swinger had used words, combinations of words, and expressions that I had only the slightest idea of their meaning. I remembered Swinger mentioning that Slick had told him to make sure that I did not "gob"* myself. I soon found out that the term *gob* covered an immense amount of territory with Swinger. "Deep enough," that was another mystery, what was that about? When I left, Swinger did not say anything like "goodbye" or "see you later"; he simply said, "Tap 'er light, kid."

It was obvious during that run down the canyon that something had to change. I needed more time up in Alta with that man that called himself Swinger and everything that may go with that. My transportation situation was the big obstacle. I did not want to be faced with a time schedule that required early, too early, departures from Alta. There was no doubt as to where this line of thought led, and that was to my old GMC—General Mess of Crap. That four-wheeled disaster had to, somehow, be put into a running, road-worthy state, if such a thing were even possible.

* Technically an obscure and seldom-used term describing waste rock, in most cases in coal mining. It also means to do oneself harm or to die. For miners, it can describe so many things as to require a full chapter to itemize them. It is the most versatile word in their vocabulary and to truly appreciate this term, it has to be experienced.

5

The General Mess of Crap

BECAUSE OF THE major role the old GMC played in this story, that old truck's history will follow here. That truck came into my possession in the early spring of 1957, and it was by then a 16-year-old, extremely worn-out and dilapidated 1941 General Motors truck. I was still working as a painter at the time, and between my wife and me, we had income enough to pay all the bills and still have a small amount to do with as we pleased, and the acquisition of a second vehicle seemed manageable without extending ourselves too far. I started looking around town for a truck that would not create a financial disaster and had no luck in locating something that we could comfortably afford. I spent quite a number of unproductive Saturdays walking through various used-car lots.

Then one Saturday morning, on my way back from another unsuccessful hunt, I found it. I probably should have just went on by South State Auto Wrecking, but I did not. The thing was sitting out near the front fence, along with some other junk that made it look good, so into the yard I went. Once again, the time had come to go through all the ceremonial bickering that was standard when dealing with the proprietor, my old friend, Vince Julian. The color combination was green and black, the paint was still in reasonably good condition, and there was little body damage, just a few dings. A not-so-minor problem was the fact that the old truck had no bed on it. All it amounted to was a cab and chassis.

At this stage, I told Vince that maybe it would be a good idea to see if the thing would start. That sent Vince into his big building to forage about for a battery to install in the thing then told me to jump in and give it a try. So into the beast I went, turned the key, and tried to turn the engine and start the thing.

Well, turn over the engine it did, but that was the extent of it, as the engine refused to start. Vince told me, as he put it, to quit grinding, as he was going to have to "prime the hell out of the carburetor," and off he went in search of some gasoline. Shortly Vince returned carrying a spouted can that may have held a quart of gasoline, lifted up the left side of the hood, took the air cleaner off, and dribbled a little gasoline into the top of the carburetor. He told me to try it. I did. Same result: nothing happened. Vince gave it another dribble and told me to try it again. I did, and this time there was a reaction. There was a coughing sound followed by a belch of flame shooting up from the carburetor. Vince could move exceptionally fast and did so, saving his scalp by a hair, while tossing the container of gasoline out into the yard. When he got his breath back, he told me to try it again. This time the old engine started, stumbled a bit, then smoothed out. It smoked a little. Actually, the old clunker smoked a great deal, the blue smoke pouring out of what served as a tailpipe. None was right with the old GMC.

That done, it was time to proceed to negotiations. I pointed out to Vince that the thing was no damn good without a bed! Vince said that was probably true, but then it would cost more money. Instead, good old Vince piled a nondescript short-box pickup bed on the frame and we wired it in place as a temporary measure to get it out of the yard. The color of the bed did not exactly compliment the rest of the truck's paint; "shit-brittle brown" described it. The frame of the truck originally accommodated a long-bed model, so the fit was not ideal. There existed between the front of the bed and the back of the truck's cab a two-foot gap. At that point, one would think that the pinnacle of ugliness had been reached, but that did not happen to be true.

The newly mounted bed, I pointed out to Vince, seemed to be lacking fenders, and that was not desirable. Another discussion ensued involving that deficiency, and Vince finally threw two fenders off a Model A Ford pickup bed into the deal. He said he did that because he was such a "nice guy" and offered suggestions on how to put them in place so they would not fall off. When I left the yard at South State Auto Wrecking with that pile of iron, it was not running too well. Vince told me not to worry about it; it most likely just needed a valve job. It needed something, and that was for sure. All the way home, as the old GMC coughed back through the carburetor and let loose a few backfires, Vincent's valve job boiled through my head. Unknown to me, I was taking my first steps into a lifetime of regret, as far as trucks were concerned.

I was now the proud owner of a one-hundred-dollar truck that became a hobby of sorts. The sad truth of the matter was the fact that in reality, it owned me. Therefore, with few tools and even less knowledge, I embarked on the "valve job" and hauled the cylinder head to Lambert and Company in Sugar House for the machine work. If I had only guessed at the time where this act would ultimately lead, I would have burned the old General Mess of Crap to the ground.

With the help of the machine shop, I put it back together and things were looking up. Till the damn thing would not even start. I tried many things, all of them wrong, and I drove many people nuts with questions regarding timing, cylinder-firing order, and other incidentals. It took little time before people were out when I came looking for them.

One fellow could not escape too easily. His name was Richard Christianson, more commonly known by his nickname Cris, and he ran the shop at Lambert and Company. I was down at that shop constantly with questions, and one day, Cris finally had enough and summoned one of the men working there. Ross Montgomery came over while I was in the middle of the latest "whys" and "how comes." Cris instructed Ross to take what he thought he needed, follow me home, and not to come back until that engine started and "built smoke." When Ross left, the old GMC was doing both, particularly the smoke part. Still, the junk pile was finally able to move under its own power again.

Through long days and longer nights, a lot of profane oaths and experimenting, I was about to end up with a mobile wreck that might possibly limp to and from Alta. In the gap between the cab and the bed, I put together a plywood box covered with tin in which to stash my mining gear and other incidentals. I will have to say this about the old clunker: it never quit on me completely, though I had some interesting rides in it. Had I been an older man at the time, I probably would have had several strokes dealing with its idiosyncrasies.

The old GMC had owned me for a couple of months prior to my meeting Swinger, and I had worked long and hard on that pile of iron when August of 1957 arrived. It was then I quit the painting business and the money troubles began. The only work that I'd found was as a service station attendant that paid less than half what I was making as a painter's apprentice. A holdup on the old truck became necessary, as I did not have money enough to finish the job. When I finally got the old truck in shape for its first run to Alta, I ended up owing my uncle Fred of F. G. Ferre and Sons $50. I owed that money for too long a time, and it took me forever to pay that bill.

6

The First Trip, and Other Things

THE WEEK FOLLOWING the one I met Swinger and received the car-dumping lesson, I was able to go up to the mine only one time. I had spent most of the week trying to get the General Mess of Crap in good enough condition to try a run to Alta. It was late afternoon, and Swinger was just coming out of the mine with two loaded cars when I arrived. I declined his invitation to dump them and told him I needed to get back to the valley and that I would be up Tuesday of the next week. He said that it was good with him, and he would look forward to it. I headed back for town, as I needed to pick up my wife from work, hoping that would be the last of that one-car business. It all depended on that old cobbled-together GMC, and confident I was not.

When Tuesday finally saw fit to arrive, it was time to find out if the General Mess of Crap was worth the time, aggravation, and money or should be pounded into small pieces with a sledgehammer. My wife had possession of the nice new Ford Fairlane that we could not afford, and I was about to take the venerable General Mess of Crap, which we also could not afford, and attempt a maiden voyage. It was one of my days off, so I had the entirety to see how this might turn out. The previous evening, I had loaded all my gear in the shabby-looking tin-covered box between the bed and the truck's cab. The gear consisted of my fishing boots, my hard-boiled hat with its homemade lamp bracket, a carbide lamp,* carbide,† and a couple of candles. There was a possibility that this whole plot just might work out.

A relaxing trip up that steep Little Cottonwood Canyon that morning it was not. The exhaust barked, the transmission whined, and everything rattled as that old mobile junkyard clattered up the canyon. But things quieted down considerably when I turned the ignition key to off at the mine. I pried my left hand off the steering wheel and released the death grip on the seat that my hind end had established. Damn, the old iron pile had not even boiled over climbing that canyon, but it was still very hot according to the gauge. The first half of the maiden voyage went well, but the fact remained that this rolling potential disaster still had to take me home at the end of the shift. I got Swinger to come out and look it over.

Swinger put his hands behind his back, gripping one wrist with the other hand like a British Field Officer, and commenced his inspection. He walked around it full circle once, reversed direction, walked around it again, peered inside, unloaded a big spit of Cope on the ground, and said, "Jesus Christ and little Rizzi kid, who in hell hated you bad enough to unload that whoopee on you?" Then he broke out with that familiar grin, gave a chuckle, and announced, "Coffee's built kid, let's get after it."

I gathered up my gear and piled it up just off the side of the big step in front of the shack's door. Swinger looked it over a bit but said nothing, just suggested we go in and have some coffee. We sat down at the table for a couple of cups of good strong coffee, and that was when I found out how he acquired the moniker of Swinger and a

* For many years, these lamps were the primary source of light in mines. Acetylene gas powered the flame, intensified by a reflector surrounding the burner orifice. Carbide filled the screw-on cup on the lower part of the lamp. Water added to a separate compartment, above the carbide, controlled by a drip lever, allowed a measured amount of water to reach the carbide and determine the amount of light.

† Calcium carbide, known simply as "carbide" to a miner. When exposed to water, it produces acetylene gas that is extremely flammable and explosive.

lot of other interesting information. The following is the general run of how he explained the origin of his nickname.

"Well, kid," he started out in his usual fashion, "I am sometimes called Jack, but my good little Mormon mother gave me the name of John T. Campbell, the T standing for Thomas. I was hatched out in Silver City, that's a little south of Eureka and Mammoth. Like most imps growing up in a mining town like that, I ended up as a miner. I started out skinning mules in the old Colorado Mine up out of Knightsville working for my old grandpa Bean. I had committed another nasty crime in class at the old Knightsville School and got mucked out at the tender age of twelve. Now, that has nothin' to do with how I came by the handle of Swinger so I better just stick with that tale.

"It happened in the later years and at the time I was breaking rock in the old Chief Consolidated Mine in Eureka. Now, in those days, actually for a long while before, I had developed a great love for whiskey but anything with alcohol was good with me. One day after we had come up out of the hole, me and another sonofabitch or three or four decided to have a few drinks. The first two or three went down real smooth so that called for going deeper into the project to see if we could improve. Well, that set us off on a real pippin and we stayed drunk for several days. It was a remarkable outing I guess. What I could remember of it, which wasn't much. When all of us sobered up, my chums were calling me Swinging Door. I asked where the hell they had come up with that one. You see most of the guys called me Lefty, that being from our ball-playing days in Mammoth. They said they hung the name Swinging Door on me because I could make the bar doors swing so good. Anyhow, that is how I came by the name Swinger which is Swinging Door shortened up some."

I still had half a cup of coffee left when he ended that little tale, and he still seemed interested in more talk, which in most cases he was. Swinger's coffee was not gone either, so I figured I would get a little more out of him. I asked him, then, if he had come up to Alta from Eureka, and he said no and that he had not worked in Tintic for some time. He said he had been playing round all over the

West with different outfits and on his own. He said he had landed in Tooele, where he had a place to hole up when he was not floating, and it was there that the Bull had tracked him down. The next thing out of me was the question of just who was the Bull. This is what he told me.

"Well, kid, the Bull is the super of the drain tunnel project down the hill from where we are sitting."

I told him that I had seen it and described what it looked like, and he agreed we were talking about the same place.

"So, what happened, kid, was the Bull tracked me down in Tooele and explained to me that my loafing days were over and to pack up my gear. He would see me at the Wasatch Drain Tunnel Monday of the next week. The Bull said he needed a good man on the grass.* Wouldn't be anything in the hole—well, maybe a little and I had better figure on being there for a while. Then the Bull, being the Bull, he just had to get in his usual poke at you just to make sure you were paying attention. He informed me that I was to bring my own bed, as he knew that would hold my oversize carcass off the floor. The penthouse I would be living in had some bunks, six of them, but he said if I climbed in one she would come in† for sure."

Swinger said he did load up his junk, including his bed, and headed for Alta and the Wasatch Drain Tunnel project. He told me that he and the Bull had worked together all over the country. He went on to say that the Bull had always been the boss, and every time it had ended the same way. Without fail, he went on, he and the Bull would get into a few arguments and then one that was a real "pippin." At that point, they would break their picks‡ with

* A slang term describing the surface plant and processing area of a mine on the outside of the tunnel. It actually has nothing to do with grass. The workers outside the underground workings were said to be "on the grass."

† Describes a collapse of any kind, especially a cave-in. Example: *The timber gave way, and half the stope came in. Three men were caught under it and got gobbed.*

‡ A slang term for two or more individuals that have reached their end of association with one another, usually under unfavorable or hostile circumstances.

each other, and it would be down the horseshit trail. Swinger then explained that the Bull always referred to firing a worker as "putting them down the horseshit trail."

"It took about three months this time before the usual blow-up took place, not bad for me and the Bull," Swinger said. "Back in the old days, sometimes we didn't make a week before the fuse hit the primer. Same deal all over again, just another pippin of an argument and I don't even remember what the hell we went at it over. Hell, I don't remember if the Bull sent me down the horseshit trail or if I went on my own.

"Slick Hansen showed up at the drain tunnel shortly after I moved in. He said that he had secured a lease in this hole and wanted me to know. Slick said that when the big blow-up took place it was just short of a mile up to the next job. Old slick was some familiar with the history of me and the Bull."

Swinger put a couple of small lumps of coal in the stove, and we went out of the shack.

7

Into the Mine

THE MORNING I climbed into the General Mess of Crap for my first run into the cold, wet darkness of the old Columbus-Rexall, I had no idea of what lay ahead. The Columbus-Rexall Mine has approximately 15,000 feet of workings. At the time of this story, less than one-half of those 15,000 feet were accessible, and I worked only a small section of that. The Columbus-Rexall Tunnel begins at a point 350 feet in from the Howland Tunnel's portal.

Originally this branch off the Howland was known as the Enterprise drift,* driven to access the old Enterprise ore zone below its deepest workings. The Enterprise drift, in 1906, became the Columbus-Extension. It carried that name until 1915, when it was renamed the Columbus-Rexall, and so it remains to this day. Two separate blocks of ground were under lease agreements when I became involved with the mine in 1957. Whitney C. Hansen (a.k.a. Slick) was a lessee as was a fellow with the name of Frank Reedy. The leased areas were a considerable distance from each other and created very little conflict between the operations.

The first 300 feet of the Columbus-Rexall Tunnel was heavily timbered, much of it in bad condition. The drift that branched off the Columbus-Rexall Tunnel leading to Frank's lease was in solid limestone that required no timbering.

Proceeding 200 feet more from the point where the drift to Reedy's lease branches off, another junction appears. One branch of the tunnel runs straight ahead; the other makes an abrupt left

* Often-used term to describe a tunnel, typically used when following an ore vein. Example: *They were driving a drift following a tight mineralized fissure.*

turn. A station opened up in this area and, as it was in quartzite, required no timbering to hold the ground. The first sight of this would make one wonder what the purpose of all this was. There were switches and tracks, the rails seemingly going every direction and would make no sense to the uninformed, such as I at that time.

There was in that station a critical piece of equipment that both Hansen's and Reedy's operations were very dependent on. This thing—which was known by many names, most of which were exceedingly foul and profane in nature—was an air compressor. The compressor run on 220-volt electricity, and a cable brought the power in from a substation outside the mine. The compressor was far from being new. It was, in fact, almost an antique at the time and prone to short out. The shorting out was due to not just its age but the extremely wet environment it inhabited. This old worn-out piece of equipment was the only source of compressed air to operate drills and other air-powered equipment, so when it shorted out both Whitney Hansen's and Frank Reedy's work came to a halt until it was running again.

Most of the timber work in that section some distance beyond the compressor was less than 10 years old at the time, but the constant shifting of the ground, the water flows coming in that varied from drips to streams, caused the heavy timber to shift and the lagging* to give way. Broken posts, caps, and lagging that had opened up due to the shifting or breaking would allow rock falls. The rocks and muck would dam the ditch and flood the tracks, making it necessary to clear, by shoveling, the affected railbed and rails. The rails themselves were in bad shape, the ties soaked through with water and the spikes holding the rails loosened constantly. The havoc created

* Rough, unplaned planking used in the construction of timber supports, most often 2 by 10 inches or 2 by 12 inches. Lagging put in place above the cap timbers and between the ribs (walls) and posts of timber sets prevents small rocks and other loose material from falling into the tunnel. It is also used as bridging (see photo insert).

by broken timber and lagging that dammed the ditch and blocked the tracks needed catching up* continuously.

The presence of great quantities of sulfides in the mine was another problem. The dissolving sulfides created sulfuric acid that attacked all that was iron, such as airlines and rails. The rails, particularly the ones that run through the sulfide zone if they were old (and most were, being a lightweight 18-pound rail), would sometimes collapse under the weight of the train, the web of the rails holed through by the acidic water. This would cause a derailment at the very least and sometimes other collateral damage. This kind of problem generated unbelievable, although very colorful, language unique in its foulness. Not to mention the intense labor that followed such an event.

Farther into the mine, there was a junction switch, and the main rail line run to the end of the tunnel. Here in the working face of the tunnel, the fissure† followed by the miners stood vertical and easily seen, measuring three-quarters of an inch wide. The fissure, according to Slick, run 900 ounces of silver (Ag) to the ton, a considerable rich ore. It would not have mattered if it had run 2,000 ounces to the ton; there was no way to mine it due to its narrowness. The only real value existing in that particular fissure (and the value it allegedly contained was a good story) was, hopefully, its use to mine the pockets of unwary investors.

The Columbus-Rexall was wet and cold throughout its 15,000 feet of underground workings. Water dripped constantly from everything overhead and in many places was well beyond the category of drips, instead turning into running rivulets from fissures. All the timbering was wet and slippery, and that held true for ladders in any of the raises anywhere in the mine. All of the workings, with few exceptions, that went below the tunnel level‡ were water filled.

* A miner's term for that which needs serious attention.

† A narrow break or crack in the rock. Many fissures will carry mineralization that may have exploration drifts driven on them. Assay values determine if this occurs or does not.

‡ The elevation of the workings below the shaft or mine entrance—that is, *700 level* is 700 feet below the collar of the shaft.

Rubber work clothes and boots were a necessity along with heavy rubber work gloves. Swinger had said, more than once, "The water in the hole is so goddamn cold it is stiff."

Another sometimes-disturbing trait the mine had was its overall darkness—the term *darkness* in this case not meaning the absence of artificial light. The mine was a place of dark and dismal coloration. The quartzite for the most part was dark brown; the shales that dominated much of the mine's country rock were dark in color ation. They varied in color from dark purple to almost black and a very dark green. The shale zones, particularly those with the darkest coloration, would exhibit an unsettling contrast of colors. The shales were rife with fissuring that allowed mineral-laden water consisting of sulfides of iron to stain the dark background rock. The fissures appeared to be oozing semicoagulated blood. It was a happy place.

Swinger told me what he and Slick had been doing since he came on the job was mostly cleanup work. No one had done any serious work in that section of the mine for about six years. Things like broken airlines or other leaks in the air system needed fixing between the compressor station and the work area. Sagging and broken timbers needed replacing, along with the broken lagging between the timber sets. The ditch* in several places required shoveling to remove material that was backing up the water and diverting it down the track bed. One of the three carloads of muck, which I went to car-dumping school on, carried the last of the material shoveled out of the ditch. The tracks themselves had to be respiked and their ties replaced, but as the near future would show, not nearly enough of them were. Rock falls blocked the tracks in many places and so on.

We finished off our coffee, and Swinger stared into his cup for a second or two, then announced, "Let's get off our dead asses kid,

* The ditch carries the water encountered in a mining operation. Ditches require ongoing maintenance, as the mine rails and other low-mounted utilities must be as water-free as possible. Clearing them is not a sought-after job in a mine.

things need doing in the hole. Now, Slick ain't paying me sixteen dollars a shift to sit around telling lies and drinking coffee so let's go play in the dark for a while."

Finally, the time had arrived, and I was about to go underground for the first time to do actual work. Swinger already had his work boots on; they were knee high, all rubber with steel toes, the nametags on the front identifying their brand as Goodall. He looked over my pile by the step and remarked that the "lid" looked fine and the light was good too. He gave my hip-high fishing boots a nudge with his toe and said there would not be much fishing in the hole. He said that the boots might get me by until something better came along. He picked up one of the boots and inspected it from top to bottom. Why he did that, I did not have any idea and would not figure out until sometime later. I did not know this man very well at the time and could not read him then, as I would be able to in the years to come. He handed me the boot and said, "I see you ain't got no rubber but then I didn't figure you would, so grab the coat off the hook next to where mine is hanging. That's Slick's tuxedo but he won't be coming around today anyhow."

By the time I got my boots on and borrowed Slick's coat and had it on, Swinger was suited up in his rubber gear, his hat perched on his head. He then rummaged around in an old dynamite box, came up with a pair of heavy rubber gloves, and tossed them to me. Holding his lamp in his hand, he waited until I had my hat on and my lamp in hand. I reached for my little can of carbide, but he told me to leave it alone. Swinger said that Slick had plenty of carbide on the project and that Slick could furnish all that I would need. We walked to the trammer, he unhooked the charger leads from the trammer's batteries, and the train was ready to go. With that accomplished, it was time to get our lamps ready to go into the mine.

To get our lamps fired up, we both did it the same way, the usual way, except for one thing Swinger did that was just a typical Swinging Door bit of eccentricity. Before the bottoms of the lamps were unscrewed to take their load of carbide, we simply dipped the lamps, with the filler cap snapped back, into the water in the ditch coming out of the mine. When the lamp was full of water, the bottom was removed, and in went the carbide. With the bottom screwed back in place, the water-flow control lever on the top of the lamp was opened. I always opened the water flow to about the halfway point, gave it a few seconds to do its job on the carbide, then thumbed the striker wheel, sparking a nice two-inch flame.

Swinger's method was interesting. Immediately before attaching the lamp's bottom to its top, he'd spit a stream of Copenhagen juice into the carbide and then screw the lamp together. He turned the water control full on, put his hand completely over the reflector, in the center of which was the burner orifice, waited a second or two, and then rolled the striker wheel with the heel of his hand as it cleared the reflector. There was a loud pop followed by three inches of flame. He then turned the water control back to center. I was thinking I was going to have to try that myself next time, except I lacked the charge of Copenhagen juice. (A disastrous Copenhagen tobacco business was not too far in the future for me, and it was a dandy.)

Swinger settled himself down on the seat of the trammer and said, "Climb in one of the cars kid, it is time to get this circus underway. Now, don't put your hands on the rim of the car, keep them away from that. You see, she will scrape against the rib* in a lot of places, and you don't want to come up short of fingers. That would be bad, but what would be worse is if you lost your nose-picking finger."

With that warning, we headed into the mountain. Going into that hole felt like I was going home after a long absence. The experiences that lay ahead of me would never be forgotten and, to me, were priceless.

The project of the day, Swinger had said, was to see what we could do with a hung chute, but the work began before we reached the chute's location. On one of the turns going in, trouble came in

* A slang term for the side or wall of a tunnel (see "back" in the glossary for origin).

the form of a derailment when the last car of the train jumped the rails. There were to be many episodes of this particular aggravation. Next to the derailment, the water in the ditch was deep and there was no lack of iron-stained mud. Swinger referred to the mud as *gob*, thus adding to the term's versatility. The empty car was no problem to get back on the rails. Had it been loaded—or worse, if the heavy trammer had left the rails—it would have been no fun at all. Unfortunately, that event was in the future too.

Swinger pulled the train beyond the chute and past the switch that would open the way into the side drift. The cars were unhooked from the trammer and one at a time moved down the drift beyond the switch. The switch was changed, and the cars pushed into the side drift, and the switch changed back to the main run.

Swinger went back, got on the trammer and announced, "Be right back kid, got to make a little run back to where the compressor is to turn this whore around. It's a better system there than that stubby-legged wye outside by a long way. Now should I come walking back instead of riding, that will mean this damn thing jumped the rails and we don't need that kind of fun."

Off he went down the tracks, and now I knew what the rail layout was all about down at the compressor's location. Swinger was back in a short time, we hand trammed the cars and hooked them behind the trammer, and once again, we had a train. Swinger told me he was going to back the train up and to stop him when the first car behind the trammer was beneath the chute.

8

The Hung Chute

A DESCRIPTION OF the chute, its construction, and the raise itself would be in order here. The chute occupied the right side of the raise; the man way* with the ladder was on the left side. The wall of the chute, on the ladder side, was a solid wall of lagging (2-by-12-inch planking) securely spiked to the inner side of the timber posts wedged into the raise at a right angle to the run of the chute. Swinger called these timbers anchoring the chute stulls†—another word he would employ with wide diversity. The other three sides of the chute were solid rock. The ladder was anchored to four-inch square timbers that were tightly wedged across the bottom side of the raise between the stulls that the chute walls attached to; the raise itself rose upward not vertically but at an angle of about 60 degrees. Anchored to the stulls near their top ends was a three-inch diameter pipe. This pipe carried compressed air to the workings above.

The chute dropped into the drift high enough that the lowest point was above the upper rim of a car. The bottom of the chute, the lip, extended above and about a foot inside the box of a car. It was nearly the same width as the car box was long. The gates on this particular chute were simply two lengths of 2-by-12-inch lagging

* Man way refers to a mining lane of traffic in an adit or raise reserved for the passage of miners. In this case, there was a chute occupying the right side. In adits, there may be one or two lanes for rails with a man way adjacent for the miners to climb or descend safely and so as to not impede the flow of ore or muck traffic.

† A single support timber. It can be mill-cut timber like a post or simply a tree trunk cut to length, as was the practice in early mining days. In the jargon of miners, such things as canes and crutches are also called stulls (see photo insert).

that fit into channels on each side of the chute. The flow of muck or ore was controlled by lifting the lagging upward in increments. With the two lengths of lagging stacked one above the other, it made a gate 24 inches in height. Essentially, they became the upper and lower gate. The upper gate would be raised first, then when the muck was level with the top of the lower, that one was raised, thus clearing the chute.

Swinger was at the side of the car across from the chute, between it and the rib. It was a tight fit for his bulk, but there he stood looking at the chute. He spit Copenhagen at a load that was ready for unloading into the car and said, "Looks tight, kid, sorta like wet concrete. I think that we are going to have fun with this shit as I suppose it's been there for some years. I think I could pull both gates and not get much, but for right now, I'll just jerk the upper. We'll get her moving one way or another 'cause it's got to be done. There is more than one way to clear up a case of constipation."

He grabbed a long bar off the trammer, and with it, he pried the top half of the gate up and out. A few pieces of the material behind the gate rattled into the car, but nothing else came down. Swinger worked the bar into the muck in the chute, got some more to break loose, which fell into the car, and that was it. The rest of it stayed where it was, so he pried up the bottom half of the gate. The muck in the chute never moved, and Swinger told me to hand him the shovel that was on my side of the drift.

Swinger went after the jam with the shovel and then the steel bar and finally a good-sized chunk of rock slid out of the chute into the car. The stuff was like partially set-up concrete but broke up fairly well when it landed. With a bit more prodding, enough then turned loose, and we ended up with half a carload. A solid wall of muck remained stuck in the chute. It lay about six feet up, and it would take considerable more persuasion to get it loose. Swinger worked himself out of the spot he was in and came around to where I was standing. He pulled a hammer out of a cluster of different items that were around his seat and set it on top of the trammer. That intrigued me, owing to the fact that I had no idea what was coming next.

"Okay chum," he started, "this is what we are going to do next. You need to go up the ladder, won't be much, and pack this single jack with you until I say stop."

He handed me the hammer.

"Let's see, your head will probably be even with that second stull up, puttin' you shoulder height with the plug. You will be swingin' that single jack with your right hand and hanging on to a rung with your left. You will figure out which one when you get in position. Make sure your feet are solid on a rung and you feel stable. When you are solid, lay into the chute wall with the hammer. It will take more than one whack I have to say and that damn four-pound hammer is going to feel like a twelve-pounder after the first few hits. I will play with the bar from here and give it some pokes. Give her some good hits but watch your footing and keep yourself locked in good. Now, a goddamn dive out of a raise is something you don't want to do."

After grabbing hold of the hammer that Swinger called a single jack, up the raise I went. Hanging on to the four-pound hammer with its 18-inch handle and climbing up that ladder felt awkward. An extra hand and arm would have been good. The single jack did not feel too heavy; it just seemed to be in the way. I made it up to where Swinger told me I had to be and yelled down I was in place. He told me to start banging on the wall of the chute, and he went to work with the bar. It did not take too many hits with the single jack and with Swinger working the bar till the plug turned loose with a rumbling roar. By that stage of the game, that single jack weighed about 20 pounds if it weighed an ounce.

I climbed down and walked over to where Swinger stood looking at the load that had hit the car. It had filled the car completely, leaving some still in the chute. The chute appeared to be clear, with no muck in sight, so I figured we had the job done up to this point. Swinger took the shovel and moved the muck into the corners of the car. That finished clearing the chute and left the car loaded to capacity. Swinger moved the trammer and loaded car down the track, leaving the chute unobstructed. When he got off the trammer he was carrying a battery-powered light that had been cached somewhere around the seat.

He announced he was going to look up the chute and make sure it was clear. Swinger squatted down a bit and leaned into the chute some to get the light and his line of sight where it needed to be. It probably took less than 10 seconds before he pulled back, shut off the light, and stood there shaking his head, then spit and said, "Jesus Christ and little Rizzi kid, we've got another plug up there like I was afraid of. I went up the raise a couple days ago with a small hammer, did a little sounding on the chute wall in some places, and figured that sure as hell I had found another crapshoot to deal with. Well, there she is if you want to take a look, which I don't think is too good an idea but go ahead. If you hear any sound at all or even a pebble rattles down that hole, get the hell out of the way and damn quick. If that turns loose it will come out of there like a mad God after a Lamanite."

I took my look and wasted no time getting out of the line of fall. It was a nasty-looking proposition and I said so, although I had never seen a plugged chute before. Swinger decided we might as well go on out with the one car, put on a pot of coffee, and rustle up a sandwich. I looked at my watch for the first time that day and could not believe the time. Hell, it could not be that time yet, but it was. The clock always moved quick in the mine. I could put down a fast cup of coffee but then needed to get myself down the hill. I had been late for that evening shift in that damned service station too many times. Hate that job I surely did, but we needed the paycheck at home and if I managed to get myself fired, there would be some unpleasant times in my future.

9

The Plug Turns Loose

WHEN I HEADED up to Alta the next morning, I was ready for anything that might come up. I had managed to get about five hours' sleep because my quitting time at the hated Phillips 66 service station was midnight. That shortage of time in bed did not seem to matter, as I had that day and the following as my two days off that week. What made it even better was the fact that my wife had to work those days, thus avoiding even more disagreements involving my interests in Alta. I got to the mine about 7:30 in the morning, unloaded my gear next to the big step into the shack, and then walked in. Swinger and I exchanged good mornings, and I sat down at the table. He got up off his chair and took the coffeepot off the stove; the cups were already on the table.

It was the usual good brew, dark in color and strong—the only way Swinger would make it, which suited me. He said that after I had left, he dumped the single car we had brought out and got everything ready to go back in the mine. The trammer sat parked at the charging station, the cables still attached. It was just a matter of getting suited up, gathering a few miscellaneous items, and unhooking the charging cables from the trammer. With that accomplished, we would be ready to head into the mine. Swinger was as usual in no big rush, as coffee was the immediate priority. As I suspected, the first order of business when we got in would be to go after the hung chute. He was, as usual, in a talkative mood, and the chute was the main subject.

Swinger said there were any number of ways to getting gobbed in a mine, and a couple of the bad ones were a hung chute and a missed hole. He just passed on by the missed hole without further comment and spent the time on hung chutes. I had no idea of what a missed hole was but later, down the road, I would become familiar with that problem too.

"That chute, kid, is most likely plugged up tighter than a bull's ass in fly time. What I am hoping is that we can shake her loose without having to give her a Herc enema, which is nothing more than a 60 percent suppository."

I got lost on most of what he said immediately. What the hell was a Herc enema? What in hell was a 60 percent suppository? The explanation was already on its way before I could ask questions.

Swinger said that in most cases, some hard hits with a double jack on the chute wall would shake the plug loose. How many times that wall may have to be hit ranged from a few to enough to wear out the arms of the man wielding the hammer. Another way was to drag an air hose up the ladder and use compressed air to break things loose. Most of the time, that involved opening small holes in the chute wall so a hose with a nozzle could reach the plug. That system, most of the time, did not work well, and he said he liked to leave that alone. There was always the Herc way he said, and if done right, most of the time, nobody was killed.

"I guess I better break a few things down for you kid," he started out. "You looked kind of jammed up when I mentioned a Herc enema, a 60 percent suppository, and such. Okay, this is what that is all about just so you know. On this job, we are using dynamite made by Hercules Powder at 60 percent strength. That sixty stuff is the amount of nitroglycerin in that stick of powder. It gets complicated trying to explain the reason for different strengths of powder, but you can look it up if you want."

"Okay, Swing," I said, "I guess I've got it now. Herc is short for Hercules, and the 60 percent suppository is the strength of the powder. So, a Herc enema and a 60 percent suppository are all the same thing. It cleans out a plugged-up asshole, I have to guess."

"You've got her down kid," he said with a grin. "Let's get after it."

We put everything together, headed into the mountain, and got to the chute without any derailments or other aggravating problems.

Swinger said he intended to leave the gates out of the chute, as it was a sure bet that when that plug upstairs came down, it would tear any gating right out of the chute. It all sounded reasonable to me simply because I had no idea concerning any part of an operation as this.

"What's going to happen now kid, is this: I'm goin' up the ladder with the double jack, and I'll thump the hell out of the chute and see if it will shake that plug loose. I don't want you anywhere near that car under the chute or the back of the trammer. I am hoping that there isn't a whole bunch of shit hanging up there. If there is more than a carload, we are going to have some fun down here."

"How about I go up there and give it a try," I replied. "I managed to shake the one loose yesterday; why not this one?"

"I don't think it is a good idea at all kid. First off, you will be a lot higher up that ladder on this one. If you had come loose from that ladder yesterday, you would have got banged up some, but if you came down out of there from where you have to be today, it would not be good, I can tell you for sure. No, I don't think so kid."

After more back and forth, Swinger relented and told me to go ahead and try it. When I started up that ladder, I had some serious misgivings start to go to work on me. I commenced wondering just how damn smart this idea had been. I went on up to where my head was even with the sixth stull, some 20 feet or more above the tunnel level.

Looking down from my perch, I had the notion I was 100 feet up that raise. Then the idea popped up that the best thing would be to give it up, but being young and stupid, not to mention full of pride, I discarded the notion. With that, I figured I had better give it a try, which I did. I took a few whacks at the chute wall, swinging with my right arm like the day before and hanging on with my left. I felt a little shaky but put a little more effort into the hammer blows. Nothing happened, shit! OK, what the hell. I put more effort into a couple more, but my arm felt like it was turning to rubber. The position I was in and the close quarters of the raise made it necessary to swing the hammer overhead. So far, the plug had given not a sign that it was going to move.

I gave my right arm some time to rest and relaxed my left as much as I dared, which was not much. I was frustrated and disgusted when I decided to try again, putting all I dared into the swing. I did not want to come loose and come down out of that raise like a mad God after a Lamanite, as Swinger liked to describe such a thing. That next one did the trick, and with what seemed like an impossible roar, the plug broke loose. It seemed like the whole raise was heading for the tunnel level, which of course it was not. The noise quickly subsided, my legs felt rubbery, and I started, shakily, down the ladder. The goddamned single jack felt like it weighed 100 pounds by the time I got down. I got to the tunnel level, dropped the single jack, looked at my partner, and said, "Jesus Christ and little Rizzi, Swing!"

"Yeah!" he said—that was all.

There was more than a carload, little doubt about that, and we were definitely going to have fun with the mess. The car was filled, and muck was backed all the way into the chute; we could not tell how far up it went. There were some pieces of timber hung up in the mess, and they were the first things we worked out of the muck and laid aside. Swinger unloaded an impressive spit of Copenhagen and looked over the chaos.

He managed another good spit, shook his head, and said, "Well, I have seen worse, but it has been a while. Make sure there is no crap on the tracks between the two cars so we don't have a runoff to deal with. Then what I am going to do is pull a car switch as quick as it can be done and hope to get by with the stunt."

"What in hell is a car switch?" I inquired.

"What that is all about kid, is I will move the second car under the chute as fast as I can get her there. With any kind of shithouse luck, it will catch the next gob that comes down. We don't need to have things get any more interesting than they are now."

Swinger got on the trammer and moved the second car under the chute as fast as the trammer could do it. Some of the muck went between the cars but not enough to jam things up and cause a derailment. The second car topped itself to the rim, and fortunately, the chute quit running. We still had the third car, but the cleanup around the chute area would nearly top that one too.

We had three fully loaded cars when we headed for the outside. We had great hope that there would be no cars jumping the track and our luck held good all the way out, and making it through the nasty section known as the Brain Fissure was beyond good luck. That run of tunnel, with its "floating track"* and other things just lying in wait to jam everything up, would later get its revenge many times over. That damned nightmare stretch was just biding its time to create havoc with the operation.

When we got to sunlight, as Swinger at times referred to getting out of the mine, we did the usual switching around and dumping of cars. With the trammer back on the charger, the outfit was ready to go back in the next morning. The coffeepot went on the stove, and we got out of our gear and had a couple of cups of coffee and a fast sandwich of cheese and ham. I looked at my watch for the first time since I arrived at the mine that morning. It was 4:30—where had the time gone?

Swinger announced, "She is deep enough kid. We will call it done for this day. You comin' up tomorrow?"

"Hell yes! See you for coffee first thing." That was my answer for that question.

I left my boots, my hard-boiled hat, and my lamp at the mine, as there seemed to be no use in packing that stuff in the GMC's junk box. I hung Slick's coat up by its hood, said goodbye to my friend, went out, climbed into the General Mess of Crap, and headed down the hill. It had been an interesting day and then some. Another good thing about the day was the fact that I did not have to be at the damned Phillips station that afternoon.

* A section of track that will not stay in place. This generally occurs in mines that produce large amounts of water. Spikes hold the tracks of the rail system securely to wooden ties (sleepers) keeping them in position and at the proper gauge. If the ties deteriorate due to water saturation, the spikes will loosen, shift easily, and pull out completely at times. The "floating track" is the result and makes derailments a certainty. Poor ditch maintenance is the usual cause of this problem.

10
Tommyknocker Boots

THE WEEK FOLLOWING the hung chute project, some repairs to that chute along with other things needed some attention, so I headed up. As usual, I was driving the old General Mess of Crap. The old clunker had managed to get us, meaning the old truck and myself, up and down the canyon several times, in two pieces. I got there around 7:30, and I wanted to make the best of it, as that Phillips station nightmare required my presence in time for the start of the swing shift. I was determined to get in a good half day plus a little more before I had to head down the hill. I pulled onto the mine property and did not like what I was looking at. Instead of the Chevrolet sedan that was usually there, a good-looking Ford pickup had taken its place. It was a well-cared-for 1955 Ford F-100, blue in color.

All kinds of things run through my mind, the biggest of which was, whose truck was that? I did not want to consider that maybe Swinger was gone and somebody I did not know was on the job now. I sat there in the old GMC contemplating what a lousy deal that would be. About that time, Swinger walked out of the snowshed door and waved me in. I got out of the wreck, and we went into the shack. There were two cups on the table; Swinger removed the coffeepot from the top of the stove, and filled them both. He sat down and took a sip before laying it out in Swinger fashion.

"About that truck out there kid. That is mine and the crate that has been here since you showed up belongs to Slug. Now, that is my son whose real name, well, the one used most is Bud. He needed a truck for a while so I traded with him, which wasn't good because he needed the truck longer than he said which smelled bad to me.

Anyhow, I have my whoopee back and he has that goddamn worthless kite.* Christ, kid, I wouldn't have that thing stuffed in my ass if I had room for a ten-car muck train and that's along with the trammer."

There were more surprises in store for me that morning. Coming inside, I'd noticed Slick's coat hanging in its usual place next to Swinger's. What was out of place was another set of what Swinger referred to as "diggers" hanging next to his. This outfit did not have the usual iron-colored mud smears all over it, so I asked if somebody else had come on the project.

"That set of rubber out there now belongs to you. You might call it a present from the Bull down at the drain tunnel except he don't know about it. I don't think it is too likely that he ever will. Nobody was using them diggers and probably was somebody's that went down the horseshit trail or quit. The Bull does that to people now and again one way or another if he decides he don't like them.

"I go down about twice a week at night after the night shift goes in the hole to take a shower in the dry† and fill up my water barrel. The water up here kinda tastes like a rusty spoon. The water down there is some better. Somehow, the rubber got hung up on my water barrel and I had to get the works back up here to separate the diggers from the barrel. There are two outside guys that know me down there and let me into the dry for my clean up. And they fill up my barrel while I am douching off and load her too."

All I could do was shake my head. I took another sip of coffee and shook my head again. "Goddamn, Swinger, I have listened to some bullshit tales in my short time but rubber gear getting stuck to a water barrel kind of sits high in the tree. You sure that's how it happened?"

* Another name for an automobile or a pickup truck. It is commonly used by a mining individual to create confusion in the mind of the listener.

† The staging area near a mine entrance for miners to prep for or derig after working a shift.

"Well, something like that kid. Anyhow, they got stole anyway you want to look at it."

That was not the end of the bullshit stories. The best came a short time later after we finished our coffee. I told Swinger I would go get my boots out of the junk box and get ready for whatever we were going to do that day. I told him I had to be out of the hole and down the hill by 2:00 so I could pretend to kiss some asses. I pushed away from the table and got up.

"Better hang on for a minute kid, while I get out of this chair, and forget about going after those dainty things you call boots."

Now what? I thought as he walked over next to his bed and started rummaging around under it with one foot. There was a scraping noise and out came a boot, more rummaging and out came another boot. He kicked them one at a time toward me and said, "Pull them on kid, they should fit just fine."

There lay a brand-new pair of Goodall miner's boots, knee high and steel toed.

"They are yours kid. Use those others for fishing, them things are no damn good in a mine."

That rather stopped me in my tracks for a bit. Then I told him I appreciated the boots, but I did not have any money to buy a pair of boots like that. He told me there was no money involved in the deal and that I had better make sure they fit. They did. Then I had to commence on him from a different angle and said, "Hell, Swinger these things are brand new, somebody had to buy them, and that requires money."

"No, that's not how it happened. You ever hear of Tommyknockers?"

"No, never heard of such a thing, Swinger. What in hell is a Tommyknocker?"

"Well, a Tommyknocker is what gave those boots to you. Dropped them in last night sometime. Most likely two of them. Anyhow kid, the Tommyknockers are little, really small guys that can't never be seen. They live in the mines and raise all kinds of hell if that happens to be their notion. Tools disappear; stuff gets moved around and can't be found where it was left. Then it turns up someplace else, usually a bad someplace. If you listen you can hear them tapping at the rock with their little hammers. If they start tapping real loud and there are more than one at it you better watch out. There is goin' to be some kind of accident on its way, maybe a cave-in or another thing or two that ain't good. Every once in a while they pull off a good thing like them boots you've got on. That is rare. Must like you kid."

What a story. Only Swinger could come up with a bullshit yarn like that. Then he went on some more about the Tommyknocker business just to back up the tale even better.

"Now there are going to be a lot of people that will say there ain't no such a thing as a Tommyknocker. If somebody tries to tell a Cousin Jack* that it is all horseshit, there most likely will be a problem. There is one hell of a lot of old miners in this country that know damn well these little folk are real. The Tommyknockers came over to this country from Cornwall with the Cousin Jacks, who by the way, taught the boys in this country how to mine deep and do it right. Cornwall had the best miners in the world years before mining started in this country on any big scale."

With that last, I decided that I had heard some interesting things and needed time to try to put it all together. Tommyknockers were one thing, but the boot business was another. He was reluctant to tell me how it came about, but finally he did.

This is how I ended up with that pair of boots. I tried to figure out how Swinger had known what size boot I wore and drew a blank first thing off. After working with that question for a short time, I finally got it. I remembered the first day I had brought those fishing boots in the building, and Swinger had picked one up and looked it all over. It would seem that he had the idea he was going to buy

* The nickname bestowed on the immigrant Cornish miner. Cousin Jenny designated the immigrant women from Cornwall. It is usually considered a compliment, not a slight.

me a pair of real miner's boots when he seen how serious I would be about working in that mine.

Slick had come up the Saturday before the week I got the diggers and the boots. He wanted to talk about how things were shaping up in the mine, and Swinger laid it all out for him, the works, hung chute, and all. Swinger told him he was headed down the canyon to Midvale to bullshit with the Tame Ape. The Tame Ape was, in reality, Mickey Ross who owned a mining equipment business that carried about everything needed on a mine project. If he didn't have something he could get it. Slick knew him by both names and referred to him as the Tame Ape most of the time. With nothing else pressing them, they both headed for the Tame Ape's establishment.

The usual banter back and forth surely took place, and at some point Swinger announced he needed a pair of boots. That created a question from Slick who wanted to know what was wrong with the boots he already had. Swinger apparently told him they were not for him, as he was going to buy the boots for me. The Tame Ape decided he needed to know the story of why Swinger would do such a thing. I suppose he must have told the Tame Ape the story about some "Boo-Coo" kid who was nuts enough to work in the hole for no pay just to learn something about the game. Slick thought that was a grand idea and announced he would go for half the cost. It seems that the Tame Ape thought that business with the Boo-Coo kid was more than interesting and announced that the bill was going three ways, and they each would chip in one-third of the total.

When we finally went into the hole, it amounted to mostly cleanup work that filled two cars that we dumped when we came out. We accomplished the work on a steady but not rushed basis, and I suppose that fit the classification of a leisurely day's operation. That was a good thing for me, as I still had an evening shift ahead in that damned Phillips 66 station. I got down the hill and to work actually a little early, which looked good for once to the manager of that location.

11

Copenhagen and Derailments

ONE DAY, ABOUT midafternoon, Swinger had me on the operating end of a drill that employed an auger bit. We were working in crushed but tightly packed ground in a fissure. It was in the mineralized area to the side of the mostly caved Olympic Stope, 75 feet above the tunnel level. I was just a beginner at this to start with and at the time was not in any way proficient in the use of this machine. We both had cotton stuffed in our ears to dampen the noise the drill created. Because of the hearing restriction, it was necessary to use hand signals and the occasional rap on my hard-boiled hat to get my attention.

On this particular afternoon, there occurred no hand signal and no rap on my hat; Swinger just simply closed the valve that cut off the air supply to the drill. *Now what?* I thought. *What the hell did I do that caused that?* But that was not the case at all. I pulled the cotton out of my ears, and he did likewise and announced, "Shift's done, kid, she is deep enough for today and we are going to shut her down."

That made no sense at all to me because it was just midafternoon. The explanation came before I could ever start the question. "We are out of Cope kid, and that means we are headed out for the day."

Apparently, Swinger had used up the last of his Copenhagen through some miscalculation on his part. Not that it mattered; it simply ended the shift in his eyes, and that was it for the day. She was deep enough.

Copenhagen snuff was the most common form of smokeless tobacco favored in the mining community. Most of the miners I knew in the Cottonwoods and elsewhere were users of the product.

It follows, of course, that I figured it was past time to try it and see for myself what the great attraction was. I decided that if I got into that stuff, I would fit in better with the rest of the stiffs.

The time came late one afternoon a week after the early shutdown. We were ready to head out into the sunshine with a four-car muck train. This amounted to one car more than usual, as we had loaded a lot of waste rock into the chute. I asked Swinger if I could borrow a pinch just for the hell of it, and he fished the can out of his shirt pocket.

"Are you sure about this kid?"

I told him I was good and dipped out a moderate pinch from the open container and tucked it in my lower lip. No trick to that, as I had watched Swinger do it countless times.

"What now?" I asked.

"It will take care of itself so just play with it but not too hard."

What he meant by that, I had no idea but thought, *Well, it's in so I will see what happens now, I guess.*

At that point, Swinger decided to issue a warning: "Now whatever the hell you do, make sure you don't swallow any of the stuff and in particular the whole damn plug. I can tell you that won't work out well."

I ended up doing exactly that.

When we moved a loaded train out, I always walked behind it, never walking alongside any cars. I was kind of like a caboose, keeping watch on the train ahead for anything that did not look right. I really had no idea of what I was supposed to do with that loaded lip, and it did not taste too good either. It was just a short time before the first step in the disaster to come was set up. A few feet ahead of me, right in the middle of the first turn, the train stopped. Swinger could feel it when the car derailed because the pull on the train changed. The second car behind the trammer had run off the rails. We got lucky on that one because, for some reason, only the two leading wheels were off the rails. A very unusual occurrence, Swinger had said later.

The runoff would not be too much trouble to get back on the tracks. Some wedges under the wheels would bring them back up to track level as Swinger eased the train slowly forward. The big scaling bar,* used as a lever and anchored on the inside of the rail as the wheels came up, would shift the car back into alignment with the rails. The car went back on with a hard push on the bar, which was good.

Something else occurred that was not so good. The effort on the bar and forgetting the Cope loaded in my lower lip somehow put most of the plug, one might say, down the hatch. That "spit" (lit) the fuse, and how long that fuse would burn was the question here. I spit the little remaining in my mouth into the ditch and thought, *Shit!*

Swinger had missed all the blue-faced choking and gagging that had occurred behind him and slowly moved the train ahead. When we got on the next turn, the train did fine but the individual walking behind knew he was in big trouble. An ominous bubbling and churning was going on in my lower regions, and I was getting cold flashes. When we got through the last turn that put us on the main Columbus-Rexall Tunnel, Swinger stopped the train. He probably could not believe something had not jumped the tracks, and it was time to check everything. He was about to witness another kind of episode that would find its way into a number of bullshit sessions over the years.

Employing the miner's jargon for what came next would describe what happened very well. That the fuse spit at the derail site hit the primer, and the primer shot the powder, well describes what came next. I was gripping the rim of one of the cars when everything came up, one heave after another into the ditch. This was definitely the measuring stick for sick! Swinger came walking back to where the excitement was going on.

"What in the hell?" he started.

* A bar, usually varying in length from four feet to eight feet. These bars have a chisel point at one end and a straight point of various designs at the opposite end. The primary use of this tool is to remove loose rock from the back and ribs after blasting, but it can also serve as a pry bar or lever. The scaling bar is a most versatile tool.

"Swallowed some of the goddamned Cope," I managed to croak out.

He gave a low whistle, kind of grinned, and walked back up to the trammer, nodding his head a couple of times. He had figured on it.

When we had everything outside and shuffled around, I got through helping dump the cars but that was it. Unusual as it would be, I did not feel like sticking around for some good coffee, and it was without a doubt deep enough for that day. Swinger put it all together with no problem and made an announcement having to do with the incident saying, "Christ kid, I think that you had better just keep on being a loose lip [someone who doesn't use dip] here on out. You don't look none too healthy."

It was an epic understatement and one hell of a piece of good advice, and I stayed with it throughout the years. That ended the Copenhagen adventure for the first and last time. I have never had any inclination to play with it again.

12

The Baptism

ONE MORNING, WE headed into the hole with the train to bring out what should amount to three carloads. The day before, we had drilled out a round and shot it (set and detonated a dynamite charge) at the end of the day, so this day, we would go muck it out and dump it. It was only a short way to the collar* of the chute, so we loaded the muck into a wheelbarrow to get it there. I called that piece of equipment a wheelbarrow just one time before Swinger straightened me out as to what it really was. He called the thing an "Irish buggy."† It was hard work, but that was how a "poor boy operation," as Swinger called it, had to work when money was thin. We cleaned up the muck pile and, after uncounted trips with the Irish buggy, had it all down the chute.

The contents of the chute filled two cars to capacity and the third about three-fourths. The whole operation was unfolding well, and we figured that we would be outside with time to spare. It would seem that the Tommyknockers had a different idea.

We passed through the first stretch without any problem. That felt good because many times we had to put cars back on the rails in that stretch. From there, the 100 feet of timbered and tightly lagged drift run to the Columbus-Rexall main tunnel, and that's where the Tommyknockers were.

Had this not been, as Swinger called it, a poor boy operation,

* The point at which a shaft intersects the surface or where a raise intersects an upper level.

† The Cornish miner supposedly is responsible for giving this name to the wheelbarrow. They did this simply to aggravate "they bleddy paddy," or Irishman. It became a well-used designation throughout the mining industry.

this section, known as the run of the floating track, would have ended up with all the rails being replaced along with most of the ties. As it was, it was a cobbled-together nightmare. Because the ties were half rotten and water saturated the spikes, the section had a habit of allowing the rails to move outward. The wheel flanges of the trammer and the cars were on the inside of the wheels, which allowed the track to move outward rather than inward.

That is what happened. The train come to a halt, and I heard Swinger loudly utter, "You rotten dirty whore!"

Instead of a car this time, the trammer had fallen victim to the displacement of a rail. Somehow, and it was a small bit of luck, the wheels on the left side of the trammer stayed on the rail, and we managed to get the disaster fixed with a jack. That took care of the trammer problem, but that did not end the difficulties. The second car back had come off the rails also, so out came the wedges and the scaling bar. The bar was about seven feet in length, with a tapered dull point on one end and a curved chisel on the other. These things were heavy and made a good stout lever.

We put the wedges in place where they needed to be on both sides of the car. The wheels on the right side of the car had to come up high enough so the flange would clear the rail. The left side would not be as big a problem because the flanges were on the inside of the wheels.

Given the situation, Swinger very slowly would ease the train forward and pull the wheels up the ramps of wedges. My job was to take the bar and put the curved end inside of the rail and against the car's bed. It took a lot of force against the bar to move that heavy car off the wedges to line up with the rails. That was how it was supposed to work, and it did, but not without cost, and I paid that bill.

Because of the height of the bed's bottom off the rails, the leverage was not ideal. The smart thing for me to have done was, when the wheel came up to the proper elevation, have Swinger stop pulling, grab the other scaling bar we had, and have both of us lever that car where it needed to go. Unfortunately, smart I am not at times. I was right next to the ditch and standing on that red mud that covered everything in the bottom of that tunnel. That mud was as efficient as any grease ever produced and was a good part of what occurred next. The train inched forward, and I put everything I had against that bar, all seven feet of it, with both hands near the top end. I have no idea what happened next, the only clear thing was the fact that with that push on the bar, my feet went out from under me. The bar seemed to work against me, put me into a half twist, and dumped me into the ditch with an explosion of water and gob.

That water was so cold, it should have been stiff, as Swinger had once said. I shot up out of that ditch like a ricocheting bullet off a steel plate. That dunking had taken my breath away, and my hat and light had disappeared. Then my breath came back.

"GODDAMN SONOFABITCH, SHIT, JESUS H. CHRIST!" I bellowed. "I'll be a sad bastard, GODDAMN!"

That bit of noise had Swinger down off the trammer and headed my direction as quick as he could move. I got most of what he was saying except for the first word or so and it went something like this.

"—Christ and little Rizzi chum! Are you still in one hunk or what?"

I was standing up in the ditch, so I guessed most things were still intact, but the next thing out of my mouth was "I lost my goddamn lid, got no light. I don't know where the hell they got off to."

"The lid is all hung up on your legs kid, but I think the light kinda got drowned a little. I'll grab the works out before it gets on its way to sunshine. Now don't waltz out of there just yet."

The light got drowned! *Now how the hell could that be?* I wondered but did not say. My gloves were full of water, and my diggers had plenty inside too. There I stood in the ditch taking inventory of what damage might be present in my water-soaked carcass. Nothing seemed out of order, so I climbed out of the ditch and then discovered my head hurt a little. I must have hit a post on my way into the water, my hat taking the blow and, in the process, getting knocked off my head. Swinger got started again.

"Well, your lid's full of water and a good load of gob. I will have your light burning in a couple of minutes. For some reason it was still on your hat and why I don't know."

I still had my hat and light, so that was good. Swinger got the lamp burning, set it on the muck in the front car, and said, "You ought to douche the gob out of your lid, and while you're at it, you might want to dump a hatful over your gourd because you're all mudded up. Hell, you are painted up like a war whoop"—one of Swinger's names for an Indian—"but then again that water is running red so maybe not. Goddamn kid, that was a pippin. John the Baptist ain't got nothin' on you when it comes to dippin.'"

I was fairly well squared away, my hat back on with the lamp in place and the flame strong, and I was not feeling too bad considering I was wet and cold. I leaned on one of the cars for a minute or two, wondering how it had all come about.

"Well, I'll be damned!" Swinger said. "Sonofabitch! The car is back on, kid. That has to be something. At least that went all right for some reason."

Sure enough, it was. How, I could not imagine, because I thought I had lost the force on the bar when I made the dive into that damned ditch. However, why question it? We headed on out to the sunshine, with me following the last car like a damn caboose. What an experience! Then a thought crept in as to how lucky I had been that when I made that dive into the ditch there had been no sprag* in that area. If I had fallen across one of those things, I most likely would not be walking out of that hole. Then another idea crept in after the sprag deal. I got to thinking that I was not too sure that the Tommyknocker business was all bullshit. And if they were real, they'd called it deep enough for that day and finally left us alone.

* A miner's name for a horizontal brace, usually running from the post of a timber set to stabilize or render immovable various objects such as floating rails. Like other terms in the miner's vocabulary, sprag can cover nonrelated items. Such an example would be in order to keep a loaded car from overrunning the mule on a downgrade, the skinner (mule driver) would sprag the last pair of wheels on the last car (see photo insert).

13

Things Change

I ARRIVED EARLY at the mine one morning and pulled in alongside Swinger's truck. Two others arrived right behind me, one occupied by Slick Hansen driving his usual Chevrolet flatbed. The other truck, a pickup containing two men, pulled up close behind Hansen. I thought to myself, *Now what the hell do we have here?* We all got out of our junk, all three of our rigs easily qualifying to meet that designation. Of course, my cobbled-together old General Mess of Crap made the others look a little better. Everybody headed for Swinger's little palace.

Five of us in that place made for a crowd, and we came up short one chair. Swinger did not make it a habit of being the entertainer for anything over three visitors. Coffee cups would come up short also, but fortunately one of the two unknown to me had a thermos with him, and that cured that problem. Slick made the introductions mostly for my benefit, as Swinger already knew both of them. One of them had a last name of Smith, and the other I did not quite get. Swinger, never one for true names, straightened that out immediately, and I came to know Tokyo Joe and Alimony Bill. That stuck; it was all I needed to know.

Tokyo Joe and Alimony Bill had been working part time for Slick in a mine located in a side canyon of Butterfield Canyon in the Bingham mining district. Slick had done fairly well with that lease, but it was nearing its end. Slick intended to put his efforts into the Columbus-Rexall lease, and he said that Tokyo and Alimony were going to work on that project a couple of days a week along with Swinger while the mine out west shut down. That put all five of us in the hole that morning. It was obvious to me that I would just be in the way, as they all knew the business, and I was just a working observer. That is when I decided it was time for something else. It was time to look around a little more in that vast underground kingdom, places that I had never been.

I got Swinger off to the side and told him that I was going to do some looking around in other parts of the hole. He knew what the deal was and told me to do what I thought best but it would be a good idea if I came around the shack about noontime, so he knew I was all right. To that, I immediately agreed, and that was what I did. I went on back where the compressor was located and looked around that area and soon found myself in completely unfamiliar territory. I did not venture too far, as all I had was my carbide lamp for light. If I were going to play this kind of game, I knew from former experience that I needed three sources of lighting available. That would include my usual carbide lamp, extra carbide, a good flashlight, and at least two candles along with waterproof matches. The candles would have a dual purpose, the more important being checking for bad air and the other as a light source.

I had all I needed in the junk box of the old GMC, but after the noontime meeting, I felt somewhat left out. I went back in with the guys after the noon break as far as the raise but did not go up to the workings above with them. I got Swinger aside and told him I thought I would head on out to sunshine, look around the buildings out there, and then head down the hill. Swinger knew that this was not going to work out much longer, as there would not be a lot for me to do in the hole. Things were changing and I knew it. Had I been a miner on Slick's payroll as an official employee, I would have had a place there. The thing that I still had, however, was unfettered access to the mine where Slick had the lease and anywhere else I decided I wanted to go. That was worth a lot.

I went back up to the mine the next day with no intention of spending any time with Swinger, Slick, and the two others. I had some coffee in a thermos and a sandwich with me in my old lunch bucket that would stay in the General Mess of Crap. When I decided I was hungry, I would come out after it. What I had laid out to occupy my time that day involved the Howland Tunnel. When I got out of the old General Mess of Crap, I got my bag of necessary gear out of the junk box and brought it with me. The junk bag was simply a stout canvass-fishing creel with a shoulder strap. Contained in the bag were a flashlight, candles, pocket carbide cans with carbide, and spare batteries for the flashlight. We all met where the trammer was hooked to the charger, made a little small talk about nothing of importance, and they got all set to head into the hole and I figured I would follow them in. Swinger was the motorman as usual, and the other three walked behind the train.

During the time spent thus far at the Columbus-Rexall, I had heard references from both Slick and Swinger about a place in that old mine identified as the Sulfide Stope. The Sulfide Stope is for good reason more often referred to as the Jewel Stope. The Jacobson family controlled Mineral Veins Coalition, and it was a Jacobson that granted the lease to Slick, and it was years later that I found out which Jacobson did that. The Jacobson family had been in that district since the late 1860s, knew all the stories, and had lived most of them. To see the Jewel Stope, I decided, was something I absolutely had to do.

Prior to the time I became involved in the old Columbus-Rexall—actually while still incarcerated in that damned high school—I had heard about a publication by the United States Geological Survey. The title of the publication, Professional Paper 201, is *Geology, and Ore Deposits of the Cottonwood-American Fork Mining Area, Utah*. It has an abbreviated section concerning the history of the district but more valuable to me, it contained maps of many of the district mines' underground workings. It was not up to date on work after about 1940, but it is of immense value to individuals like myself and included maps of the Columbus-Consolidated, the Columbus-Rexall, and the Cardiff. The location of the Sulfide/Jewel Stope appears clearly on the maps.

On that morning, I followed the four into the hole until they turned off the Howland and into the Columbus-Rexall. I kept walking straight ahead along the Howland's run as I had planned. This would be all new territory to me, and I was looking forward to the exploration. At that time, I knew who Frank Reedy was, and we had exchanged hellos but never talked other than that. That week, on the first day of the two I was to put in underground, I made two new acquaintances. At the Howland Tunnel's 350-foot mark, where the Columbus-Rexall starts its run, another 175 feet along the Howland itself, there's a crosscut* that goes left. There I found two husky-looking men hard at work. With shovels in hand, they were busy loading muck into a single car. It appeared to be a cleanup job like Swinger and I had been doing when I first came on the job. One look at those two and their outfits left no doubt they were very much at home in that mine. Those two, I would soon find out, were experienced hardrock miners, the real thing.

The two were brothers, Mack and Mark Jacobson, and they did not say much more about themselves as to their history. Later, somewhere in the neighborhood of two months, I would be introduced to their older brother Dan, and he would tell me as to Mack and Mark that they had spent almost all their lives as miners, starting when they were old enough to hold a shovel, as had he. Mack and Mark were curious as to what brought me into the mine and why. I told them what I had been involved in with Hansen and what I was doing now. During the short conversation, Mack said that if I was going to play explorer and wanted to take the chances involved, there was a place I needed to see. Here once again, the Jewel Stope came up. Both brothers had been there countless times and pulled a little decent ore off the stope fringes. *They* had firsthand knowledge, Slick and Swinger only had the story.

The immediate area the brothers were clearing out was across from the crosscut that headed left coming in. I made inquiries concerning it and Mack told me that it connected with the Columbus-Rexall Tunnel in a short distance. There were several side drifts off it that all came together before it got back to the Columbus-Rexall. He mentioned that I needed to look out for a shaft that was

* A level tunnel/drift driven across a mineral vein.

just off the main run but on the right side. He said it went down to the 400 level of the Columbus-Consolidated workings. I noticed that when either brother referred to the two mines, they called them the Col-Rex and the Col-Con. I immediately adopted those shortened names and have used them ever since, so they will appear from here on in this story as such. I made the short walk from the Howland to the Col-Rex and back again to the Howland.

I got a look at that vertical shaft, and it made the hair on the back of my neck stand up. It was open to a degree—well, sort of. Looking down that hole as far as my three-cell flashlight would penetrate revealed a jumbled mass of displaced timber and lagging. There was muck hanging on to some of the timber, those without angle enough to shed the rock. Had the shaft been clear enough, its bottom would have been beyond the reach of the flashlight's beam. The thought of falling into and down that shaft was unnerving to contemplate, and I closely watched my footing at the collar. I returned to the Howland and, waving at the Jacobson brothers, set off following the straight run of the tunnel.

14

Howland Connections

I FOLLOWED THE Howland's straight run for a good distance, then it curved gently to the right and soon arrived at an intersection. A crosscut run to the left with the Howland continuing straight ahead. I decided to have a look into the crosscut and follow it out to wherever it might lead. The workings of the Howland, so far, were wet but did not have a ditch with running water. That was in stark contrast with the Col-Rex and the heavy flow its ditch carried. That fact was definitely not a disappointment to me. The water dripping down out of the back* was minimal, but the rubber work gear and boots kept me warm and comfortable. I very much appreciated those Goodall boots and the stolen diggers I was wearing.

I had not progressed very far along the crosscut when I came to a place where another drift came in from the left. Another decision to make, so I did, and remained on the straight-ahead course I had been following. It did not stay straight for long before it started wandering around through constantly changing colors in the rock and geologic structure. I had no idea at that time what I was looking at. I would later consult my map of the area to find out what I had seen. I did not attempt to pace off and record the distance I was traveling. The U.S. Geological Survey (USGS) map of the mine would have that information readily available.

I followed the drift with all its turns until I arrived at a cave-in

* The top or roof on the inside of a tunnel mine. In the earliest days of mining in England, the miners considered the mines to be snakes due to the way they wove through the earth. Back, like rib and belly (the floor of a mine tunnel), referred to the part of the snake. Eventually, these terms found their way to the United States via Cousin Jacks.

that would not allow passage beyond that point. I had encountered no raises in that stretch or any prospect holes off either side of the tunnel. At the cave-in, I turned back and decided to have a look into the drift that had opened to my left a short distance after I left the Howland. Everything I had passed through still had rails in place—and better ones, by far—than what was in the Col-Rex section. When I turned into the drift I wanted to follow, the rails were in good condition also. So far, I had not encountered any of the heavy sulfide concentrations that existed in the Col-Rex. This, of course, had direct bearing on the condition of the rails in the area I was in now. That was about to change. I soon entered into a zone that required occasional timber sets and, in some parts, lagging in the back and at the ribs. Here I began encountering sulfides (mostly iron, the good old "fool's gold"), but not in the quantities that existed in the Col-Rex. Soon I started coming across areas where loose muck buried the tracks having come from the back and ribs. This created dams, backing up water but none of it more than a foot in depth and easily passed through. Everything was wet, but it was just from drips off the back and nothing more than that. I had no idea how far I had come along that drift, but in time I came to another junction that looked familiar. A drift was coming in from the right that had a ditch, and it carried a heavy flow of water. For the time being, I bypassed that and proceeded ahead. It was a short distance traveled when I found out why things had looked vaguely familiar. I came to a halt looking at the reason, which was that notoriously unreliable compressor. I was only feet away from the Col-Rex Tunnel that led, eventually, to the raise going up into the Olympic Stope area. I was standing on the main tunnel run and had just passed where it turned and headed for the Jewel Stope location and the Cardiff workings beyond. I decided that I was not interested in going on out to sunshine following the Col-Rex Tunnel and decided to backtrack to the Howland. The crosscut that connected the Howland and the Col-Rex had followed the Brain Fissure and which way it was driven I had no idea. At that stage of my journey, I did not know I was on the Brain Fissure; that information came from my map, later consulted. The timbered and lagged sections of that crosscut, along with the sulfides showing up, should have made me suspect this. I was, at that time, far too inexperienced to make connections along those lines.

Arriving back at the Howland, I decided to follow its course rather than turn right and head out of the mine. In a short distance, I found a drift taking off to my right and followed it until I came to the old working face. There was not much to see along the drift's run, so I headed on.

Immediately I found myself in another stope, so it became very apparent that they had opened up considerable ore in these areas. There were more prospect drifts off the stope that showed tight mineralized fissures but had not opened up into minable quantities of ore. Much work for nothing. I headed back to where the main run of the Howland Tunnel had entered the stope. It was immediately apparent that the tunnel extended beyond the stope. That interested me, but what was more interesting was another section of tunnel going right. This section widened in width to about three times the breadth of the normal drift and had two sets of rails disappearing into the darkness ahead.

I figured there had to be something worth seeing back in that darkness, and it turned out there was. I had seen nothing like it in the Col-Rex. I also had no idea at that time that shortly before I walked into that first stope, I had passed into the Columbus-Consolidated Mine (Col-Con). I soon arrived at the collar of a three-compartment inclined shaft. It appeared to go down on about a 45-degree angle. The beam of my good old three-cell flashlight showed me nothing but blackness. This incline had to go deep, and my urge to try to go down into its depths was very strong. I did not do it that day or soon thereafter. That extremely foolish act was yet over a year ahead of me.

Using the flashlight, I probed the incline rib to rib and as far down as it could penetrate the darkness. There was no timbering of any consequence other than a few stulls here and there. There were indications that at one time a double set of tracks had existed going down into the depths. To the right of where they had been, a ladder that followed the angle of the incline down appeared to be intact. There was a heavy electrical cable going down, tied tightly to the ribs against the back. Alongside the ladder against the ribs were pipes that appeared to be three-inch in diameter and, along with them, a pipe that had to be over four inches in diameter. They lay side by side and disappeared into the blackness like everything in that incline. I just had to go down that shaft and see where it ended up. However, as said previously, not that day. One thing that all these items running down that incline had in common was a coating of that damned red-orange mud. It covered everything along with the bottom of the incline shaft. I spent a little more time pondering some of these things, then headed for the main run of the Howland Tunnel. I found out later that the Howland had been the main working tunnel for the Col-Con during its productive period.

But it was time to head out for sunshine; I was running low on my supply of carbide, not to mention energy. I told the Jacobson brothers, when I passed them, I was headed outside; they said they would be right behind me. *What the hell*, I thought, *are those two quitting early?* That was not the case at all. When I got out, I looked at my watch for the first time. It was 3:30 in the afternoon. Where the hell had the time slipped off? Once again, I found myself thinking time has no meaning in the underground world. My thermos of coffee was only lukewarm but tasted so good, and I devoured my sorry little sandwich. I finished it off just as Swinger, Slick, Tokyo, and Alimony emerged from the mine.

They came out with four loaded cars that afternoon, loaded to the rims. This time, those cars did not go outside for dumping. The four cars were loaded with ore that went straight to the ore bin for unloading. I soon found out from Swinger that these cars were not the first ones to go into the bin. To me that sounded encouraging, and I hoped that the work was starting to produce something besides waste rock. Swinger said to me, out of hearing range of the other three, that he thought the ore was of marginal shipping grade, just a little better than muck. It would still be some time before there was enough in the bins to ship to the smelter. It would go to Midvale,

Utah, to the smelter operated by United States Smelting, Refining, and Mining Company.

I stayed around until the cars were unloaded and everything switched around behind the trammer for the next morning. When they decided to head into the shack, I said my goodbyes and pointed the rattling old General Mess of Crap down the canyon. The old wreck had not quit up to this point, but I wondered how long that old truck would keep going before it called it deep enough.

15
Going Deeper

IT WAS NOW near the end of November 1957, and so far, I'd had to chain up the old truck twice. If my tires had any decent tread on them, I probably could have made it up the canyon without chains on those two occasions. Swinger remarked, at one time, that the tires on the old GMC were nothing but regrooved inner tubes. I could not afford decent tires, and the only reason I had a set of chains was the fact I had talked my dad out of them. The chains fell into the classification of "well experienced," yet they were to last as long as the old GMC owned me.

The journey to the Jewel Stope was still at the top of my "have-to-do" list and something I needed to do. The week following my explorations in parts of the Howland/Col-Con and a small part of the Col-Rex, the time had arrived to, once more, attempt that journey. I had two days off in the middle of the week, and my wife was working both of those days, so I headed to Alta to try to get to the Jewel Stope. The location of that obsession was just over a mile into the mountain from the Howland portal, and I had no idea of what I might encounter.

The Jacobson brothers had given me just the barest of information during our first conversation about the Jewel Stope, but one of them made a remark that might have been a warning when he mentioned something along the line of my being willing to take chances. I thought little of that at the time but had good reason later to recall what he had said. That came months later, when I became acquainted with their older brother Dan. He told me in detail where I had passed through in my attempts to reach the Jewel Stope.

When I described what I encountered in the long stretch of heavily timbered and lagged tunnel and other dangerous places in the area, he apparently knew exactly where I had been. I told him I had named the area Spook Alley for lack of a better one. He told me I had been in the section of the mine known as Death Valley, a name acquired during the original driving of the tunnel by the Columbus-Extension Company. The length of it was well over 1,000 feet, and it earned the name through many casualties, claiming its last victim in 1952. Five years after that event, I walked into Death Valley for my first time.

I arrived at the mine just before Slick, Tokyo, and Alimony showed up and told Swinger what I was going to attempt. Swinger had the coffee on and we had put away about half a cup each when the boys came through the door. The usual small talk took place, I finished my coffee and headed out to the old GMC to get my gear together, and Swinger followed me out. While I pulled on my boots and got suited up in my rubberized tuxedo, Swinger delivered himself of a lecture. That short lecture included his opinion that it was the worst kind of an idea to make that trip by myself. He had no illusions about my not doing it, though, and told me to remember the things he had taught me and be damn careful.

I had all I needed, probably more, stuffed in pockets, some of it in a shoulder bag that was nothing more than just a canvas fish creel that worked just fine. The sack was waterproof, a definite advantage in itself. Inside it was my three-cell flashlight, extra batteries, extra bulb, waterproof matches, and two new miners' candles. In my back pants pockets, protected by my rubber overalls, were two cans of carbide. The two metal Justrite pocket cans were sealed tight and waterproof unless underwater for some time. If that occurred, it would be a sure sign that I would not be leaving that old mine. The carbide contained in the two cans would refill my lamp six times, easily, and the lamp was already loaded with carbide. I filled the lamp with water, struck the flame, and headed into the mine well ahead of the four men. I figured three of them were still working on drying out Swinger's pot of coffee.

I went on back to the compressor location and turned right instead of the familiar straight-ahead route. I very soon arrived at a junction where the Col-Rex main turned left and entered unfamiliar territory that would, I hoped, eventually take me to the Jewel Stope. The venture soon became a stress-filled journey involving a fool's good luck or something within that category. Here in the Col-Rex, I was back in lots of red-orange mud; it was everywhere along the tracks and the bottom. There was plenty of water, and not just confined to the ditch due to countless piles of muck creating dams across the bottom. I had to appreciate the Goodall boots that the Tommyknockers had provided and the rubber overalls and coat that the Bull had so kindly and unwittingly donated to the cause.

Water dripped constantly off the back, and in some places, small rivulets seeped out of fissures in the ribs. There was not a dry spot in that hole, and as I went farther, it did not get any dryer; if anything it got wetter. Three hundred feet along after that right turn, I came to a drift to the left and thought I better check it out. The time spent doing that had shown me nothing of interest. I suppose the boys were simply running a prospect drift on something I could not see. There had to be something though, as no miner would open up a drift like that just to have fun.

Another 500 feet past that drift, still heading generally north, another drift came in on the left. A few feet into this one, my progress came to a halt. This drift proved as interesting as the prior one was not. There was a wall just over waist height constructed of rock from the area, well mortared and watertight. Backed up, as far as my three-cell flashlight would carry, was water, almost reaching the top of the dam.

There were two three-inch pipes coming through the dam's wall about a foot above the base and tightly capped. I suspected it was a culinary water source from when the mine had employed and housed many miners in the early days. An item caught my eye also; it was hanging from a spike driven into a tight fissure. It was an old-fashioned enameled cup with a few rust spots where the enamel had chipped away. I took it off the spike and turned it over several times, then dipped it into the water filling it.

I drained the cup dry. The water was cold and tasted good, so good I drank another full cup of it before hanging the cup back on its spike. That would not be the last time, as over the years, those cups of water became a ritual. During those later explorations, sometimes alone and later, in the early 1960s, with another man, one who had no problems with danger and hard, slow going. We both drank a couple of cups going in for luck and a couple more to celebrate on the way out, because each time, somehow, we had come through unscathed. Had to be luck.

16

Death Valley

STARTING DOWN THE main run, I came into a section of tunnel that was extensively timbered and tightly lagged. But the lagging was buckling down from the back and inward from the ribs. In places it had opened up, allowing muck to come into the tunnel, backing up water. I climbed over one dam and found myself nearly to the top of my boots in that cold water and facing a pile of broken timber, lagging, and rocks that completely blocked the tunnel. The water, as it usually does with a cave-in like that, had found its way through, but nothing else, including myself, was going to get past that plug.

Stopped by that massive cave-in, I turned back to where a drift had come in from my right and decided to look into that area. It was slow going because the scum on top of that still water would not allow me to see the drift's bottom clearly. There were drifts branching off the run I was on, and I spent the time to check them up to their old working faces. That took more time than I expected, but I wanted to make a thorough inspection as I went along. When I got back on the main run, I followed another short drift to the right that ended at a water-filled winze,* so I came back and turned right through another area tightly lagged and heavily timbered. I was back on the main run of the Col-Rex, and the water steadily deepened until it was almost to the top of my boots and I gave up on that idea.

* A shaft put down on an angle that starts underground. It is used to follow a lead to see if it will open up into a minable ore deposit. In many cases, it will be used to intersect another level of the mine or in some cases, by mutual agreement, another mine's workings.

Taking my flashlight out of the bag, I directed the beam ahead of where I was standing. Sure enough, there was a cave-in ahead of me, the tunnel plugged tight. I had made so many twists and turns in various short tunnels, I was not certain where I was. Retracing the steps in my mind, I figured it out. I was on the backside of the cave-in I had run into coming in. One could sure as hell get lost in these labyrinths with little problem.

I turned back and found myself again in the location of the notorious old air compressor, carrying, in one hand, a lighted candle. This began to amount to an irksome aggravation because of having to deal with hot melting candle wax. It had covered my fingers and glued a couple of them together. It was warm, approaching hot, but tolerable. It was a necessary thing, as I had no idea of the quality of the air as I went deeper into that mountain. I put up with that to be as safe as I could be, which was laughable considering everything else involved. There was, of course, nothing safe about anything inside this mountain.

Coming out of the last explored drift, once again, I headed what I now supposed to be north, and I quickly found myself entering another run of heavily timbered and lagged tunnel, its condition just as bad as the prior one.

Getting through this, I found myself in another stretch of tunnel without any timber whatsoever. Then it was back into another run of timbered ground, more Spook Alley stuff for sure. This was getting more stressful all the time. Then into another short timberless run. There were raises going upward on both sides of the stretch, just a few feet apart from each other. This had been a serious undertaking, as both had descending chutes and ladders alongside them. The ladders looked solid and substantial but wet and slippery. Then I got into the bad stuff, and Spook Alley did not come close to describing the mess. Being young and stupid was a large factor in what happened along with the fact that there was no more room in hell that day for another damn fool.

There was no lack of that red-orange mud everywhere, and it left a scum floating on that still water, making it nearly opaque and rendering the drift bottom invisible. Immediately upon entering that drift, I noticed a wooden shaft propped against the rib. When I picked it up, I was holding in my hand a common wooden-handled hoe. I decided to use the hoe handle as a probe to check the hidden bottom of the drift, a condition I did not care for at all. The Tommyknockers were really starting to raise hell. I tried to stay on the railheads* to keep the water below the tops of my boots. It was slow going, and soon I came to a branch going off to my right and the water was at the top of my boots.

I had focused all my attention on the probing and the water problem and not enough elsewhere. I felt an icy-cold uneasiness settling over me as I looked around. The back and ribs were crumbling, and there was no timber in the area, and that should not have been. There was a cave-in ahead of me, and I thought, *What the hell is wrong here?* There was no voice, at least there could not have been, but what came through in my head was just as plain as the spoken word. It was my friend Swinger: "It's the goddamn ground kid! She is goin' to come in! Get the hell out from under it."

That I did, as fast as I could. I started back to the drift I had turned off, and another chill set upon me. Now what? I was still trying to stay on the railheads and using the hoe handle with my right, and as I turned slightly to my left, the probe descended into nothing just off my right side.

That woke me up even more, stopping me dead in my tracks, and I looked up and to my right. There it was. I needed no ghostly word spoken into my mind; I knew instinctively what the probe had found hidden by the scum on top of the water. The stout ring anchored to the right wall by a rod of iron driven into it told the tale: there must be a shaft directly below it. How deep? There was no telling, but it could have been deep enough to do the trick. That was still not to be the end of it. I started back toward the main tunnel, still spooked and probing ahead with my hoe handle. Nearing the

* The part of a rail that the wheels of the cars run on. The T rail consists of the base, the web, and the head.

main tunnel that was in view ahead of me, I saw to my right, on the back close to a timber rib, was another anchor and ring. Sure enough, just below it, the good old handle of that hoe once again found no bottom. The scum floating on the water had effectively hidden that trap also.

By this time, when I came into the main tunnel with its timberwork, the whole layout looked like something that I could not deal with anymore. I was tired, stressed badly with what had occurred. My candle was still burning, the second one of the day—that made for one good thing anyhow. I had used up one spare can of carbide by this time, and my lamp had a very weak flame. The time had arrived to charge the lamp again with fresh carbide and fill it with water from one of the drips off the back. It was time to call it deep enough for that adventure. I felt so used up that sitting down, even in that cold water, sounded like a good idea, which it was not.

The recharged lamp burned with a flame strong and bright—it was much stronger and brighter than I was by this time. I directed the flashlight's beam down the run of the tunnel, which I had not yet passed through. It was more of the same as far as the beam would carry, heavily timbered and tightly lagged. The question I was asking myself while looking at that which lay before me was, *Do I really want to play with this nightmare again?* I did not. That was it; I had had enough for the day, and I parked that old hoe there at that junction, leaning it against the rib. I looked at that old tool and said a silent thanks to it. The chances were very good that without it, I very well might have set up permanent residence in one of those two hidden shafts. I rolled back my sleeve and cast the lamp's light onto my watch for the first time that day. *That is not possible*, I thought. *Three thirty in the afternoon?* I walked out of the portal of the Howland at 4:45, and four sets of diggers were hanging on their spikes outside the shack. I put the lamp out, took off my diggers, and hung them up, leaving my hat and shoulder bag outside. I kept my boots on, too tired to pull them off, I decided. I knocked once on the door and walked in, finding Swinger sitting at the table, no coffee cup, just sitting there. He took a long look at me and said, "Jesus Christ and little Rizzi kid. I was starting to get pretty damned worried. You look like hell. Must have been kind of a rough run. Did you make it to the Jewel?"

"Hell no! That damned hole is one mean sonofabitch. Don't know if I even want to try for it another time. Hell, I don't know how close I was, and I will have to try and track that little stroll on my map when I get home."

After talking a short time, I headed out to the old General Mess of Crap. I stowed all my gear in the junk box and left my boots on; my sandwich had sat there all day along with my thermos of, now cold, coffee. None of that interested me, so I fired up the junk pile and headed for home. It was snowing lightly.

The next morning, the second day off from work, I found I could not generate enough ambition or desire to go up to the mine. I stayed home and was glad to do it, although my original intention had been to use both days, if needed, to get to the Jewel Stope. Instead, I opened up the map of the Howland/Col-Rex workings to see if I could track where I had been the day before. I retraced my steps on the map to determine where I had turned back. What I determined was not to my liking. I had turned back far short of the Jewel Stope, so short of that goal that I double-checked everything, and both times, it came up the same. The day before, I had reached the 3,400-foot mark in the Col-Rex. From my turn-back point, I would have had to travel nearly 2,000 feet more to reach the Jewel Stope. Shit!

17

A Brief Slowdown

THE WEEK FOLLOWING the unforgettable venture that took me into Death Valley, November was in its last week of existence before December 1957 took its place. I did not get to Alta that week, as an unexpected shift change put my two days off over the weekend. It was probably a good thing, as I was still arguing with myself about the advisability of trying for the Jewel Stope. Common sense almost won out, but the young and stupid part overcame that. What had occurred in the Death Valley section of the mine that day, I never told anyone outside of Swinger. Had I been foolish enough to tell my wife, she would have thrown a fit. She was nearing the end of any form of tolerance when it came to my obsession with mining and the time involved.

I got to the mine just behind Slick, and the other two, Tokyo and Alimony, were together in Tokyo's truck. Swinger should have run us all off before we emptied his big coffeepot, leaving him half a cup. However, Swinger was just not that kind of fellow. I probably would have been, and I felt bad that I had not brought my thermos in.

I went into the hole with them as far as where the compressor was, and we parted company. I headed into the crosscut for the Howland/Col-Con workings and arrived at the Howland Tunnel shortly. Looking down its run, I spotted Mack and Mark Jacobson hard at work as always and headed down to say hello. Things were different there that day, and they had, as Mack told me, put a couple of rounds in and had opened up about 10 feet more of drift. In that 10 feet, the fissure containing the sulfides had opened up, and galena*

* Sulfide of lead, a type of ore.

was coming in with the pyrite. I heard later from several men that if there were a pound of ore in the country, a Jacobson would find it. How true that had proven over many years, at times causing much head-scratching by others.

I went on my way deeper into the mine and soon passed into the first stope of the Col-Con. I spent some time going over the area but turned up little of interest and went on into the next stoped area. I spent more time in that one looking at everything, some of it twice. I turned up pieces of an old lantern, the remains of two mangled carbide lamps, and an old ax head. I left it all there and traveled on until I came to the big, inclined shaft. I was tempted to try to go down, at least for a short distance, but then all the nasty experiences in the Col-Rex seeped into my head. Years later, in another setting, that one military, there was a saying describing fear, unease, nervousness, and such: "shit in your neck." That is what I had now as I looked down that shaft. Any thought of making my way down that incline vanished at that point. For that day, at least.

After looking around that entire area, I decided to head on out by way of the Howland Tunnel. It seemed like a good idea to have some coffee and a sandwich for once around noontime. The last few trips, I came out so long after lunchtime that I could not get interested in a sandwich and the, by then, cold coffee. Another thing involved in my decision was the fact that back in the Col-Con, I decided also that I did not want to try to find the Jewel Stope that day. For that attempt, the day was too far gone, not to mention I was still hesitant to try because of Death Valley. I had just sat down in the cab of the old General Mess of Crap, opened my lunch box, and started to unscrew the cap of my thermos. I did not get that accomplished because about then Swinger and the other three walked into sight, passing the door opening into the snowshed. Swinger spotted me and waved me to come on in, that putting five of us in his palace.

What happened during that lunchtime sit-down was typical when it came to keeping company with the likes of Slick, Tokyo Joe, Alimony Bill, and Swinging Door Campbell. It involved a pair of binoculars that belonged to Swinger, an interested Slick, and two individuals who had heard the bullshit stories from the master of such things, one Swinging Door Campbell. Swinger had a good solid foundation for the tale he had told the other three. Because of the shack's location at the top of the dump level and the two windows facing the Peruvian Lodge, it would make the story ring true. Apparently, Swinger had really laid it on about the entertainment available looking into the lodge's upper windows. Those windows were about 75 yards distant from those of the shack.

Swinger had told in detail what one would see in the lodge's rooms with a good pair of binoculars. The events described, of course, consisted of tales of wild orgies, all manner of "weenie-hiding and hosing party" episodes, and other fascinating antics involving all kinds of interesting deviations among the involved participants. Tokyo got to the binoculars first, which did not sit well with Alimony, and with that, the fun began. Tokyo braced himself against the wall next to the window and focused on the upper level of the Peruvian Lodge. He looked the whole section over slowly and then said, "Holy shit! Some poor bastard is over there and his clothes are missing. Holy shit! There are two really lumpy women, they got no wrappers on them either, and they are really going over that poor dumb sonofabitch. Hope he survives. Holy shit!"

Alimony started, as Swinger liked to say, going boo-coo and demanding the binoculars so he could look the situation over. Tokyo, being Tokyo, would not turn them over and just kept on with the *holy shit* routine. Alimony then shorted out (another Swinger term) and howled, "Gimme them fuckin' spy glasses, Tok, or I am a-goin' to kill ya!"

Tokyo simply refused to comply with Alimony's demand and came up with a couple more *holy shit*s, which by that time had Alimony going completely crazy.

"Goddamn it, Tok, I will kill ya unless you hand over them glasses."

Swinger and Slick just sat there, smiled, and nodded their heads, and I was considering the sincerity of Alimony's threat to send Tokyo to the other side. Tokyo finally relented, as he figured he had old

Alimony tuned up good, passed him the binoculars, and said, "All right, All right! You horny little bastard, go ahead and have a stroke, I don't give a rat's ass."

Alimony grabbed the binoculars, nearly dropped them, braced himself against the wall, and commenced his scan of the Peruvian Lodge.

Alimony went over the target fast then slowed down and tried it again, this time slower. He then slowed down even more and made another complete scan. He finally turned away from the window, the binoculars clutched in one hand, gave Tokyo a hard stare, and held it.

"Tok, ya dirty rotten sonofabitch, I am really a-goin' to kill ya now, and really I am! There ain't nothin' over there, goddamn it!"

"Well, hell, Bill" Tokyo started out. "Nobody knows as well as you do that I am the world's biggest liar. Got you with that one, didn't I?"

Tokyo looked at the scowling Alimony Bill and started grinning. Alimony kept his hard stare on Tokyo, and he started to grin. Tokyo started to chuckle, then Alimony commenced laughing. Swinger and Slick came up with a couple of guffaws, joining the other two. I just sat there in my chair and shook my head asking myself where in hell these kind of characters came from. Slick threw his bit into the situation by announcing, "We need to get some lunch down, gents. We need to finish pulling that chute, get the cars out and unloaded in the bin."

"Now, if you two kids," Swinger started out, "had busted up my binoculars during a killing try, I would have had to put the remains over the dump and both of you with them. So, let's do what Slick here has said."

What chance there might have been that I would try for the Jewel that day was ended. I decided to go in the mine with them, but I was going to spend the time around the area where the compressor was located. There were drifts in the area and at least two raises, things I wanted to spend more time looking over. I figured that would make for a good afternoon.

It did not take too long to go over this section, and rather than go on to where the men were working, I followed the Col-Rex Tunnel until I got to the water tank drift, took the old enamel cup off its spike, and sat down on the dam. I filled that old cup twice with that icy water and spent considerable time enjoying it. Sitting there, I started thinking about that damned Jewel Stope and the route through all the bad areas that I had encountered. For some reason, my reluctance to deal with that ground again seemed to diminish considerably. When I hung the cup back up on the spike, I knew that I would be going after that old stope, and it would be soon.

I decided to head out for sunshine, which that day was not an entirely accurate way of describing what was outside the mine. When we were all in the shack for lunch and the entertainment, the light snow that had been falling when we first arrived had decided to quit. The clouds were down on all the high peaks, obscuring them. When I got outside, the conditions were the same: cloudy and a dismal grayness lay over all. I had removed my diggers and hung them on their spike when I heard the rumbling and clanking of the train coming out of the hole.

Swinger was operating the trammer and the other three, following it out, walking behind the rattling train. I waved and went on out to secure the necessary items out of the General Mess of Crap as the train came to a halt. While the crew set about making the necessary switching and got the cars ready to unload in the bin, I changed boots. I already had my heavy coat on, so I just stood around and observed, as there was plenty of help to get the job done. There was no reason to get involved in that business, and besides I was somewhat worn out from my wanderings. Things were wound up in short order and everything put back in line for the next day. It was time to head on down the canyon, and I decided to leave the chains on just in case. I headed out to the old junk pile, saying as I left, "Don't go bustin' John T.'s binoculars. I will check in the morning."

18

The Search Continues

WHEN I LEFT the mine the day before, I could have removed the chains before I pulled out, as the road was clear. I stopped near Tanners Flat, took them off, and stowed them in the junk box. I was tired of listening to them, not to mention the vibration that carried through the old GMC. The old crate did not need any more vibrations than it already had. That morning it looked like I had clear road ahead of me when I got above Wasatch Resort, so the chains stayed put in the junk box. I considered that as a good sign. That helped because this day was the day that I would get to the Jewel Stope, at least that was my hope. Everything felt right. A clear road and high clouds and confidence that I would get to that old stope. Sometimes you just know.

I got to the mine before the other three, and Swinger, as usual, had the coffee built, as he termed the act. I did not pass that up, and he poured me a cup and I told him what I intended to do with the day. Swinger told me I was nuts, it just was not smart to try that journey alone, but regardless of what he said, he knew I would do it anyway. He added to it with a statement comparing the hardness of my head to a block of Little Cottonwood granite. Swinger reminded me once again about what to look out for when it came to sagging timber, bad air, and half dozen other things that could gob me in the blink of an eye. We sat drinking coffee and talked for a while before the trio from down in the valley came clunking into the shack.

I spent enough time to say good morning to the three men, then headed out to the General Mess of Crap for my mine boots and the war sack, which was now its official name, instead of fish sack. I left my coat in the truck, grabbed my hard-boiled hat, and headed back inside the snowshed and got suited up. I run through the contents of my war sack in my head. In a crushproof—well, crush-resistant—container, was a sandwich. There was no room for the thermos though, as it was too big to fit in with the other necessities. I had no four-leaf clovers or a rabbit's foot for luck, just my young and stupid confidence, and that would have to suffice in the luck department. I got the lamp burning and headed for the portal.

It was a quick and easy trip to where the old enamel cup hung from its spike at the water tank drift. The ritual must continue, and I took the old cup off the spike, filled it, and drank it dry. I would repeat that ritual on my way out because it was now required. I then came to a fork in the tunnel, and I was positive that I needed to go right but went left to assure myself where I was. Sure enough, I ran into the cave-in I was sure I would find. I turned back and took the right turn.

In a short distance, I was back at the beginning of the section of the mine I had first called Spook Alley, but its true old-timers' name of course was Death Valley. The fact that I could see nothing but timbered ground still ahead of me when I'd turned back on the first trip was still unsettling. The experience with the two water-filled shafts, hidden by that scum on the water, of course, had much to do with that.

There would be no side trips on this day, and I walked at a much faster pace than the time before. I had not started a candle burning yet, as I knew from the last time that the air was good in this section. I passed by all the side drifts and arrived soon where a drift broke off to my right. There at that junction, leaning against the rib, stood my guardian angel, the old hoe that most likely had saved my life. It was here, looking at that old tool, that I put the first of my candles to flame. All ahead of me would be unfamiliar territory now, as this was where I had turned back that first trip. The time had come to head north.

I still felt reasonably good about going on even though standing there, I felt a little slip in my confidence. Up to this point in Death Valley, nothing had seemed as dangerous as on the first foray. It seems that after the first venture into a questionable situation, each succeeding one loses much of its frightening character. It was true for at least that moment, and I headed deeper into that mountain with little trepidation. The timber sets were in reasonably good condition, with little sagging of the caps; the posts stood firm and exhibited no sign of buckling inward. The lagging was, however, broken inward in a number of places, letting in enough material to back up the ditch in places.

Things were looking up when, after a distance of roughly 200 feet, I passed into a solid structure without a stick of timber in sight. Midway through that timbered and lagged stretch there was a gentle curve to the left. I hoped that I had made it through all the bad stuff I was going to get into. I still had nearly 2,000 feet ahead of me until I got to the Jewel Stope. By this time, the flame of my carbide lamp was at a very low point. It was time to replace the carbide and top off the water compartment. With the candle parked on a handy little ledge on the rib for illumination, I completed that chore quickly. With a good flame burning, everything looked much brighter, and picking up the candle, I proceeded, once again, in a generally north direction.

In the area I was passing through now, there were only minor rock falls, and they did not create any problems involving backed-up water. There was no lack of water, but the ditch easily carried the flow. The bottom between the rails and off to the sides of them, with the exception of the flowing ditch, was covered with the ever-present red-orange mud. The source of it still had to be somewhere up ahead of me, as there was no indication of it in the back or the ribs of the tunnel. The mud was deep enough that my tracks in it were well defined, and mine were the only tracks visible. Tommy-knockers, of course, left no tracks.

Shortly I came into a junction with drifts running both to my left and right, but I passed them by. I did not want to use up time to explore them, because my goal for that day was the Jewel Stope. Going on for what I calculated must have been about 200 feet, I came onto another drift running left off the main, but I stayed straight ahead and soon came into what appeared to be the second edition of Death Valley. I was soon into timbered and lagged ground and had to pass over a blockage backing up water. The water was deep enough that it was just two inches below the tops of my boots. As I looked things over, a feeling of unease, bordering on fear, started coming over me.

This was heavy ground, the timber sets were starting to buckle, and the lagging was breaking inward from the back and ribs. I came on to a partial cave-in that left a muck pile almost up to my waist in height. That today's business was now deep enough was more than convincing. More convincing yet was what I was able to see from the top of that muck pile. The flashlight's beam showed deep water on the other side and another cave-in ahead of that. Beyond that, nearly invisible, a chute came into the tunnel indicating workings above that had likely contributed to the caving ground. Trying to get through that would be nearly impossible and extremely dangerous, likely leaving anyone that attempted it a permanent resident of the neighborhood.

I turned back from that mess, wondering if I would ever get to that elusive stope. The thing to do now would be to follow the drift that had been on my left coming in, a distance of less than 50 feet away. Once in it, my flashlight showed the drift continuing on, straight, as far as the beam could penetrate. I left it alone and decided to continue following the straight run ahead of me instead. I went straight for about 200 feet, and the drift started a slow, gentle turn to the left. Ahead of me, a very short distance after making the turn, was what appeared to be a low dike.

This was no rock fall or cave-in and when I looked at what was on the other side the reason it existed was very apparent. The dike, that was what it was, channeled a heavy-flowing ditch into another drift. I knew where I was and if I followed that drift, I would be on the backside of the cave-ins and deep water previously encountered. The accumulation of that damned red-orange mud helped confirm that thought. I crossed the dike and started walking in ankle-deep mud till I found a set of heavy wooden stairs on the left side of the tunnel.

The stairs went up to a point that would have been halfway up the rib. There they ended, and so did the rib. Iron pyrite crystals were everywhere in the bottom of the tunnel. Above the level of the rib and the ladder, the weak flame of my carbide lamp disappeared into a black void. The break in the rib extended for a distance beyond the range of my dim lamp. For a short time, I stood in place, convinced I had finally found what I had been searching for, the Jewel Stope. An abundance of water in the form of drips falling from the back would furnish water for my lamp. I still had ample carbide in reserve in my two pocket containers, though one was nearing empty. By the light of my half-burned candle, the second of the day, I recharged the lamp, and it produced a good flame. With the candle in one hand and the indispensable flashlight in the other, I climbed those wet stairs to the top step.

19

The Jewel Stope

THE BRIGHT FLAME of my lamp and the sweeping beam of the flashlight revealed, what to me, was a stunning sight. My lights would reach into the stope some distance but could not penetrate the blackness of the far reaches. With the exceptions of a few dark, drab, and widely dispersed sections of country rock,* every surface glittered, reflecting back brilliant points of light. The small, isolated sections of country rock seemed to intensify the sparkling brilliance of the pyrite due to the contrasts between the two. The impression I had was of being inside a cocoon of iron sulfide—often labeled "fool's gold," "iron pyrites," or just plain "pyrite"—and the sight forever burned into my memory. The map of the mine labeled this unbelievable place the Sulfide Stope, a misnomer if there ever was one.

I wanted to spend some time looking around and was about to get started on that when it occurred to me that I had a sandwich in my war sack. The sandwich sounded like the better idea of the moment, as I realized I was hungry, and I had ample time to attend to that chore. I never bothered to consult my watch because time meant little underground. I looked around for something that looked like a good soft rock to sit on and soon located it. The rock, if it could be called such a thing, was an enormous boulder of brilliant iron pyrite made up of crystals all bound together. The boulder was such size that it would have to be broken into pieces to fit into a one-ton mine car, and it would require more than one. I estimated it might weigh, as it was now, well over 2,000 pounds but likely much more.

* Any rock that is in the surrounding mountain but not holding ore or value.

I sat down on top of that monster and devoured my sandwich, wishing I'd had enough room for my thermos of hot coffee. I finished the sandwich in short order because I was more than ready to explore that stope. The Jewel Stope contained an amazing display of iron pyrites in quantities that most people could not begin to imagine, let alone ever see in a lifetime. The stope was in such a stable structure that its back, with few exceptions, needed only stulls for support. The base of the stulls were set in what the miners called hitches, simply pockets cut into solid rock. Most of these stulls were nothing more than long, sturdy tree trunks with all their branches removed—simple poles, really. At their contact point on the back, wedges tightly driven between the end of the stull and the back held them solidly in place. In many instances, short lengths of lagging along with wedges helped close the gap between the stulls' end and the back.

The main purpose of stulls in the case of stopes was to hold slabs of rock in place rather than support heavier ground. Crib supports constructed in three locations in the Jewel Stope had a far different purpose than did stulling. Crib timbering was capable of holding tremendous weight and would greatly reduce chances of a catastrophic cave-in of a large area. The cribs were 12-by-12-inch timber, 8 feet in length, laid at right angles to one another to form the box-like structure known to miners as a crib set.* The outside dimension measured 8 by 8 feet, the inside 6 by 6 feet. Waste rock, mostly iron sulfide, filled the interiors of the crib sets in the Jewel Stope, increasing their load-bearing capability.

I slowly worked my way around the stope, closely looking at each stull I came near, visually verifying it was not buckling or that any loose slabs existed in the rock nearby. So far, I had seen nothing to be alarmed about, but I did not bump or lean against any stull, as

* A box-like structure made up of heavy timbers laid at right angles to one another. Used to support the back (roof) in large excavated areas such as stopes. The timbers used in construction are usually eight feet in length and eight inches square. Filling these structures with waste rock is common practice. This increases the load-bearing capacity of the crib set (see photo insert).

that kind of foolishness could bring heavy things down on my head. The crib sets were an entirely different matter, as they were so solidly in place, 10 men could lounge against one without a concern. In many places around the perimeter of the stope prospect tunnels had been driven and all ended in barren country rock. In the northern end of the stope, I found the big inclined raise that connected the Col-Rex with the Cardiff Mine. The rails were still in place, and a manway ladder went up at their side. Along the side of the ladder were three runs of pipe, at least one of which would be an airline. I had no idea what the others were for, as all three ended where they came into the stope.

I estimated the dimensions of the raise were eight feet by eight feet, which indicated it had been intended as a haulage or production raise. Outside of knowing, by looking at the Cardiff map, that the 600 level of that mine was at the top of this raise, everything else was unknown. The rock of the structure the raise was in looked solid as far as the beam of my flashlight could reach. Only an occasional stull appeared within the light's range. I was tempted to go up that raise but set that aside after some thought. I decided to go back to the main tunnel of the Col-Rex and follow it to its end. Having consulted the map, I knew I had another 800 feet to traverse. The map showed a number of winzes sunk below the level of the tunnel along that 800 feet and other things that looked interesting.

All of the winzes with the exception of two were filled with water to their collars; the overflow joined the water of the ditch. There would be no point in going down the two that were dry, as I could see their bottoms with the flashlight. Everything about those winzes indicated a lot of prospecting had taken place at depth. There was no indication of ore in the loose material around the collars of the winze, and so with little reason to spend much time in the area, I moved on along the tunnel's run.

In a short distance, the tunnel split into a series of Y-shaped drifts, each coming back into the other, and there were what appeared to be caved stopes above. That area did not look like anything I wanted to look deeper into that day, and I moved on along the main.

The tunnel ended, and there I found another winze, identified as the D winze on the mine map, going down from its right side. The water level in this winze stood at about 30 feet below the collar, and it was clear as crystal. It was deep, deep enough that my flashlight's beam could not penetrate far enough to see any bottom. A set of tracks run down into the depths of the water, and to the side of them, pipes did the same. Two of the pipes looked to be airlines and one of much larger diameter was probably a water line, the water being pushed up from a pumping station at the bottom of the winze. This layout represented a serious undertaking years earlier by someone with good financial backing. Mounted on a concrete foundation was a compressed air-powered hoist of heavy capacity. The drum of the hoist had a number of wraps of cable still on it, the free end running down the winze between the track rails.

Once again, my good old carbide lamp was dimming, the carbide and water due for replenishing. All that remained of my candle, the second, was a stub that was getting too close to my fingers, and the heat was increasing. The first, then the second candle, had been burning since I left the water tank drift and had entered Death Valley. I would need no burning candle to get out to sunshine, as the air had proven safe for the entire distance traveled.

With the lamp recharged and producing a good flame, I started on the return trip. When I turned away from that hoist and the D winze, I had well over 6,000 feet to traverse to reach the portal of the Howland Tunnel. That distance in daylight over flat ground or even gently rolling terrain would not take a long time; most people could walk that distance in about a half hour. That isn't how it works in the underground world, especially when the passage is through unfamiliar and often dangerous conditions. Although I would be passing through most of Death Valley for the second time, I did it at a slow pace. There was nothing about that stretch that I trusted.

When I arrived at the water tank drift, I filled the old enamel cup with the icy water and took my time drinking it. I was feeling good, satisfied that I had finally reached the Jewel Stope and took even more time with the second cup. With those cups of water, I also gave silent thanks regarding my good fortune in not getting, as my friend Swinger would say, gobbed in the process. When I came to the location of the notorious air compressor, the train and the men were just ahead of me, and I fell in behind them about 20 feet back. Swinger was operating the trammer and had four cars in tow. Slick, Tokyo, and Alimony trundled along close behind. The conversations between the three, along with the clanking and rumbling of the cars would drown out any noise I might make. They had no idea I was there behind them, although I had closed the distance between us.

I stayed silent until we passed out of the portal, where Swinger slowed to a stop. That was the ideal moment, and I shouted out a loud howdy, which resulted in noisy retorts like "Jesus Christ!" "Goddamn! What the hell?" "Scared the supreme shit out of me!" (Whitney's usual response to such things). All that came from Swinger was the usual "Hello kid! How's she hummin', chum?"

Tokyo and Alimony got busy shuffling cars, Swinger tending to his job with the trammer, while Slick stood out of the way looking proud. Tokyo and Alimony were doing the heavy work; they did not seem to care in the least, it was simply how things worked around that operation. During the time this was going on, I had taken off and hung up my rubber, pulled off my Goodalls, and put on my leather boots. I walked out to the old General Mess of Crap and stashed my gear in the junk box, then followed the crew into the shack. They all sat down. I remained standing, and Swinger took a hard look at me, not bothering to voice the question. I just looked at my friend and said, "I made it, Swing, I made the Jewel Stope, and it is a pippin. I guess I will head on down the hill and will see you next week, as this week is done for me."

I went on out, fired up the old GMC, and pulled out onto the canyon road. It looked like snow was on its way. What a day!

20

Over the Dump

DECEMBER 1957 WAS now at its midpoint, and during the first week of it I never had made it up to the mine due to certain conflicts on the home front and the canyon being closed by snow. Finally, about a week and a half before Christmas, I made it up to the mine with no particular agenda in mind. When I headed up the canyon, it looked like snow would be a sure thing but had not started yet. I arrived at the mine early, and the only thing parked in the cleared-out space, which five vehicles could be crammed into, was Swinger's pickup. The Jacobson brothers had not made it up yet, and as it turned out, they would not on this day. Clearing the snow around the parking area was a constant job. This morning, it was six feet on the level. That was nothing, the Jacobsons said—just wait until it really decided to put snow down.

I went in through the snowshed and on to the shack, knocked once, and went on in. Swinger was sitting at the table, I could smell coffee, and that was a welcome thing. It went as it usually did when I walked in.

"Hello kid! How's she hummin', chum?"

I came up with my usual also, which consisted of a good morning wish to my good friend.

"The coffee's built, kid, and your cup is on the table. Just loaded mine so you have some catching up to do."

I went over to the stove, grabbed the pot, filled my cup, sat back down, and took a small sip. As usual, it was dark, strong, and hot, so hot it nearly burned my tongue, which I had anticipated. It was perfect. We sat for a few minutes without anything said, and then he told me what was going on. It seemed that since the beginning of the week, with threats of increasingly bad weather, things had changed. Slick had dispatched Tokyo Joe and Alimony Bill out to the Bingham area, where he was finishing a lease.

It all came down to the fact that the project up here at the Col-Rex was short two men. Swinger said he did not expect to see Slick until just before noon, and that is how it worked out. We decided that we would just mess around on the outside until Slick made his appearance.

The trammer was on the charger with four cars coupled behind it, so we just straightened up a few things around the ore bins and spent more time talking than working, and I told Swinger, in some detail, what the trip to the Jewel Stope was like. Swinger did not come out and directly call me crazy; he did not have to because I knew what he was thinking. On a few occasions during the telling of the story, he would break in and go over the myriad of ways one could get gobbed playing around in old holes.

Somewhere around 11:00, we were getting cold and went back into the shack, put on a fresh pot of coffee, and had some lunch. I had brought a sandwich up with me, and Swinger had a couple of boiled eggs and a cheese sandwich. We had just finished everything other than our coffee when Slick walked through the door, said howdy and something about the goddamn weather. It was 11:30. Swinger handed him a cup of coffee that Slick took a big gulp of immediately. Instantly following that, when he got his breath back, came "Burned the supreme shit out of my tongue!" Slick was really into that "supreme shit" business; it covered a lot of territory for him. It could not have been 10 minutes after the tongue burning that the "goddamn weather" arrived.

It started with a furious gust of wind that shook the building, seeming to get worse with each passing minute. I got up and went to the west-facing window for a look and seen something that I had heard about but never witnessed. A solid white wall completely obscuring the canyon moved toward us, driven by the howling wind. The wind-driven snow hit the window, hit it hard, and I thought to myself, *Oh shit!*

The shack, showing its age, trembled and creaked. Whitney uttered, "Goddamn!"

At the same moment, Swinger announced his thought: "Jesus Christ and little Rizzi, kids!"

I simply stayed with my silent *Oh shit* and nodded once.

The time had come to get some work done in the mine. There were at least four carloads of plain old muck waiting in the chute. We got into where we were going, accomplished the usual switching around to put the cars behind the trammer. The four cars, filled to capacity with a crown of muck above their tops, were ready to go.

When we got out of the hole, the wind had slowed down. The snow had not, still coming down heavy enough, it was hard to see where the rails ended out on the dump. That country in winter months required the dumping of loaded cars when they came out of the mine. Loaded cars full of wet muck, if left overnight, would freeze solid. There was a fix for that, but it involved dynamite, and that was something to avoid at all costs. We got the usual switching around done, and Swinger and I went out on the dump to clear the rails of snow. There was about a foot on the tracks, and the snow was still falling heavily. Slick stayed under cover to do his part, which involved unhooking the chains between the cars and wedging the wheels, allowing them to come out one at a time. Slick could easily move one out by himself, as it was a downhill grade to the dump's end. The cars could roll by themselves but had to be controlled.

When we went out to shovel off the rails, Swinger told Slick he would holler when they were clear of snow, and we'd made sure the stop chain* was in place. The chain would be about four feet back from the end of the rails. It was not there we discovered, and that was not a good thing, and it was about to get worse, as we heard a rumbling clatter approaching. Swinger had not yet yelled back to Slick to start a loaded car out, so that made little sense as to the

* A length of chain wrapped tightly around both rails at the end of their run. It is a simple and effective way to prevent any runaway ore cars from leaving the tracks.

why of it. We looked back as the why of it was coming toward us, no Slick hanging off it.

"Jesus Christ and little Rizzi, kid, the slaphappy sonofabitch has turned one loose. Just let her go, kid, somebody will get hurt trying to stop that bastard."

We stood off to the side of the rails letting it go by, watching as it reached the end and disappear over the dump.

Swinger, being who he was, decided to have some fun with this deal as we watched Slick walk slowly toward us. Swinger bellowed out in his direction something only Swinger was capable of on the spur of a moment: "Goddamn, Slick, that was a pippin! Now get back in there and get another one comin' like that one. That sonofabitch that just made it over the dump landed on the hood of some ski queer's Cadillac. The rear end of that goddamn Cadillac is sticking up in the air like a stinkbug's ass. Now when that next one comes out, me and the kid here will put a little drift on her just as she goes over. If we do it right, the car should end up in the trunk of the Cadillac. That'll settle the bastard back down level again."

Whitney had slowed his pace even more, his lamp was out, and his head was moving like a chicken, kind of back and forth with his steps, and looked comical as could be. He was walking funny too. Slick walked out to the end of the dump, and the wind started up again while he was looking down into the Peruvian parking lot. He had his look, turned back to where we were standing, and commenced. It was a noisy tirade, loud enough that the wind could not tone it down.

"GODDAMN! Swinging Door, you SONOFABITCH! I lost twenty years of my life on that little walk out here. JESUS! Of all the damned stunts you have pulled off over the years, this is one that damn near put me in the ground. That business of the smashed Caddy scared the ABSOLUTE supreme shit out of me! Well, you two assholes can bring out the other three because I've got to head for the shithouse."

"Well," replied Swinger, "that is not surprising Hansen [Slick]. I would suppose you worked up a good shit with that runaway you pulled off, so you best go get it done. Just so you know, your masterpiece damn near caused two loaded diapers out here when that runaway came rolling down the tracks." Swinger said all this while half laughing and trying to keep a straight face.

At that, Slick got started again: "I don't have to take a shit GODDAMN IT! I already did that! I got to go scrape my leg is what the deal is now. DAMN!"

With the conversations now at their end, Slick turned and walked toward the buildings. The chicken head thing was past, but he still walked kind of funny, a little bowlegged actually. There was little doubt that he needed to go scrape his leg, as he so delicately put it. Swinger put it well when he said, "Old Slick Sheet walks like he's got a stovepipe up his ass, kid."

As we watched him go, Swinger started laughing, and that set me off on the same business. We enjoyed a good laugh at Whitney's expense, and Swinger announced as he headed for the buildings for me to wait out there while he rustled up a length of chain to bring out and make sure there was no repeat of the flying car stunt. He soon showed up with the chain, and we did a double wrap around the rails, then headed for the loaded cars. We brought them out one at a time, there being no other way, and both of us hung on to keep them on a slow roll. It was still snowing hard, and the footing was not good because the ties were wet and slippery under the snow. That might be the reason the car got away from Slick.

Whitney got back from his little leg scraping project, and we worked to get the switching done to line up the cars, the three we still had, and tied them and the trammer together. It was not yet 4:00 but nearly there, and it was time for coffee, as we were all cold from the outside work. No one said much until we each had a cup of coffee in front of us. Slick then started on the tale of how the flying car came about.

"I decided that I would get one car started out and had a wedge on the muck in the car to block it if I was too early. I see you two give up on the shoveling and figured it would be about right timewise. Yeah, I know, Swinger, you told me you would holler when things were cleaned up. Anyhow, I was moving along slow-like and then I fell on my ass, lost my hold on the car. Didn't have no chance to wedge her and she was off. Well, that part you know about. But when I went down things in the lower reaches got some shook up and started moving. I didn't think that I was too bad off and then you got started on the smashed Caddy and I dumped my chute. That Caddy bullshit is what popped the round. Goddamn it, Swinger!"

We could not decide whether to laugh or feel bad for Slick, so we simplified the operation and folded up in our chairs in a laughing fit at poor old Slick, and he could not see what was so funny.

By the time we warmed up and were ready to face the run for home, it was still snowing. The wind had let up a little but was blowing hard yet. I did not think the crate would fire up, but eventually it did, just before the battery gave up. We pulled out and headed down the hill, Whitney in the lead.

We left the chains on until well out of the canyon and onto Wasatch Boulevard, which the snowplows had cleared of snow. Although I had the next day off from that service station job there was, probably, little chance the canyon would be open for most of that day. And things were about to change considerably. I had no idea when I left the mine that day, it would be my last working day in that old hole.

Col-Rex from west. Sectioned out of larger photograph of M. R. Evans camp, circa 1920. Photographer unknown. From G. W. Hansen collection.

Col-Rex ore bin, looking north, circa 1950. Photographer William Kastelic. From G. W. Hansen collection.

Jacobson family on porch at old lower Flagstaff boarding house, circa 1929. Photographer unknown. Given to author by Dan Jacobson.

Main tunnel of Cardiff 600 level, 1972. Author's photo.

Bedded iron sulfide (fool's gold) in Jewel Stope, also showing use of stull supports, 1970. Author's photo.

Dick Fluehe and crib set support, Jewel Stope, 1970. Author's photo.

Wasatch Drain Tunnel buildings, looking east, 1963. Photographer Laurence P. James. From G. W. Hansen collection.

Wasatch Drain Tunnel from Old Peruvian Road, looking west, 1916. Photographer F. C. Calkins, USGS. Author's collection.

Jay Woodward loading ore for trip to smelter with Banana Wagon at right, looking east, circa 1958. Author's photo.

Dan Jacobson operating trammer in Wasatch Drain Tunnel, circa 1960. Photographer unknown. Given to author by Dan Jacobson.

View downward of Cardiff inclined shaft from the 800 level, 1975.
Author's photo.

Dick Fluehe at left with John T. "Swinging Door"
Campbell, 1960. Author's photo.

21
Major Change Takes Place

IT WAS ABOUT four days before Christmas before I headed up Little Cottonwood Canyon to the Col-Rex again. The road did not look bad, but considering the worn-out tires on the old General Mess of Crap, I chained up at my usual place. When I got up to Tanners Flat, I was glad I had done that, as they would have had to go on at that point. From there, the grade of the road steepens and in a short distance, there is a sharp turn to the right and an additional increase in grade. All this was now snow covered, and that old GMC with its almost bald tires would not have made it up that section without chains. When I arrived at the mine, there was only one truck parked in the cleared-out space by the snowshed. I figured it belonged to Frank Reedy and had been there all night, as there were no tire tracks in the new snow.

I did not like how this was looking, nothing about the situation felt right, especially the absence of Swinger's truck. I got out of the old GMC and headed in through the snowshed door. The trammer was at the charging station with just one car hooked to it, the other two down toward the ore bins. Four sets of diggers were hanging on the spikes outside the door going into the shack. I knocked on the door once, just out of habit, and walked in. The table and three chairs were in their usual place, as was the little refrigerator, though it had been unplugged from its power source. Without the familiar coffeepot sitting on the stove, the room was just an empty, dismal, and forlorn place; nothing of my friend Swinger remained in that room.

I stood there, looking around the place, feeling worse by the minute. I walked out, closed the door, and stood on the small porch, attempting to come to grips with my darkening mood and the depressing situation. I heard a door slam down in the area where the ore bins were and turned my attention in that direction. I had heard that there was a small, cramped living quarters of sorts on the other side of the ore bins sometimes used by Frank Reedy. That proved true as Frank came across the walkway from his hideout, moving toward where I was standing. He walked up, looked me over as if he had never seen me before, and said, "You must be that kid."

I was already disgusted with what I had found, my mood was not the best, and what he said hit me wrong. It really had no reason to do so, but it did, and I came back at him with, "Well, I might be, but there is only one man that has ever been able to get away with calling me that."

Things were not progressing well. He just glared at me, and I knew I had really messed up this encounter. Before he could come back at me, which he was about to do, I spoke up quickly: "Aw shit, man, I am really sorry about that last. I am just not thinking right at all. Coming up here and finding my old friend Swinger gone has turned me into one sour asshole, and it ain't your doin' so you didn't have that coming."

That calmed things down. We just stood there, both of us looking down at the rails for a bit, and Frank said, "Yeah, I guess that would be some upsetting, just walking in and finding your amigo has vanished. Swinger told me you would be comin' around and to say he didn't know how to get ahold of you. He just said the kid would be up and if I was to see you to give you a message. He hasn't gone far, pard, just down the canyon to the drain tunnel and back to his old job down there. He said if I was to see you to point you in that direction. So, there you have it."

I thanked him and once again repeated my regret for talking to him as I had. He told me to forget it and he headed back to his hideout.

I walked out to the General Mess of Crap. It was starting to snow heavily, and after starting the old crate, I knew exactly where I had to get to: off the highway and down to the Wasatch Drain

Tunnel operation, having seen its turnoff each time I had come up the canyon.

At the turnoff, all the usual signs were in evidence concerning keeping out, private property, and the sin of trespassing, and another one proclaiming "Cardiff Mining and Milling Company" with another "Keep Out" notice below. I did my usual and ignored them, starting down the road, only to find an International Harvester dozer coming toward me, pushing snow off the road. There was no way of getting around that thing, as it occupied the middle of the road.

The machine stopped and so did I, with about 20 feet of distance between us. I thought, *Oh shit!* The International had a closed cab. The door opened, and a man stepped out onto the track, then down onto the road. He was a big fellow, warmly dressed, and he walked toward me as I sat in the cab of the old GMC. I rolled the window down as he came up next to the door and stopped and said in a loud voice, "Hullo kid! How's she hummin', chum?"

The day brightened up as if the sun had just come out, which of course it had not, but things were where they should be now.

"Goddamn, Swinger, am I glad to see you! I figured you had quit the country, but old Frank up at the mine set me on the trail down here. And so here you are. I'll be a sad bastard—no, make that a happy bastard."

"It's a long story, kid," Swinger said.

Swinger said he would get off to the side so I could get by. He told me that the first building that came up was where I could park with the other outfits close to the building. He said I would find two doors, one on the west and one on the east. The one on the east side went into the office, and if I went in that one, I would find the Bull and two of his slaves inside. The door on the west just opened up into the dry. What was a dry? I thought to myself but did not ask. He went on saying that if I did not want to go inside, just wait a little, as he was just going to the highway and then straight back to the main area. I had not been down that road since 1955, when I had walked down because of a locked gate. At that time, the buildings were still under construction.

The flat areas around the buildings down the road from us—the big one, a smaller one, and another farther east—were almost snow-free. Swinger had been a busy fellow, and it was obvious. The buildings here were all of steel construction, with no wood evident on any of the outside walls, unlike the structures up at the Col-Rex, which were constructed entirely of wood. Back at the time of their construction, wood was the only material available.

There were three or four cars, as I remember now, parked next to the building. I decided not to wait until Swinger got back and figured I might as well go on in and see what I would run into. When I went in through the door, I found a long counter running the width of the room with a swinging door just off-center to the right. The counter and the door were about waist high, and to the right of it behind the door was a desk with a man sitting behind it. He did not look like he was dangerous in the least, but that could not be said for the craggy-faced individual who sat at a desk to the left of the door. He was not a small fellow; he had an old-time fedora hat on his head and wore a pair of glasses that were sitting low on his nose. The eyes looking at me over the top of those glasses had a hard look in them. I figured this had to be the Bull, and he looked it. The fellow to the right stood up, and he rather smiled as he inquired as to what he might do for me.

I answered his question with one eye on the man I suspected could be the Bull, soon to be confirmed.

"Well," I started out, "there is a guy out there pushing snow around and will be here very shortly, he pointed me down and said to go on in or I could wait for him to come back, which, as you can see, I didn't. He is a good friend of mine and I put in some time up in the old Col-Rex getting an education, he being the professor."

With that said, the big fellow at the other desk got up, pushed his glasses back up where they should be, walked over to the swinging door, and stuck his hand out—and he had a grin on his face when he did it.

"You have got to be the one Swinger calls 'the kid,' I would have to say. He has talked about you several times. I'm glad you came by.

Now, we both know how Swinger is with names and I suppose he knows your real one, but he is way too damn good with nicknames. Your real name would be good to know because you may be young but you're no kid, from what he told me."

We shook hands and his paw was nothing you would find on a piano player. His grip was something to be respectful of as there was a lot of strength in it. I told the Bull my real name, and he said his was Al Wondershek. There was no doubt that we had made a tight connection, Al and I. It would prove out over the next two years.

22

Becoming Acquainted

ABOUT THAT TIME, Swinger came in through the door, making a show of stomping the snow off his boots. When he came in, we had not arrived at the point that I had any idea who the other fellow was. I had been looking around and noticed another man in the back of the area who was standing at a large table. His attention was on something on that table. Swinger put his cap on the counter, looked at the Bull and me, and said, "Looks like you and the Bull are doing all right. That fellow over there, that's just standing there, is Sweet Pea, and in the back there, that is a slide-rule kid called Matt."

The fellow back at the big table just raised his hand and started up to the counter area. He was about the same size as Sweet Pea, and he was a friendly looking individual. The Bull decided it was time for real names and introductions, so he commenced to do that. "Swinger is up to his usual, so I guess I better straighten out just who these two guys really are. The one he just called Sweet Pea is really Vern Barr and the other is Matt. The slide-rule tag is what Swinger hangs on anybody that made it past sixth grade and went on to college. Matt is an engineer along with knowing how to survey. His real name is Martinson."

Swinger just stood there and took it all in, a grin on his face, and when the Bull was finished, he spoke up. "I've been at it, Bull, since two hours before you and Sweet Pea got up here, so me and the kid are going upstairs for a pot of coffee."

"I figured that was comin'," the Bull said, "so go ahead and get after it, and if you ain't done when the muck train comes out, Gus and whoever is on the motor can dump the cars. That most likely won't be a problem because we probably have two hours yet. Well, the penthouse and the coffee is a waitin'. Get the hell out of here."

With that, I followed Swinger left along the counter and through a doorway. To the right was a flight of wooden stairs that went up to another level. At the top of the stairs a large room opened up that I figured was the so-called penthouse. The layout was a presidential suite compared to Swinger's former quarters up at the Col-Rex. Over at the east wall of the room was Swinger's big bed, made up as usual, with a chest of drawers next to it and a big wardrobe cabinet alongside of that.

Against the north wall was a refrigerator, twice the size of the one up at the Col-Rex. To the right of it sat an electric range with four heating coils on its top and an oven located midway down its front. The familiar old coffeepot sat on one of the heating elements. Next to the stove to the right was a double sink, the faucet having both hot and cold water available. An inclined drain board was on the right side. The old single-spigot water barrel that had been the water source up at the Col-Rex was now permanently retired. A sturdy wood table occupied space a few feet away from the stove toward the center of the room. There were four chairs in place around the table.

The west wall of the room, which had the stairway on the other side, rose up to and was anchored to a cross beam. Two bunk beds were located, end to end, against and firmly attached to the wall. There were mattresses on them and would accommodate four individuals if the need arose. I would later find out that there were a number of folding cots stored in the storage area on the first level. Apparently, when the plans for the building were put together, those doing it were familiar with the many times the canyon could be closed due to snowslides, stranding those caught behind them for a couple of days. Heating for the room came in through ducting from the oil-burning forced-air furnace located in the dry. That furnace heated the entire building, and it did very well at its job. It was a comfortable place.

In a short time, the coffee was ready, and we sat down at the table and went to work on it. That was when I got the story of how Swinger came to be back at the drain tunnel. Swinger wanted to hang the whole thing on the Bull, but I think that is not quite how it happened. Apparently, Swinger had run into the Bull on occasion when he went down to get his water and have a shower. On other occasions, the Bull came up to the Col-Rex, catching Swinger outside the mine. Some of the conversations had involved the Bull asking Swinger why he did not come back down to work at the drain tunnel, as things were sure a lot fancier in the penthouse.

"Well kid, this is how it went and why I am back here living fancy again. Can't say I'm not liking it either. I came out of the hole one day and didn't have no cars to dump because I had been catching up on a few things. I see the Bull's kite sitting outside the snowshed and Sweet Pea plopped down in the pilot's seat. The Bull had flopped down in a chair at the table waiting and he got right to it. He said that the game was over. That him, Sweet Pea, and Gus would be up first thing in the morning to load up everything that was mine and it was going down to the drain tunnel and get set up in the penthouse. He said it had to happen because I had been on the payroll for a week already. He said Slick knew all about it and had no problem with it as he was going to shut down up there for a while. That is how it happened, kid, and so here I am. I am getting a buck and a half more per day and get paid for seven days a week, as I will be living on the job and also will be watching over things on the weekends. This gives me a good place to hole up, no rent, and all I have to buy is my groceries."

We probably sat there for over an hour and put away a lot of coffee. When my last cup was half gone, I started thinking that I ought to be on my way. It was a workday for Swinger, and I was uneasy about hanging around due to that situation. Of all the things I did not want to do, I did not want to mess up what looked like would be a good deal for me. I had taken an instant liking to the Bull, and it appeared to run the same line with him. I did not want to take a chance on lousing it up, and that is what prompted me to get on down the hill, so I told my friend that I had better be getting off the mountain.

We left the penthouse and headed toward the door, both of us with our outside gear on; it was snowing heavily when I looked out the window.

"You two calling it deep enough already?" the Bull started out. "I figured you'd piss away the whole afternoon up there telling lies."

When he said that, there was no indication that he was saying anything sarcastic at all. Swinger said he was going out and see if the road needed attention, and he did not think it would, so his next stop would be the building at the portal of the mine. He said he would give the kids a hand dumping the cars of the muck train that was due out soon. He told me to be careful going down the canyon and headed out into the snow. I told the Bull, Sweet Pea, and Matt that I was glad I had met them. Matt just waved from his place at the back of the room, and Sweet Pea mentioned he was happy for the chance to meet me. The Bull sat back in his chair a little and said, "I am glad from my end to get to know you, as I have heard some of the stories from Swinger and he sure thinks a hell of a lot of you. You are welcome up here anytime you can make it and the next go around I'll make sure Swinger can break loose and take you on a show-and-tell tour around this project. He has before and will in the future put in some damn long days, especially now that we are in deep winter up here. I take that all into consideration. Watch it close going down and have a safe trip."

I made it out to the highway with no trouble. The old General Mess of Crap, chained up as it was, went through the new-fallen snow easily. Over eight inches of snow had fallen on the mine road since I had come in. The amount of snow that could come down in that canyon had always been a source of conversation. The only way, however, to begin to understand how fast it could accumulate was to experience it firsthand. The canyon highway had seen little traffic during the middle of the day, but when the skiers started down, it would be a different story. I wanted to be out of that canyon before that business started.

If those people skied as they drove, they would not have gotten off the mountain alive. Lunatic drivers were about to overrun the country, and the road would soon be jammed up good, but that business is for another story. I made it out OK and pulled the chains off at a turnout on Wasatch Boulevard between Big and Little Cottonwood Canyons.

December of 1957 was almost at its end, with Christmas just a short few days away, and a new year would open up and bring some interesting times along with it. Some of it would occur by chance, and one event that was coming would have nothing to do with chance. The plotting of that event, quietly done, had one goal: my departure from Phillips Petroleum Company. No one but myself knew what was going to take place, and no one ever heard what did—until now, as this piece of writing will lay it out.

23

First Trip—New Year

IT WAS THE second week of January 1958 before I got back up to Alta. The day started out with the necessary precaution of putting the chains on the old GMC at the usual spot, and as was usually the case, it was a good thing because of the snow. My intention was to go in the Col-Rex to make note of and put on my map of the mine things that were not on it. This map came with the USGS Professional Paper 201 that I had obtained. I would use pace count for the distances involved through the timbered sections and for any drifts or crosscuts off the main run of the Col-Rex. I intended to mark on the map the locations of the most hazardous places I had encountered like hidden water-filled shafts, caving ground, and impassable sections of the mine. This project would take in the Col-Rex from the portal of the Howland Tunnel to the D winze. Over 6,000 feet lay between those two points, with hundreds of feet of workings off the main tunnel.

I had the USGS 201 map in a waterproof folder, and it would only come out of that if I had to refer to something that only it contained. That map, along with all the other gear I deemed necessary, would be in an old military rucksack along with a sandwich and my thermos of coffee. The thermos of coffee took up space and was a luxury, not a necessity, but what the hell? I had a clipboard that had about a dozen sheets of paper to record reference points, paces made, and the features in the mine I wanted to put on the map. These sheets of paper would be full of rust-colored water spots before the job was completed.

To undertake this planned trip underground alone was not a smart thing to do. To somewhat mitigate the situation, I planned to stop at the drain tunnel, look up Swinger, and tell him what I was up to so somebody would have an idea of where my carcass might be found. His reaction was the usual and reminded me that I had to have some kind of a head problem to pull off a stunt like that. To that assessment of my mental capabilities, he told me to check in when I came down so he did not go boo-coo wondering how I came out. I assured him that would happen.

Another thing that he brought up in the midst of his little lecture was he wondered if I could even get into the mine considering the snow. Both of us knew that old Slick had temporarily shut down his operation. Frank Reedy was unlikely to be up there, and that left Mack and Mark Jacobson as the only ones doing anything in the Col-Rex at the time. When I got up to where the road leveled out, the snow had buried the snowshed from the bridge to the buildings of the mine with just an occasional patch of roof showing through. A silent *Oh shit* run through my mind, then I spotted the pickup the Jacobsons came up the canyon in.

They had parked their truck in a turnout on the north side of the highway, just west of where the now completely buried snowshed run from the highway bridge to the portal of the Howland Tunnel. It looked doable to me, although I had no idea of what getting down to the snowshed door would entail.

I went back to the truck, exchanged my leather boots for my Goodall's, put on my rubber tuxedo and hard-boiled hat with lamp, got the loaded pack out onto the road, and locked all my other things in the truck. It required a major adjustment to the shoulder straps of the pack so it would fit over the bulky rubber coat I was wearing now. There were going to be problems with this layout, but it had to go in with me regardless.

As I neared the snowshed, I noticed something I had not been able to see from the highway. At the end of the path, a welcome sight appeared in the form of a heavy ladder with just the top three or four rungs showing above the hardpacked snow. The ladder had heavy rungs and rails, making it look just like the ladder in a raise. In all probability, it was just that. Being familiar with wet ladder rungs,

I had no problem going down the thing. I went into the shack and found no one in sight but found the stove almost hot. There were various items of clothing hanging on spikes in the walls and a few boxes on the floor near the east wall. It looked like Mack and Mark were making good use of the place, but they were not as fussy about keeping it cleaned up as Swinger had been. It was time to get my lamp burning and I simply borrowed what I needed in the way of carbide from Hansen's big can then put the lid securely back in place. I dipped the lamp in the ditch to fill the water chamber and got it fired up.

Originally, I had intended to leave the Howland where the Columbus-Rexall Tunnel branched off it. When I reached that point, I decided to make a short detour until I arrived where the Jacobsons were hard at work. I figured it would be a good idea to let them know I was in the hole and what I intended to do. They did not expect to see me or anyone else that day, and it surprised them when I showed up. I told them that I intended to head for the Jewel Stope area and would probably be back out when they shut down for the day. Mark told me I looked like a mine inspector because of the clipboard.

Mack told me to watch myself and asked if I had a candle. I told him I did, and it was handy but that I was not too worried as the last trip showed no problem with the air. Mack told me that regardless, it would be best to carry a lighted candle all the way through the long-timbered section. He added to that by explaining that changes in atmospheric pressure could make dangerous changes in the air quality of that stretch.

I left the Jacobsons and took the crosscut over to the Col-Rex, where I found myself in heavily timbered ground, which I already knew was there. I made my ritual stop at the water tank drift and had my cup of icy water using the old enamel cup, rehanging it on its spike, and then heading on.

I put a match to the candle when I got to the first of the timber, and that candle would keep burning until I came out at the end of Death Valley's run, a distance of over 1,000 feet. Carrying the candle in one hand and the clipboard in the other was a monumentally aggravating job, and it added, considerably, to the time involved to roughly map everything I wanted to put onto the 201 map.

When I finally got to the end of Death Valley, I was feeling considerably worn down. The flame of my lamp was again low enough that another recharge was in order. The candle was burned down now to a stub, and I did not have a spare, which was a bad miscalculation on my part. I got the lamp going again and left the candle stub burning on a small ledge on the rib. It occurred to me at that time that I was a little hungry—more than a little, actually. There was not a nice soft rock to sit on anywhere in sight, so I devoured the sandwich standing up. Two cups of coffee out of the thermos followed the sandwich while I leaned against the rib.

I decided to carry the flashlight in one hand going out, so that stayed out of the pack. The clipboard with its water-splotched sheets of paper, with all the scribbled notes and drawings on them, went into the pack with the rest of the gear. There was a lot of time invested in those sheets of paper, and I hoped that they would be decipherable enough that I could make out what was on them.

When I passed by the old cranky compressor, I was close to the cutoff to the area I had worked in. Worn out from the short six hours I had already put in, I went on out the Howland's portal under the highway bridge, stopped, and sat down on a handy empty powder box. I drained the water out of the lamp, unscrewed the bottom, and knocked what was left of the carbide out of it. Then I just sat there.

I was just getting up to head outside for the old General Mess of Crap when Mack and Mark Jacobson came out of the hole. They said they were glad I had made it outside and wondered how things went, and I told them. Mark said they were out a bit early and were going to get the fire back up in the old Monarch and put some coffee on. Did I want to stay and have a cup? I declined, saying that I had promised Swinger to stop by the drain tunnel to let him know I was still among the living.

When I got to the drain tunnel, the Bull, Sweet Pea, and the day shift had already headed for the valley, and the night shift was heading into the hole. I found Swinger up in the penthouse when

I went up the stairs. I could smell the coffee and decided I was not going to pass on a cup of that, and as usual, Swinger immediately made the offer. He asked how things had gone, and I told him it was a good trip but had kicked the hell out of me for some reason. I told him about the Jacobsons and that access to the mine was not bad at all. This all seemed to be good news to him, so we just sat there for a while and enjoyed our coffee. It was getting dark and still snowing when I got back in the old General Mess of Crap and headed for home. It had been an interesting run.

I had the next day off and planned on heading to Alta to do more exploring in the Col-Rex. I intended to do more work toward the updating of the USGS map of the mine. That idea did not go over well on the home front. My wife also had the next day off work. An interesting session followed my announcing my plan for that particular day. The term *domestic dispute* is a somewhat gentle way of putting what came next. I had pushed things to the limit, and I had to admit that, considering the immense amount of time I spent in Alta, virtually ignoring the home front. Among other things, the suggestion, by her, came up that maybe I should just move out and live up there.

That forceful suggestion, among the rest of the things mentioned, caused an awakening on my part. I realized that I needed to take a strong look at what I had been doing and make some changes. So along with that, plus the fact the day's escapade had worn me down, I discarded the plan for the next day. It turned out it was easy to do, as the next morning, heavy snow was falling in the valley and snow would close the Little Cottonwood Canyon highway.

24
At the Drain Tunnel and Col-Rex

I MISSED GETTING up to Alta the next week even though I had two midweek days off from my beloved job with Phillips, the end of which was getting close. There was timing involved in making my departure from that organization a workable thing. It was the last week of January 1958 when I made it up the canyon, and that was just for one day. My wife worked that day, so as long as I was home by 6:00, things would work well. I decided to stop at the drain tunnel before going on up to the Col-Rex so Swinger would know what I intended to do. When I got off the canyon highway and started toward the mine buildings, there was a fellow doing something on the gate at the start of the road going to the mine. He had the gate closed across the road; the Bull's truck was behind him. I knew immediately that it was not the Bull because this gent had a very dark complexion and I had never seen him before. He waved me to stop and walked up to the truck as I rolled the window down. He got right to it without any type of greeting, so I just listened.

It was the usual run of dialogue that entailed what the "No Trespassing," "Keep Out," and "Private Property" signs meant. He was not nasty about it but tried his best to speak with authority and just about pulled it off. I decided not to argue with him, so I tried a different tack just to see where it went.

"All right," I started out, "now this is the deal from my end. I promise to pay attention to the signs and you and back this crate out to the highway. But there is something you need to do to get me to do that."

With that, he inquired as to what I wanted him to do but made no commitment.

"When you get done with what you are doing and go back to the office, I would like you to tell the Bull and Swinger that you just run the kid and his old pile of junk off the property. Will you do that?"

That gave him pause, and he looked hard at me and said, "Aw shit! You must know Mister Al and Mister Swinger. You must be the one I have heard talk about by those two. Now let me get the gate out of your way. I think you can get past the truck okay."

I thanked the fellow, got through the now open gate and parked where I would be out of the way, got out of the truck, and went into the office. I found the Bull at his desk and Sweet Pea at his post, and spotted Matt in the back at his big table. We got all the greetings done. I told the Bull that a dark-colored fellow had stopped me and explained what the no-entry signs meant. The Bull kind of laughed and said that I had just met Gus. He added that Gus sometimes worked in the mine and sometimes as an outside man. I told the Bull that I had to drop a couple of names on him to get past the gate, but the two I used got me a pass immediately. Another chuckle came out of the Bull, then he said Swinger was down at the portal building, and he told Sweet Pea to go fetch him. Sweet Pea got by without that little walk, as Swinger came in through the door. It was the usual.

"Hullo kid! How's she hummin', chum?"

We just talked for a bit, and I told them I was headed for the Col-Rex to play around for a while and I would be stopping on my way down to let them know I had not managed to gob myself up there. With that and a few more things said between us, I walked out to the old General Mess of Crap and headed up the canyon. When I arrived at the Col-Rex there was no truck parked in the turnout. That indicated that the Jacobsons were not there that day.

I made the walk from the highway over to and down the ladder and found the door into the snowshed closed. The snow had drifted against the door and piled up about two feet deep. It took some hard pushing with my shoulder to get it to open; when it swung inward, I went inside. The place felt hollow and lonely, and some of my enthusiasm started to wane. I was tempted to turn around, head back to the truck, and give it up for that day. I gave it some more thought, and figured, well, I was there, and I ought to do something other than just walk away.

My original intent had been to head back to the Jewel Stope and beyond where the D winze was located, as there were things back there I wanted to add to the 201 map. The idea at that moment did not seem like a good one at all. Going through Death Valley was the big item that made me discard the venture for that day.

I walked under the old bridge and through the snowshed to the portal. I was still considering what I wanted to do that day. When I got to the portal timber set, I had it figured out. I got the clipboard with its paper out and paced off the distance from the portal set to the last timber set where the solid limestone started. I made note of this so I could draw it in on the 201 map accurately. At the point where the Col-Rex branched off the Howland, the pace counts commenced once again.

All that went down on paper with the most simple of illustrations of how the two tunnels lay in relation to each other. This would make it a simple job to transfer the information to the 201 map at home. Done with that section, I headed on into the location of the tired old compressor, noted that, and went on to the drift along the Brain Fissure. Following this drift would take me to the familiar raise to the Olympic Stope. The drift along the Brain Fissure was timbered and lagged tight all the way to the unforgettable Baptist Bend.

There was one more short-timbered section where the drift changed direction and was timbered through the bend. Beyond the last of the timbered run, I quickly came to the raise, and that area required a little time to pace and note a number of things. The 201 map did not show the raise or the extensions of the tunnel and the crosscut off it. I noted the run of the fissure along the main tunnel, the one supposedly of high grade but not minable because of its narrowness. I did not get in a hurry doing any of this. Once I was done, I headed back out of that area and in little time was at the home of the compressor, and at that point, I decided to follow the crosscut that would take me over to the Howland Tunnel. Then for some reason, that idea held little appeal, and that plot was discarded right there, so I headed for the outside.

I went out through the snowshed door and headed for the old GMC. I decided I would head for the drain tunnel, which I had promised Swinger I would do, then headed down the canyon. That left me five hours until I would have to be home. That turned out to be a good thing, as I would use the five hours almost to the minute.

25

The Two-Bit Tour

WHEN I MADE the turn onto the road to the mine, this time, there was no keeper of the gate in evidence. In the office, the Bull, Sweet Pea, and Matt were in their usual places. The Bull said that I was back sooner than he'd thought I'd be and inquired as to how things were up at the Col-Rex. I told him no one else was up there and I had the place to myself. I asked the Bull where Swinger was, and he told me that he was at the portal building doing whatever it was that Swinger did. He told me to go on over and wake Swinger's fat ass up. The Bull knew damn well that I would not find Swinger taking a nap, but he had to get that dig in. He added to that by saying I should tell Swinger to take me on the two-bit tour of the drain tunnel layout.

Here would be a good place to explain the Wasatch Drain Tunnel a bit. It was originally driven from 1912 to 1916 by the Wasatch Mines Company to drain water from the Col-Con Mine but was connected sometime later to the Col-Rex, South Columbus, South Hecla, Emily, Toledo, Flagstaff, and Frederick properties, among others. Before my time in the early 1950s, it began its effort to drain the massive Cardiff ore body (of which more will be shared in subsequent chapters), the largest body in the district by far. Most of these mines were flooded and abandoned by 1937. Now, by the time of my arrival, the Bull and his crew were working to reach the Cardiff Mine to drain it below the 1500 level.

Bull's offer sounded good to me, so I headed out the door to cross the 100 yards for the portal of the Wasatch Drain Tunnel. I was getting close when Swinger walked out of the roll-up door on the building's left front side. We met just outside the door, and I told him the Bull said I might be able to get the two-bit tour if I acted very nice. Swinger immediately agreed with that idea, and we got underway with that show-and-tell.

We walked back into the building using the doorway Swinger had just come out of. Inside was a complete woodcutting shop and store of lumber. Nearby there lay a good stack of three-inch pipe, mostly for use as airlines. There were several boxes of varied fittings for the pipe such as unions, ells,* shutoff valves, and other hardware. All the necessary equipment and tools were located here to accomplish any cutting, threading, and assembly that might be required. From there, we walked over to where the tracks came into the building out of the snowshed. Unlike any other mine in the district, all having wooden snowsheds, this version was an eight-foot diameter corrugated pipe of heavy galvanized steel. This had replaced the many-times-repaired wooden snowshed that for the most part dated back to the original built in 1916.

The new snowshed carries the track, the four-inch diameter airline, and the heavy power cable that supplies the underground workings with electrical power throughout. Swinger referred to the snowshed as the tube, as did the others that I would talk to as time went by. The Bull, however, had his own name for that run of corrugated pipe: the steel asshole. Leave it to the Bull; he had obviously spent too many years around Swinging Door Campbell. At the point the track exited the snowshed, it divided into a double track that run all the way through the building. The track terminated, stop blocks at that point, as it reached another wide doorway in the west wall of the building.

Waste rock coming out of the mine is always wet. If it hangs up while dumping, it can tip the car over unless a chain secures its underside framework to the rail it is riding on. The cars used at the Wasatch Drain Tunnel were of three-ton capacity quite unlike the ones we used up at the Col-Rex, which were one ton.

The waste rock ended up in the bed of an FWD truck, an old military surplus piece of equipment. This truck transported the

* Slang for elbow or 90-degree angle.

muck out to the dump and unloaded it. Far in the past, this truck originally was yellow, most of the paint now replaced by rust. The yellow color, what remained, prompted this thing to be designated the Banana Wagon. One Swinging Door Campbell of course, coined this name. When ore came out instead of waste rock, it was loaded into a much newer truck. This unit was a new Ford T-850, about one year old at the time.

It was well set up for ore hauling, with steel sideboards rising above the normal bed that increased the capacity considerably. When this truck was loaded to the dump bed's capacity, it is well that there were no law enforcement truck scales between the mine and the destination smelters. It would be highly doubtful that this truck ever left the mine with a legal load. The owner/operator of this truck was paid by the ton, and he had little objection to getting the most out of his investment and time. H. Jay Woodward owned that T-850. He also held the permits to haul ore out of the Cottonwood mining districts. Swinging Door, as he usually did, bestowed a nickname on H. Jay. Swinger referred to him as the Hound, whereas everyone else called him Jay.

Our last stop involved a tall, rangy dark-skinned fellow who happened to be standing in the shop area. He was the one who had played gatekeeper, the fellow who stopped me that first morning. I correctly assumed that he was the Gus that the Bull had named after my telling him of the stop. Swinger's introduction varied the man's name somewhat from the name the Bull had used.

"Kid, this is Almond Joy, the watcher of the gate—well, once in a while, that is. Now, don't hold that against him. He just likes to be a boss sometimes."

Gus—or rather, Almond Joy—and I shook hands, and I told him I was glad to make his acquaintance under better conditions. Gus said it was the same for him and said he regretted the incident that morning. I assured him I could not remember a thing about that business. Naturally, I had to wonder now what in hell this Almond Joy business was. An Almond Joy, as far as I knew, was a chocolate candy bar with two almonds in it. I spent little time pondering where that name came from, the obvious answer to that was standing next to me: Swinging Door, the master of nicknames.

We had used up a lot of time on this part of the show-and-tell, enough that when we decided to go out, the men of the day shift were out of the mine. Swinger said it was time for him to get on the other side of the wall. He said the day shift boys would be dropping their lights on the counter at the big window. With that, we went through the door that opened into the east side of the building.

I stood back out of Swinger's way, leaned against a handy wall, and watched what came next. The lamps used by the miners here at the drain tunnel were electric, the power coming from a battery pack.

When the day shift men came into the dry, the first thing they did was unhook the lamp with its cord and battery and set it on the broad counter. Swinger would take the units one at a time, clean them off, and check the water levels of the batteries, then put them on the charger. It had ample stations to hold at least 40 lamps at the same time and appeared to have at least 20 units charging at the time. This layout was very different from the Col-Rex, the carbide lamps we used, and the big can of carbide. This was a well-set-up operation, definitely not a poor boy project like the Col-Rex lease.

When the night shift started coming in, most of the day shift men were ready to go out the door and head for home. There was plenty of room for both shifts in the dry, but the Bull decided he wanted the space of 45 minutes to one hour between the shifts. The Bull always got his way, so that is how it went.

When the night shift headed for the portal, Swinger and I went into the office area and talked for a while with the Bull before him and Sweet Pea headed for the valley. I made sure I thanked the Bull for the two-bit tour and the guide.

The Bull just said, "Anytime."

The time had come for me to head for the valley also, as the day was well used up. I could have used some of Swinger's coffee, but that would need brewing, and I would definitely run out of time if I stayed.

26

Deep Enough with Phillips

AS I DROVE home after leaving the drain tunnel, I thought little about the guided tour. The foremost thing that took hold of my mind was my much-despised employment with Phillips Petroleum Company. The thing that I had not figured out was how to manage my departure from Phillips and make it look reasonable to my wife. I needed to make it believable without stretching the truth of it too thin. I had thought through several different plots and discarded each for one reason or another. This had to look right, as I was already in a big kettle of very warm water on the home front due to my obsessive interest in mining. And obsessive it was, I have to admit.

The following week after the big show-and-tell tour at the Wasatch Drain Tunnel operation would mark the end of the service station trap. The reason for this was the fact that I was to start my new job at Lambert and Company the Monday of the week after that. I had intended to give Phillips a few days' notice, four or five anyhow, but that would not be necessary. A couple of days into the following week marked the arrival of a self-important suit, his guests, and the car wash he did not approve of, which sealed my fate with Phillips Petroleum.

But first, I need to share how I came to work there in the first place. I was in the third year of a three-year apprenticeship, with about 10 months until I would be a journeyman. The company I was working for was family owned, and I worked under either my father or one uncle. We had for the first time run short of work to do, and I found myself with some time off. That was when I had decided to give up the painting trade against my father's advice.

It soon became apparent that the dropping-my-apprenticeship move I had made was not a good one. I knew I had to get back to work, and soon. I considered a career in law enforcement, but I had to be 21 years old, which I was not. I looked at a couple of sales jobs, mostly out of desperation, and knew nothing along that line would ever work for me. My father-in-law told me he had a good friend who leased a Phillips 66 service station and told me to go see him. I knew the station; it was across the street from the shopping center owned by my father-in-law. John Malmborg leased the station from Phillips Petroleum Company. It was called Malmborg's 66. With no other prospects, I went and talked to John Malmborg. I did not really want to do this, but I had to get back to work.

The order of things dictated that I would be required to pass through a three-week session of schooling operated by Phillips Petroleum Company. The first hour I spent in the classroom caused me to dub it "obedience school." Such was my rebellious attitude toward that kind of environment. In my estimation, all it amounted to was a comprehensive way of kissing peoples' asses. This was a problem, still is, and always will be for me, and it has had its cost over the years. Going in, I knew it would be only a matter of time before my way of looking at things would get me in trouble.

On finishing my education with the Phillips company school, I went to work at Malmborg's 66 along with another trainee from the same school. After three weeks, the fellow who accompanied me to Malmborg announced he was leaving. Another fellow who had gone through the training course had arranged to lease a station from Phillips and offered my cohort a job that he took straightaway. This tightly laced, overly religious individual said he would also hire me if I would clean up my language. That was not going to happen, no matter how hard I might try, because I just did not want to do it. According to that individual's way of defining things, we did not have the same values. OK with me!

During the time I worked for John, I worked mostly days, though in that time, I did sometimes catch a couple of weeks of evening shifts. But regardless, it was my good fortune that my two days off per week fell on weekdays, giving me time up in the old Col-Rex with Swinger and, on occasion, Slick. There was one thing and one thing alone that allowed me to stay as long as I did with Malmborg. One day, he mentioned that he had been a miner and had spent quite a few years working for Cardiff Mining and Milling Company. I told John about what I had been doing and still was, and as luck would have it, he knew a lot about the old Col-Rex. That held things together on a livable basis, so I lasted for a bit longer at Malmborg's 66.

However, my sense of humor was in a state of serious decline; my tolerance for the public in general had disappeared into parts unknown. The combination involving the two factors just mentioned set the stage for the final episode that ended my career in the business.

I was the lead man on the evening shift when it happened, and it was late, probably around 10:30 p.m. One of the midlevel company suits arrived with another couple whom he decided to impress with his status. He decided that his car needed a cleanup and drove it into the wash bay. This particular location made it a policy to do the best car wash in the city. I assigned two coworkers to do the job while I would take care of any customers who might come in for fuel. The suit decided to give his friends, a man and his wife, along with his own wife, a tour of the facility. He explained all the things he thought were wrong with the operation in detail.

Naturally, that critique required my presence throughout the tour so he had a subject available for finger-pointing. The only relief from this was when a customer arrived at the pumps, and I took care of them in the Phillips-approved way. At that time, policy stated that you ran, not walked, to the customer's vehicle. Policy also stated that you ask if you might fill the tank with "Flite-Fuel," which was the premium grade of gasoline. You then filled the tank or dispensed whatever amount the customer requested.

The next things in line were the washing of all the windows and sweeping of the floors unless they refused that courtesy; few did. Of course, the suit found fault with the way I did things.

The man was determined to impress his friends and his wife with his knowledge and authority when it came to operational procedure.

The suit was a professional nitpicker. Apparently, I had sinned because, after the customer departed, I had neglected to run outside with my little whisk broom and a dustpan to clean up the horrible mess I had left on the drive. Things were starting to get a little tight. That drive received a hosing down three times each shift, so I could see no point in even saying anything to that last observation, and I was ready to punch him in the mouth at that point.

The suit, along with his wife and friends and myself, were in the office standing in silence. One of the fellows from the car wash detail entered saying they were finished with the car. We all left for the wash bay so, as I had anticipated, the suit could start his inspection of the finished job. To me, it looked like the crew did a good job on the wash. They had toweled off the vehicle until it was nearly completely dry. Most customers would accept the appearance of the car, pronouncing it a job well done. Not the suit. He planted himself along with his critical eye in the front seat, pointing out a small wet streak on the windshield that was seconds from drying. He then put himself in the back seat, found another small hard-to-see wet spot, and complained about that. He was not finished yet; he removed himself from the inside of his car, did a walk around, and found more of what he called "terrible deficiencies."

I suspected that the couple accompanying him and his wife were starting to get a little uncomfortable. They were not alone, as the suit lit my fuse with his last tirade, and it was not any too long to begin with. Then he announced that he would normally require the wash job be redone. However, he added, it was late, and he was with guests. With that, in the miner's parlance, the pompous suit drilled into a miss.* It did not matter to him that all management personnel received their car washes free of charge. He was just about to start

* To drill into a miss is to drill into a previously placed dynamite charge that failed to detonate. It is one of the most dangerous events in a mine, because a charge set off by a miner's drill will almost surely kill that individual and any others working the face of a mine.

ranting about something else but did not get the chance. I beat him to it and said, "You are a goddamned asshole, you sonofabitch!"

He suddenly looked like maybe his necktie was too tight, opened his mouth, closed it, and opened it again and loudly announced, "You, young man, will not be employed by Phillips Petroleum Company tomorrow, I can guarantee."

I just grinned at him, never uttered a word, just stared.

He could not believe that someone would speak to his eminence in such a manner. He started again, "Did you hear what I said? Well, did you?"

I simply held my grin and stared at him.

He tried again: "Well? Well?"

My grin, held along with my stare, made him consider that, maybe, he was in danger of being involved in some kind of accident.

The four of them turned away and headed for the suit's nice clean car. The two women looked a little pale. The man accompanying the suit turned and looked back at me. I was still standing in place, and he gave me a friendly smile. It is possible I was wrong, but his smile seemed to say that what he had just witnessed was worth seeing. The suit would be as good as his word. When I came on shift the next afternoon, there were two suits along with the station manager waiting for me in the office.

Of course, I was familiar with the station manager and one of the suits. This fellow happened to be the one who hired me into the training program and had given the basic orientation. The fellow accompanying him could have been one or two things. He was either a suit in training or a cop, and I suspected he was most likely a cop. All he did was observe. Sure enough, as I expected, the talking suit explained to me that Phillips Petroleum Company no longer required my services. Then he waited to see if I had anything to say, which I did.

"That, sir, is the best goddamned news I have ever heard from the first day with this company until right now."

I walked out of that office feeling good. Two days from then, I would go to work for Lambert and Company, an auto parts store and automotive machine shop.

27

My Privileged Observer Status

CHANGING EMPLOYMENT FROM Phillips Petroleum Company to Lambert and Company meant weekdays off became outdated. Had I still been able to work at the old Col-Rex under the guidance of my friend Swinging Door, chances were good that I would not have left Phillips. So when Swinger left to go back to the Wasatch Drain Tunnel, that helped make up my mind that Phillips was no place for me. Another factor that entered into it was Tokyo Joe and Alimony Bill. They were now spending full weeks working for Slick in the Col-Rex. They were experienced miners, and that left no place, really, for a wet-behind-the-ears kid to be getting underfoot. Slick always told me that I was welcome to come around anytime for a visit.

February of 1958 would be the start of some interesting times for me at the Wasatch Drain Tunnel. If it were today or even 35 years ago or more, what I was able to do around that mining project would never have been possible. Albert "Bull" Wondershek threw open doors to almost anything I wanted to see or do, including the underground operation. A situation like the one I had on that property in today's world would not be possible. I would have to sign an endless number of forms, legal documents having to do with every possible release of liability imaginable.

My involvement with the Wasatch Drain Tunnel was never as a working miner or as any kind of company employee. Swinger discouraged me from even looking at the possibility of working there. He reminded me, as he had from the beginning of our association, that mining was a dying game, and those days were ending. If I were to assign myself a title around that project, it would be observer, an extremely privileged observer. There was little doubt that Swinger had pulled some chains to make my initial acceptance so smooth, something he was very good at doing. Another thing in my favor was the fact that the Bull and I made a solid connection right at the beginning. Every man I talked to over the years up there had a great respect for him. Some of that, according to Swinger, was due to the fact that nobody in their right head cared to get sideways with the Bull.

At that time, the mine employed two shifts, working alternating five- and six-day workweeks. That set things up to give the miners every other Saturday off, and that worked out very well for me in the end. Now working for Lambert and Company, our workweek included the usual Monday through Friday and half a day on Saturday. That half day Saturday was not the best for what I was doing in Alta, but it worked out fairly well.

There were no paid sick days at Lambert's, and there was no way I could afford an unpaid day anyway. My wife and I walked on the edge of financial disaster at that time, and in truth, the fault was mine. My wife was making a reasonable wage, quite unlike the man to whom she was married. When I left my apprenticeship as a painter, I took a big reduction in pay; the salary with Phillips was not much over half of what I made as a painter's apprentice. When I began my employment with Lambert and Company, my starting pay was less by far than what I had been drawing from Phillips Petroleum Company. To this day, I do not know how we made things work at all, but we did—well, sort of. At Lambert's, I learned a valuable trade as an automotive machinist. The pay was very poor at the time, but it paid off well years later.

It was near the end of February 1958 when I finally made it back up to the drain tunnel. The junk box of the General Mess of Crap held all my mining gear, which remained with the truck at all times. The only thing I had to do when I left Lambert's was head up the canyon. My wife worked Saturdays, so that did not create too much of a problem, other than that I usually got home about three hours after she did. That three hours or so was trivial compared to what I would lay in in the future, and that would cause problems at times. I had barely enough money for gas for the old clunker, sometimes getting home on luck and fumes. Consequently, there was no money to buy even a cheap sandwich for my lunch. That little problem I handled by making a sandwich before I left for work and stowing it in the truck. I did not take any coffee with me because Swinger would have an ample supply of that up in his penthouse.

The mine was working that Saturday, on the alternating five- and six-day week schedule. Swinger was pushing the waste rock that had come out of the mine over the edge of the dump with the old International bulldozer. When the muck train came out of the mine, the motorman and two of the outside men dumped the cars into the grizzly.* From that point, the conveyor system loaded the Banana Wagon. When the Banana Wagon was loaded to capacity, the conveyor shut down. After dumping its load at the edge of the dump, the driver put the truck into position for another load. Almond Joy was usually the pilot of the Banana Wagon, as he worked as an outside man along with Swinger. As the Banana Wagon had a very questionable braking system, it was too dangerous to back it to the edge of the dump for unloading. It was much safer to have Swinger push the waste rock over with the blade of the old International bulldozer.

The outside work was in full swing when I got there so I went into the office and spent some time talking with the Bull. Before we got started with that, he sent me up to the penthouse to see if there happened to be any hot coffee on the stove. There was. The Bull leaned back in his chair while I leaned on the counter and the bullshit got underway. The thing we had the most fun with was a half-cooked plot that involved a whorehouse. It went kind of like this, and the Bull started it off.

"Under the direction of the bigwigs, the armchair miners, and paper shufflers, until just recently, I didn't have any men in there for quite some time, nearly a year. What those birds wanted to do was

* A grizzly is a dump hole for waste rock.

try and develop some ore in the old workings and do some exploration work to open up new ore. We spent a lot of the stockholders' money playing that game and came up with very little and a year's delay on the drive for the Cardiff. That wasn't the only stunt they insisted on which worked even worse than inside the hill here. But those bastards had all the answers, all the money to play with, and I figured what the hell, we are all getting paid."

I just shook my head, as I'd had my own problems with suits, and I was about to tell the Bull about the last suit episode when he got started again.

"You know, Dick, I should have suggested that they finance a good whorehouse up here and give some of the guys something but rock to drill." He gave a short chuckle, then continued. "Shit, why not? Want to get in on a whorehouse operation—just kidding. The problems would be many, chief among them trying to muck the Mormon sonofabitch out of the penthouse, not to mention trying to locate talent."

I decided that I had to find out the answer as to why the Bull sometimes called Swinger the Mormon sonofabitch and so I put the question to him. I just got it out when Swinger came through the door, and the Bull said, "Now, speaking of such things, the Mormon sonofabitch has come."

"Jesus Christ!" Swinger said. "Now, if that ain't some sort of bullshit to come out of the yap of a goddamned Catholic bohunk.*"

I thought, *Oh shit!* In addition, I guess the look on my face said as much as the words would have. They both commenced laughing, as if they had just heard the king of all humorous things, and I relaxed. Between the two of them, I got the story, at least the version for that day.

As previously mentioned by Swinger, he and the Bull had worked together on several jobs, and those times stretched back over the years for a considerable number. What they could not agree on was who

* A denigrating term for an immigrant, typically a laborer, from central or southeastern Europe.

started the name-calling, each one blaming the other. I did not care who lit the fuse on this business and said so. Swinger said his mother and stepfather were both good Mormon folk, his mother being the strongest in her beliefs. He said he had managed to avoid that disease, and she was not too happy with her wayward son in that respect. There was the question of how did the Bull come into this information so he could hang the Mormon brand on Swinger.

Then the Bull had to give forth on the title Swinger had hung on him. He explained that he was a badly lapsed Catholic, not only that he was not a bohunk, even if his name sounded "sorta bohunky." They both agreed that it was during one of their many fights that each named the other, and it was not on a friendly basis. So there they were, the Mormon sonofabitch and the goddamned Catholic bohunk. I suspected there was much more to this story, but it was OK for now. I knew there would be more forthcoming from each one of them. With that business concluded Swinger and I headed up to the penthouse to get some coffee before the day shift came out of the mine.

Swinger would have to be downstairs to take in the miners' lamps as they came into the dry. There was about half an hour before the night shift would arrive, so we went out and headed for the portal building. Almond Joy was cleaning up around the grizzly and getting the empty cars arranged and hooked together. When the night shift went in, the cars went in with them, along with the man trip.*

A *man trip* is a term that is not found anywhere other than on a sizable mining operation. Here, the man trip car was simply a flatbed with a bench running the length of it down the middle. The men straddled the bench as if it were a horse and rode on it into the mine. They stacked themselves one behind the other down that bench. There was no padding of any kind on the bench, and

* A rail car that transports the miners in and out of a mine. They come in varieties, some enclosed and having individual seats for each man. In some mines, the man trip is simply a flatbed car. The flatbed has a bench running down its center, front to back. The men straddle this bench, one behind the other, usually facing forward.

nobody would ever fall asleep going into the hole. The train that Almond Joy was putting together included two man trip cars, each accommodating six men.

The night crew arrived, and we headed for the big building so Swinger could get the lamps set out for the crew. The shift would pick up their lamps after they were outfitted in their gear, then they left the dry and headed for the portal. The train would be ready for the trip into the mountain with the big trammer at the head of it. The Bull and his driver, Sweet Pea, had already pulled out when I bid Swinger goodbye with the usual "Tap 'er light" from both of us. The old General Mess of Crap fired up OK, and I headed down the canyon.

28
A Real Miner

I WAS ABLE to make it up to the drain tunnel every Saturday in March of 1958. When the mine was working, I would spend some time talking with the Bull, Swinger having work around the yard to do. The more time I spent with the Bull, the better I liked that man. He had interesting stories to tell about his time in the mining game, and time went by quickly. He spent some years in Butte, Montana, in the deep mines up there. Albert Wondershek had developed a reputation of being most valuable as a mine superintendent. During most of his years in Butte, that is what he had done, and it was there he had hired Gus Almon. Gus followed the Bull when he left Montana, and he was extremely loyal to him. When the Bull took on the superintendence of the Wasatch Drain Tunnel and the drive for the Cardiff, Gus had come with him.

During one of our conversations, the one in which the Bull told me something of the history between Gus and himself I decided to ask a question. I had thought of it on several occasions, and it was time to make an inquiry. I asked the Bull if it upset Gus to have Swinger call him Almond Joy, adding that with Gus being a colored fellow, I wondered how that set with him. The Bull explained it more or less like this, as I remember it now.

"That name don't bother Gus at all, as he thinks that Mormon sonofabitch is the greatest thing since watermelon and fried chicken. The other name Swinger has for him might get Gus some pissed, but I think there is little chance of that. Now when Gus pulls off some stunt that irritates Swinger, then he becomes the burr head instead of Almond Joy."

I never asked and the Bull never mentioned the circumstances surrounding how he came to be superintendent on the project. I had thought about it but decided to let it alone and if the Bull offered the information, all the better. Al Wondershek was a newcomer to the Alta district, never having been there before, as was Swinger. He said one of the first things he did when he took over at the drain tunnel was to try to locate the Mormon sonofabitch and get him up there. He chuckled a little and then said, "I just had to find him and get him up here on the job, as I figured he had most likely gotten fatter and even lazier than he had been when I last worked with him." Then added, "Well, that lazy stuff was a bunch of bullshit, Dick, because lazy that Mormon sonofabitch has never been. Though he has been a hell of a rum nose as long as I have known him, and that's been a while. He swore that he shut that business down. Far as I know he has stayed dried out up here as of now anyhow."

"I have never seen Swinger drink anything but coffee since I met him," I said. "He told me he had been a hard drinker during his time but was quit on it now."

Swinger always spotted the old General Mess of Crap when I came in or shortly thereafter. He would not leave anything undone before he came into the office and asked what kind of lies we had been telling before he broke things up. There was time for a cup of coffee up in the penthouse before the day shift came out, so we went after it.

On Saturdays the mine did not work, Swinger and I would have coffee as soon as I got up there—a lot of coffee and even more plain old bullshitting. I simply just listened most of the time, as Swinger had to be the most interesting storyteller I had ever run across. He had ways of explaining things that were unique and even more so when it came to expressions. I had never listened to the likes of them until I met him and to this day have never heard anything that measured up to the way he expressed himself. Until I got used to the knack he had for corrupting words, there were many times I had to get him to translate what he was saying.

One of the examples of this happened one day up at the Col-Rex when we were having some lunch before going back underground.

We got started on the Peruvian Lodge for some reason or another. The shenanigans up there observed with binoculars from the shack's window could be entertaining. Swinger, being Swinger, come up with one of his ideas, and it went like this.

"You know, kid," he started out, "now if there was any market for the damned things, we could take a couple of Irish buggies, a pair of square points [shovels] over there early on a Monday morning, go through the halls, and come up with a shipment of used conundrums. That of course would make it a requirement to find some outfit what wanted that type of thing."

"Just what in hell are conundrums?" was the question I asked.

"Well hell, kid. You know those things some people call rubbers?" he replied. "They have other names, and some of them are words too big. Well, you know how I hate big words."

Then I got it, finally. What he called conundrums were in actuality what most people called condoms. This kind of stuff from his end was ongoing and the reason why I had to call for interpretation of some of the things he said.

During March, another interesting thing came up. When Swinger went back to work for the Bull, I started watching the Cardiff Mining and Milling Company's stock, the lease owners of the Wasatch Drain Tunnel. The newspapers in the Salt Lake Stock Exchange column posted this item along with other stocks daily. The value of Cardiff's stock was low, and sales were very slow. It remained static until about mid-March, when it jumped overnight, nearly doubling in value. The stock's value continued to climb, although modestly, each day, and sales were brisk. This occurred when an impressive showing of ore in the hillside ground opened up during the drive for the Cardiff.

The Saturday I came up to the mine wanting to know what had pushed the stock up so fast, the mine was not working. It had been a scheduled five-day week. Swinger had the answer to that question and told me about the strike.* The Bull would have been happy to

* Ore discovery.

deliver the news, but he was not there that day. The Bull had immediately told Swinger about it when samples of the ore were brought out from the hillside area for assay. Swinger added that the Bull "was really cranked up" over the discovery and he described the samples as "goddamn orgasm rock." Naturally, the group of men who had put up the money to finance the expensive exploration effort were more than pleased at the news.

The strike brought on the general feeling things were where they were supposed to be around that project. The Bull had yet to put on the additional men that would be required to handle an increased workload. During this time, things started to open up for me, affording me access anywhere on the property, which usually only employees had. One of the key things happened on a Saturday toward the end of March. Swinger and I were standing outside the dry when the night shift came out and headed for the portal. The last man was leaving the dry when Swinger nudged me and said, "You want to meet a real miner, kid?"

"Hell, Swing, I know several of the best now, but yeah, sure," I replied.

"Not quite like this guy, kid," he said. "He is the real thing, one of the district's old-timers."

Then Swinger called over to that last man out of the dry and said, "Hold up a minute, Dan'l, I want you to meet someone."

The man was a husky-looking individual with a friendly face beneath the hard-boiled hat. The light was in its place in its bracket but not turned on. He wore the familiar black diggers and the ubiquitous steel-toed rubber boots. He had a dark-colored towel wrapped around his neck like a scarf, something that none of the other men were wearing. The towel was like a trademark that, among other things, made him stand out. We all came to a halt with about four feet between us. I took an immediate liking to this fellow without a word yet spoken. Then Swinger said, using my name, one of the few times he did, "Dan'l, I want you to shake hands with my good chum, Dick. Kid, this is Dan Jacobson, the real thing, make no mistake."

Dan pulled the heavy rubber glove from his right hand, and we locked our right hands together. The connection was solid, and the bond was instantaneous. It was like when Swinger and I first met with a handshake, and I knew I had just met a real friend.

Dan caught up with the other men just as they reached the portal building, and he followed them in. When they disappeared into the building, Swinger gave me some interesting information, starting with Dan. What he told me was essentially the following.

"Dan is the shifter of the crew. That's the name, other than miners, what most people call a foreman. In this game they have always been called shifters, in case you're wondering what the hell. The Bull put him on after talking him down from the Col-Rex along with his brother Mack. Mack didn't hang around long before he went back up to the Col-Rex. The Bull had heard tell of the Jacobsons and liked what he learned so he went after them.

"Well, it seems that Dan, his two brothers, and their father, Tony, had many years' time in this hole going way back. There isn't nothin' to do with the mining game that Dan doesn't know. He has done it all. It didn't take the Bull long to figure out this was the man to take over running one of the shifts. For some damn reason Dan wanted the night shift. I never asked him why though and he never brought it up.

"So, what will happen now, kid, is they will head on in and Dan will be the motorman. The day crew will have shot the drift round* at the end of the shift. By the time Dan gets his boys in there, the heading† will have been pretty well vented off—the bad stuff, blasting fumes, should be mostly gone. If there was a missed hole, the day shifter would bring the news out with him and warn Dan. A goddamn miss can be worse than deadly if drilled into. It doesn't happen often, but it does occur now and again. Nobody wants to come on to a missed hole they didn't know about."

* A drift round is the explosive charge placed at the working end of the drift.

† The end of the drift, crosscut, or tunnel, generally where the miners work. The term *working face* means the same thing and is often used in place of *heading*.

One of the men that had come out of the dry apparently did not go into the mine with the night crew. He was outside looking around the Banana Wagon parked under the conveyor belt for loading. He stood out; the main reason for this was he was not wearing the usual diggers and hard-boiled hat. I had to wonder how I had missed him when he came out with the crew, but I had. He was warmly dressed, however, as it was still very cold up at the drain tunnel. Swinger took me over where the man was so he could introduce me.

Here was another fellow I did not know, just one of several whose acquaintances I had not made up till now. It went like most times with one of Swinger's introductions; all I got was a nickname, as usual.

"Robin Hood," Swinger started out, "this is Dick, a good chum of mine. Kid, meet Robin Hood Johnson. He is on the grass like Almond Joy is most of the time along with me."

We shook hands, and I mentioned it was a pleasure to meet him. He responded likewise but added a little more, explaining the Robin Hood business.

"As you no doubt have figured out by now, this guy," he hooked his thumb toward Swinger, "has some kind of aversion to using real names, which is okay I suppose. What brought about this Robin Hood stuff happened when we first met just before he quit and went up the canyon. He actually called me by my real name at the time, which is Virgil, but not for long. Then one day he came sailing down here to clean up his carcass and swipe a barrel of water. I had come up early that day to do a little hunting and I like to hunt with a bow. The archery season for deer had opened and later when I came into the dry to get ready for shift, I had my bow and other gear with me. Well, you know how he is, Dick, he took a long look and announced that I was now Robin Hood and that is how it has been since."

29

Going in with the Shift

ON A SATURDAY morning, it was probably the first one in April 1958, my wife and I were getting ready to head off to our jobs. She had resigned herself to the fact that I would be heading for Alta when my half day at Lambert's was finished up. How she put up with these antics of mine has been a source of wonderment to this day on my part. I explained what I was going to attempt to do that day was to see if I could go in the mine with the night shift. The problem, I explained, was if that became possible, I would not be home until, probably, 2:00 a.m. Sunday morning. Happy with that she was not, but she decided not to give me a lot of trouble over it this time.

I arrived at the mine about 2:30 and spent some time talking with the Bull. There was still some snow on the dump, not much, but Almond Joy was still dumping the muck near the edge and Swinger pushing it over with the old International. The Bull told me that about a dozen truckloads of ore were now down at the Midvale Smelter. They were waiting for them to make a settlement on the value of the ore. Bull told me a man named Jay Woodward was doing the hauling and soon would have a lot more to take down. I had not met this Woodward fellow, and I wanted to make his acquaintance when I had the chance.

Swinger finished his work somewhere about 3:45, so we headed for the penthouse and coffee. I had eaten my homemade sandwich while driving up the canyon, so a few cups of good old Swinging Door coffee would set things off just right. While we were sitting there at the table and telling each other lies, as Swinger liked to describe any conversation, I finally got around to asking him if he thought there was any chance I might be able to go in the hole with the night shift. He looked at me for a few seconds, took a swallow of coffee, put down the cup, and said, "Well kid, I guess there ain't nothin' for it. If it was up to me, I would have no problem whatsoever but it ain't my place. Now you could go to the Bull and I am sure he would go for it in a minute. What you should do though is hit Dan'l with it as it is his shift and that would be the way I think you should go."

I had a few sips of coffee while I run that advice through my head and it made good sense. I was sure the Bull would give the idea his stamp of approval, but Dan Jacobson would have to be OK with the idea because he would have to assume the chore of watching over me. This would prove to be interesting, as the only time we had talked was just the short few sentences when we met. I told Swinger that his idea made good sense, and I added that I sure hoped it would work because I really wanted to see what was in that hole. We talked a little more, and the day shift came out of the mine. It was time for Swinger to go down and take care of the lights.

The day crew had finished up in the dry and were getting in their cars. As they started out of the yard, the night shift was coming into it from the highway. The men were getting out of their respective cars, headed for the dry. Dan was the last man to head for the door, and I hollered a greeting and asked him to hold up. This he did, and when I got over to him, he said howdy and asked how I was making out, at which point I told him things were good with me. I had no good idea how to approach Dan on the subject of going into the mine with his shift, so I just put the question to him straight out.

Dan never so much as blinked, and a smile appeared. "That'd be fine, Dick. Get Swinger to outfit you with rubber and anything else you need. I know Swinger will do that with no trouble at all."

I told Dan I had everything but a light and a belt for it. Told him all I had was a carbide lamp with me. I could not believe how he so easily agreed to take me in on his shift. He told me we would be heading in in about 20 minutes.

When I went in the Wasatch Drain Tunnel that evening with Dan's shift, it would be the first of many trips into that mine with the night crew. At that time, I had no idea this would go on for over two years. Most of the time I spent in that mine was with Dan's shift. I also went in during the day on a number of occasions with Swinger on Saturdays when the mine was not working, sometimes on Sunday mornings. I had only the most meager knowledge of the history of the Wasatch Drain Tunnel at that time. I gained what, to me, was a treasure trove of information, and I consider myself extremely privileged to have been given such an opportunity.

The difference between the operation at the drain tunnel and the one at the Col-Rex was stark. The Col-Rex was, in comparison to the drain tunnel, a casual operation. The first thing that night that made a lasting impression occurred after I was seated straddling the bench on one of the man trips while Dan headed the train into the mine. I had normally rode into the Col-Rex, with Swinger operating the trammer, sitting in one of the empty cars. It was a slow ride because of the narrowness of the tunnel and the none-too-reliable rails. The Col-Rex had many turns in its tunnel, nothing sharp, but no speed above a crawl was possible.

This was not the case in the Wasatch Drain Tunnel, and as Swinger liked to put it, "She runs for a mile straighter than an Indian goin' to shit." That mile was from the beginning of the snowshed to the north or Columbus lateral. From that point, the tunnel continued for another 1,000 feet on that straight line, but our turn off the main run would be at the Columbus lateral. When we entered the snowshed, Dan opened up that trammer and in we went, and I thought to myself *HOLY SHIT!* For the first few hundred feet, I figured all of us would be gobbed for sure. I was the only one who tightened up, as the crew did not even seem to notice the speed.

We must have been halfway to the lateral before I started to relax much. By the time Dan put the train into the turnoff, I decided I was not going to get gobbed.

I would like to have heard what Dan might have had to say to his crew in the dry before we went into the mine. He must have come up with some kind of semitruthful explanation as to who I was and why I was there. I suspect he must have planted the notion in everybody's head that I was some kind of privileged stockholder, maybe a type of dignitary, or some such bullshit. No one asked any questions of any kind in any of those particular directions. One thing for sure, he had outlined every man's job for that shift, as each one, when the man trip came to a halt, wordlessly headed off to carry out his assigned job. It looked obvious to me that the crew respected Dan to a great degree.

When we reached the area where the men got off the man trip, it was quite unlike any of the tunnels that we had passed through. There was a raise going up from the main tunnel on the left side. There had been some drifting off the main on both sides in this same area. I asked no questions at that time concerning any of this, as I figured Dan would let me know what was going on in the area. I suspected that this was the ore zone in the hillside ground.

For the last month, work had stopped on driving the tunnel toward the area beneath the Cardiff's flooded workings. The crews, both day and night shifts, worked at developing the ore zone of the hillside ground. The size of the ore zone had been determined, as much as possible, due to the district's complex geological structure. The raise I had observed along with the drifting at tunnel level and drifting from the raise allowed a reasonable assessment. Most of the ore developed during this time was at the smelter with some ready to ship still in the mine. This development required hiring more men, which was slow in occurring up to now, according to Dan. With a little revenue coming in, the powers that resided in higher places had once again commenced pushing to get to the Cardiff and its potential ore.

Dan did not spend much time in the area where the crew had just got off the man trip. I started to get off too, but he told me to stay put. We now headed back the way we had come in. Dan was running the trammer at a much lower speed now that he was pushing the train instead of pulling it. I had no idea of what was going on, so I just reversed my position on the car's bench so I faced the direction of travel, enjoying the ride. We traveled back down the tunnel until we came to the intersection with the crosscut, now on our right, where the old raise that led to the Columbus-Consolidated was located.

There was a crosscut running left 50 feet farther down tunnel from the one with the raise. A tail track* lay in this old drift, accessed by changing a switch on the main line. Dan changed the switch and then pushed the two man trip cars onto it and into the drift. When they were in place, he motioned me off the car, unhooked them, and pulled the trammer with the empty cars out and onto the main line. He moved the train ahead and just past the wye and the switches at the turnoff leading to the old Columbus-Consolidated raise, then pushed the cars, with the trammer, into the crosscut.

I had no idea whatsoever as to what it was all about at this point, so I just followed the trammer as Dan headed into the crosscut. He shut down the train when the trammer was just past the sill of the Columbus raise. We spent a short time here as he told me some of the history concerning that raise. Part of that little talk involved him asking me never to try making the climb up to the Col-Con level four. I decided immediately to in future times use Col-Con in place of the longer Columbus-Consolidated. Hell, I had done that using the shortened version of the Columbus-Rexall, so why not?

Dan asked me to promise him I would not try it on any of his shifts, let alone any other time. He added it was so "goddamn hairy" that he would not climb it himself unless it was a dire emergency and someone's life was at stake. I told him I would not while thinking that I would never have the chance to do it. At that moment, I had no idea of the amount of freedom I would eventually have in that mine, but I did keep the promise. Well, sort of.

Dan said we had already wasted too much time and the crew would be waiting. He was correct when he said that the men would

* A length of trackage used for the temporary or long-term parking of idle cars not in use at the time. The maximum number of cars used in the operation determines the tail track length.

be waiting for those cars. I got out of the empty car when he stopped the train and stayed out of everybody's way.

I had received quite an education that night, but I needed a lot more of it, as I still could not pull it altogether in any reasonable fashion. I decided to keep my mouth shut and simply listen and observe. All the machines I'd seen that night at the heading were unfamiliar to me. None of it had any resemblance to the things I had been around at the Col-Rex. Before I left the mine that night and while we were in the dry, Dan had this to say: "Well, Dick, you got a sniff. What do you think about what you have seen so far?" I told him I did not think I could ever get enough of it, and Dan just shook his head. He told me that barring anything out of the ordinary, he would take me in any time I wanted to go. All I had to do was say the word. Many years later, Dan would tell me that he never worried about me in the hole and always looked forward to the times I went in on his shift. I got home at 2:30 a.m. Sunday morning and did not run into as much dissension as I thought I would. Overall, I called it a worthwhile experience.

30

A Typical Shift

THE TIME I spent in the Wasatch Drain Tunnel, during the drive for the old Cardiff Mine, unlike my days in the Col-Rex, did not involve working as a miner. Because of that, the story about what I did and observed at the drain tunnel comes from a different perspective. The first few of the many times I went in with Dan's crew, we stayed in close contact. This arrangement allowed me to see firsthand how a typical shift accomplished its work. Dan was very good at narrating the hows and whys of everything involved.

The night shift followed a sequence of events that would seldom vary. On occasion, however, things could disrupt the normal run of events. The most serious of these involved the dreaded "missed hole," a dynamite-loaded drill hole that had failed to explode at the previous shift's end. Rendering harmless one of these missed holes required extreme caution, knowledge, and a steady hand. A misstep oftentimes would result in terrible, and in most cases, fatal injuries. The man who undertook the job had to know what he was doing, and the operation could consume considerable time to complete.

Normally, the start of the shift was the trip into the mine and the stops at each of the work areas. The sidetracking of the man trip cars, the use of the wye to put the trammer at the head of the train for the trip out, then the backing up of the empty cars to return to the heading for loading. Dan did this at a very slow speed to minimize the chance of a derailment due to the pushing rather than the pulling of the cars. I can remember no derailments in the drain tunnel, quite different from the almost daily derailments up in the Col-Rex. The rail was much heavier here than the old Col-Rex, probably three times the carrying capacity, and solidly in place. There were no "floating" sections of track in the Wasatch Drain Tunnel like up in the old Col-Rex.

The time involved to load all the broken rock into the six cars was to me nothing short of lightning fast. The reason for this was the fact that up in the Col-Rex, we loaded each car by hand, a hard job at best, and slow. Here the mucking machine scooped up the muck, then transferred it overhead and rearward onto a specialized conveyor system. The first car that was loaded was the car immediately behind the trammer. When that car was full, the system shifted to load the next car, and so on up the line to the last car of the train. Every component of this system, including the mucking machine, used compressed air for power. I stayed well out of the area of this activity and never got close enough to understand how the whole operation worked in any detail.

Dan would move the loaded train down the tunnel a good distance. Moving the mucking machine back and off the main track allowed the drilling jumbo[*] to be brought up to the face. When it was in the proper position, the drilling of the blast holes would commence. This particular jumbo was a "three machine," meaning it had three rock drills. The drills used hydraulics to move them into the required positions during the drilling operation. At this point, it was usually time to head for the doghouse[†] and lunch. This was always a thing to look forward to, as every man had worked at one chore or another almost nonstop.

The uninitiated, at this point, will likely ask just what the hell is a "doghouse." That which the miner termed a doghouse started out

* A machine used in underground mining to drill blasting holes. The machines use multiple drills that are in most cases controlled by one operator. In medium-sized tunneling jobs, they have from one to three drills. Miners identify them as one, two, or three machine jumbos. The earliest type of jumbo required an operator for each drill.

† The common name given to an area where the miners take their lunch breaks. It is off the main run of the mine and walled off, with a door for access. A long table with attached benches runs down the center. Most doghouses have a heat source and electrical lighting. The doghouses are relatively comfortable, and depending on the mine, some are plusher than others.

as nothing more than a short drift off the side of the main tunnel. It maintained the same dimension as the main tunnel—in this case, 8 feet by 8 feet and 12 in depth. A wall of lagging that had a door in the center closed the room off from the main tunnel.

The doghouse was a reasonably comfortable dry place in the wet, cold environment of that mine. Two tables end to end with attached benches run almost the full length of the room, with just enough room for passage around either end. Above the tables, a string of lights hung from the back—four of them, as I remember now. Two small electric heaters sat on shelves attached to the walls, one located off to the side of the door and the other in the corner where the back wall and the sidewall came together. The men could shed their heavy rubber coats, hang them on spikes driven in the walls, and be warm and comfortable.

Lunchtime typically lasted 30 or 40 minutes—never longer than 40, as 30 was the company mandate. When this well-deserved break was over, it was back to work for the men. The focus would be for the heading crew to advance (lay down) more track, any airlines with their required connections, or any other necessary items to move the tunnel deeper. Dan would look everything over at the heading before taking the loaded muck train outside for dumping. One man on the heading crew that Dan referred to as the lead would oversee the work when Dan went outside.

Before Dan got back, the crew would have finished with the utility work, brought the jumbo up to the face, and started drilling. For the times I was able to stay for the entire shift, I learned a lot by simply standing back and observing. From the start, I made an unbreakable rule I was determined to follow. That rule involved staying completely out of the way, a nearly invisible and silent observer.

The night shift had two men that made up the "on the grass" crew. They stayed busy, handling a number of chores that always existed outside the mine. They played a major part when the loaded muck train came out. One of the men was Robin Hood Johnson, previously mentioned, and usually Almond Joy, unless the Bull decided he wanted him on day shift for some reason or another.

Another man took Almond Joy's place when that occurred, as two men on the outside was the minimum. Dan would participate in the unloading also when needed, and most times, he was. There were several steps involved in dumping the cars of muck.

Dan would stop the trammer just inside the end of the snowshed a short distance from a switch. It was here that the trammer was unhooked from the train, wedges driven under a wheel of each car, and their chains unhooked from each other. The switch would open up an interesting multirail system to do several jobs. That layout of rails used three more switches in its system and a short leg wye to put the front face of the trammer pointed correctly back into the mine. While Dan was reversing the trammer, the other two men would start dumping the cars one at a time. The cars were heavy, and the rails down to the dumping hopper were on a slight downhill grade. It took two men to a car to control them, but it was not excessively hard to do.

Dan would head back into the mine, usually before the last of the cars were empty. The cars would not go back into the mine until the day shift came on, so all that went in on this trip would be Dan and the trammer. The man trip cars and the men would come out with the trammer at the shift end. It would fall to the outside men to do the necessary arranging to couple the train together to get it ready for the next shift. It took some shuffling around to put the empty cars behind the trammer and the man trip cars behind them. The last thing before they were finished for the night was to hook the charger leads to the trammer's batteries.

On occasion, I would walk behind the train until it arrived at the junction of the north lateral and the main tunnel. Dan would continue outside for the car-dumping operation. I would then look around in the number-five drift, where the raise to the Col-Con went up and the tail track was located. I had not spent any large amount of time in this area and had not walked into the number-six crosscut by that time. Several times, I looked up that raise headed for the 400 level of the Col-Con and had to tamp down the urge to go on up. I had promised Dan I would not do that, and I kept that promise, although I went two rungs up the ladder on one occasion before I quit the climb. On that two-rung climb I made, I directed my light upward and spotted what appeared to be some loose lagging blocking part of the ladder. A bad situation.

When Dan returned, he went to the heading to check on the progress of the drilling of the round. Satisfied that all was well there, he would often go back where the work was going on involving the extraction of ore in the hillside ground. This required a short ladder climb to the stope area to check progress. From there, his next chore was to go back down the tunnel to where the two explosive magazines were located.

I was standing by the trammer when he came down the ladder from the stope in the hillside ground. He told me that I might just as well climb aboard and go with him to the magazines. That sounded like a good idea to me, as I wanted to see how this particular phase of the operation went. I sat behind him on a raised section that surrounded the seat he sat on. It was far from comfortable due to there being no cushioning, just cold steel. Two grab handles were within reach, so there was no danger of sliding off my perch. We soon arrived where the north lateral intersected with the main tunnel.

At this intersection, years ago, there were two short prospect drifts driven by the old-timers, one on the right and one on the left. They were directly across from one another, and both had locked, heavy wooden doors accessible only to those who had the keys. The main blasting agent was called Anfo, a compound of ammonium nitrate and diesel fuel, and occupied the room on the left side along with the electric blasting caps. The drift on the right held only stick dynamite. Storing the blasting caps with the Anfo was not risky, as the Anfo had to be primed with a stick of dynamite to make it explosive. The two, the dynamite and Anfo, in tandem resulted in a high explosive.

One stick of dynamite with a blasting cap securely inserted into it made up what Dan called the primer. It took one primer to load each drill hole, the number of which Dan knew before making them up. The primed stick of dynamite went into each drilled hole first, then the Anfo was pneumatically loaded on top of the dynamite. This operation firmly packed the drilled holes with the explosives, a very necessary requirement. Using dynamite alone required slitting each stick open with a knife and then tamping them tight in the hole with a wooden "loading stick." This business amounted to, as can be imagined, a touchy operation at best. Using anything metal for a tamping operation would result in a sudden trip to hell.

The primers made up, it was back to the heading and time for the blasting operation. The jumbo was out of the area, pulled back while Dan and I had been at the explosive magazines. The Anfo in their canisters were back down the tunnel, a short distance, and two of the crew were on the way to the drilled face with them when we got there. I stayed well out of the way back down the tunnel while the drilled holes were loaded and the necessary wiring accomplished, a complicated operation. The long lead wire to set the charges off went back down the tunnel to what was determined to be a safe distance from the face. Dan used an electric blasting machine to set off the charges. This device also had a circuit tester as part of it to confirm all connections were good.

When a drift round was shot, it was not just one big bang. In actuality, a certain sequence of detonations took place. It was a series of timed detonations determined by the delays built into the blasting caps and using dynamite and Bickford fuse. The length of fuse determined the timing. There was no earsplitting noise connected to the detonations, just dull thumps. There would be air movement down the tunnel, but it was very gentle. Every man on the crew paid close attention to the shots of each sequence. It would be apparent if a hole misfired.

The shift was nearly over, and it was time to go outside. While the crew gathered up what needed to go out with them, Dan went down, hooked on the man trip cars, and backed up to the doghouse area. We all climbed aboard the cars, straddled the not-so-plush seating arrangement, and out we went. I still was not very comfortable early on with the speedy ride, but I soon was used to it and thought nothing of it as time went on. Outside, Dan shut the train down, and the outside men would do the rest of the necessary work. When those fellows filed into the dry, the train was ready to go back in the next morning.

Dan left a note for the day shift foreman telling him there had been no missed holes that night so that the shift going in the next day would know if they were going to have a decent shift or a nasty project dealing with a missed hole. No one looked forward to that problem. I went out into the night, climbed in the old General Mess of Crap and headed for the valley. It was 2:30 Sunday morning, and it would not be too long before my wife decided enough was enough with those kind of hours and I had better figure out a better way or else!

31
Still Stumbling Along

THE EARLY MONTHS of 1958 saw the decline of the General Mess of Crap accelerate rapidly. The tires on the old crate were finished, but I could not afford to do anything about that. Then in an effort to top off the bad tire business, the old junk pile when first started up laid out a cloud of white smoke, which cleared up after a few minutes. By this time, I was picking up the automotive machinist trade quite quickly and had a better understanding of how an engine operated and why the old GMC belched out when first started, but I didn't have money to do anything about it.

With all this going on, for some incomprehensible reason, the old General Mess of Crap was still getting up the canyon. The condition of the tires was what just about drove me crazy. It was a good thing that old truck had never seen anything over 40 miles per hour, otherwise one of those regrooved inner tubes would have blown out for sure. Then one day at Lambert's, I got lucky, and that luck came in the form of Dan Wade, one of the partners in the business. Dan must have looked at the tires on the old truck and, apparently, did not care for what he saw. One afternoon at quitting time, I was walking out to where the old GMC was waiting, and Dan followed me out.

Dan called me over to where he was standing next to a pile of who knows what under a canvas tarp. I went over as he pulled a section of the tarp back, and there were four tires in a stack sitting there. Dan was never one to put forth many words when a few would do. He just said to me, "Dick, here are four 6.00-16 tires that are a lot better than those things on your truck. They are just doing nothing but getting in the way here. Before you leave, back that truck over here, load them up, and get them out of my sight. They are yours and the price is right. Nothing!"

I was one happy fellow with that deal, and when I started to thank him, he just waved me off and told me to get loaded. I did just that, and those tires actually had a lot of tread on them yet. With those tires on the truck, that would get rid of the constant worry about the junk I was riding on.

The next trip I made up to the mine, I made sure Swinger got a look at the tires that were now on the old General Mess of Crap. Swinger made his walk around the old truck nodding his head, stopped by my side, spit some Cope, and gave forth in his typical fashion: "Well, that's more like it, kid. Now I can stop worrying about those things you were traveling on. Christ! I have seen more tread on a conundrum than was on those things you called tires. Now I can quit thinkin' about one of those damn things blowing all to hell and gobbing both you and that whoopee."

The tires on the GMC were just one of the things that were new up there that day. That is when Swinger introduced me to Corky. Corky was a midsized dog of indeterminate parentage, what Swinger called a Heinz 57 breed. Overall, he was a good-looking fellow and friendly as could be. Swinger explained that Slug, his son, had decided that his old man needed a dog and delivered him up to the mine. Swinger knew nothing of the deal in advance, he said, but he liked the mutt and took him on. Corky was to figure in some interesting stunts up there before Slug repossessed him some months later.

Virgil "Robin Hood" Johnson one night announced that he was pulling out and leaving the state to do a little farming back in the area he came from. His family still owned a lot of farmland in Kansas near a town I had never heard of, Kanorado, and it was just a spot on the Kansas map. I would miss Robin Hood at the mine, and we stayed in contact for about a year by letters. As is usually the case, we eventually lost contact with each other. One of the last letters I received from him was during the winter of 1958–59. He said he had acquired a Sinclair service station in town that would give him work when farming season was over.

Prior to the last contact with Virgil, in the early fall of 1958, I was to find out that another old digger had called it deep enough. One nonworking Saturday, I was as usual up at the mine in the penthouse. After Corky pulled off his typical enthusiastic greeting Swinger told me to get a cup poured for myself and called for Corky to shut up. As I got my coffee and sat myself in a chair, Swinger sat his cup down and started.

"Well kid, we lost one. Alimony Bill left for hell down in Taos. I found out about it earlier in the week."

"Left for hell, meaning what, shorted out, got thrown in the lockup, or some such other?" I asked.

"Well, being as he is no longer among the living, he's got to be in hell, and he had help getting it done."

I figured the best thing to do was just listen to the tale and not ask any more questions.

"From what I heard it seems Alimony decided to take on a tank full in one of the joints down there. Now, knowing Alimony Bill like I do, it was without a doubt a pippin of a load up. He could still walk they say, well, sort of, and decided to go hole up for the night and he left the joint. He was wobblin' down the sidewalk when it happened. Seems that a whole goddamn dump truck full of drunkin' war whoops came drivin' down the sidewalk and gobbed poor old Alimony right there on the spot."

I just shook my head, took a sip of coffee, and said, "Holy shit, Swing."

That took care of how Alimony Bill left for hell down in Taos, New Mexico.

About this same time, Swinger and I started what became a frequent and pleasant way to occupy some of our time on the Saturdays that the mine did not work. Swinger came up with the idea and happily financed almost all the escapades. At that time, I had no money to play around with as it took everything my wife and I had coming in to cover the essential basics. Gasoline for the old General Mess of Crap to get to and from work, let alone the fuel for the continuing runs up Little Cottonwood Canyon, required some creative monkey business. Things were so tight that the only check I ever bounced in my life was during that time. It was for the outrageous sum of two dollars. I have never forgotten that business.

On one particular nonworking Saturday, I, as usual, headed up to the mine. Swinger and I had our coffee, sat around, and talked. The weather was getting better, and the snow was starting to go down. After a while, we went outside to stretch our legs and walked around on the dump. We were standing at the edge of the dump looking down at the creek. He had his hands in the pockets of his jacket, unloaded a good stream of Cope, and said, "Tell you what kid, I'm feeling kind of lazy and don't want to rustle supper later and on top of that feel kind of fiddle footed. Let's take my kite and head for the valley. I know a hell of a good place that has a high-grade hamburger steak that they hook up with a big load of curly French fries. What you think of that idea?"

To me that sounded like one of the best ideas I had heard in a long time. It really sounded better than good. There was a problem though, and I knew I would have to back out of that deal. I had a hard time getting it out. Essentially, what I said involved the fact that I could not afford to do a thing like that. I explained that I doubted I had so much as a dollar, just some small change. Swinger just grinned in his usual fashion, spit again, and said, "What in hell makes you think you need any money kid? I have more of that damn stuff than I need right now and this business is on me so you have to get used to that. You see kid, I am a greedy bastard, need things to go my way sometimes. Let's load up and get down the hill."

That is what we did and for many times thereafter. There were times, however, it just did not feel right that I was living so well off Swinger's generosity.

The destination Swinger drove us to turned out to be a very casual place called the Center Drive In. The drive-in area was in front of the building and backed up against State Street in Sandy, Utah. It probably would accommodate 10 vehicles at the most. A small number of parking spaces existed on the north and south ends of the building. Swinger parked in front and never intended to indulge in car service. Just the way he did things. Inside, the seating area was larger than it appeared to be from outside. It was clean and neat.

When walking in through the door, the kitchen area was well in view. There was a counter with a few stools and room enough for a walkway for a server. The kitchen area was behind a waist-high wall with a long counter. The meals to go out to the customers were set out on this counter. It became immediately obvious that Swinger was no stranger in this place. A woman, about middle age, was busy over the hot grill, and a couple of younger women were in the kitchen with her. She had apparently noticed us when we came in and in a loud voice yelled out, "Swinger! Where you been hid out? It is about time you showed up. If I wasn't so busy, I'd come out there and give you a big hug."

To that, Swinger answered, "Hullo Marge! Well, here I am kid. A hug would be good but you better stay put because it would be better if nothin' ended up incinerated over a romance out here."

There was no denying that what Swinger had told me regarding the hamburger steak and the curly fries was in the same category. Excellent, absolutely. If I remember correctly, and it has been many years ago, those meals cost all of $1.25 each. Of course, I got off without having to come up with so much as a nickel. It would be years down the road before I was able to reverse this situation with Swinger. Everyone in that place knew the Swinging Door and just loved him. He was not stingy with the tips either, somewhat overboard on that, like he was on so many things.

32

No Room in Hell

DURING THE SUMMER of 1958, events were to take place that I thought would bring my adventures on Dan's night shift to an end and others that could have easily ended my days prowling around in the underground world of the Alta mining district. The first began with my leaving work at noon; it was a Saturday, and so it was a normal thing. My intention was to head for the Frederick Tunnel and just look around on the outside. It was a workday at the drain tunnel, so I would do that instead of going directly to visit with Swinger.

It was probably around 2:00 when the old junk pile and I got to Tanners Flat and an ambulance with lights flashing and siren howling shot past me heading down the canyon. That ambulance was wasting no time at all on that downhill run. As I turned off the highway onto the road leading down to the mine, two cars belonging to the Salt Lake County Sheriff's Department went past me heading for the highway.

That pretty much answered where that ambulance had come from, and I knew where to go for the news. When I walked in, I found Swinger leaning on the counter, and on the other side, doing the same thing, were Bull Wondershek, Matt Martinson, and Sweet Pea. Things were definitely not all right around that place, and on through the west door and through the big open window I noticed some of the day shift miners in the dry. I took only seconds to take all that in, and I asked, "What the hell is going on around this joint? I have to suspect that meat wagon flying down the canyon came from here."

"Sure as hell did, Dick," the Bull answered. "We had a bad one in the hole today, couple hours back."

No one had anything to say for maybe half a minute, then Swinger announced, "Let's make the climb upstairs and put on a pot of coffee and I will give you the rundown, kid."

That got the Bull started, and he looked at Swinger and said, "Muck out another cup and I'll be up in a minute, John T."

As we went up to the penthouse, the fact that the Bull had called him "John T." instead of "Swinger" or "Mormon sonofabitch" put a serious slant on things to my way of thinking.

It was a show-and-tell day, Swinger said. The visitors were men who had a financial interest in the project and most likely a couple of hangers-on to see how things worked in a mine. The group was up at the heading when the drilling of the holes for the next round was just starting. The jumbo was in place, and the men were chucking the drill steels, just minutes from starting the holes. The observers were at the rear of the jumbo and to the sides, where they had a reasonably clear view of the face.

Compressed air powers all the functions of a jumbo and requires connection to the mine's air supply. This supply line is a steel pipe, three inches in diameter. There are hookup points with on-off valves all along its run. A heavy hose the same diameter as the pipe, known as the bull hose, connects the air supply to the jumbo. Quick couplers are used to make this connection.

"Well, kid," Swinger started, "the goddamned hose coupler where it hooks to the jumbo came apart. Under pressure, that loose hose will whip around like a snake's tail on fire. It nailed one of the poor bastards that was standing a little behind it, one of the suits. The end of the hose with part of the brass coupler caught the guy in the head. Well, sort of. You see, it smacked into his light on his hard-boiled hat, smashed the light, busted the hat and done some serious work on the poor sonofabitch's head. He went down of course, and the hose was still whipping around throwing all kinds of small rock and water every goddamn direction."

With that, Swinger took a big swallow of coffee, and all I could say was my usual "Holy shit."

That was when the Bull arrived, poured some coffee in the "freshly mucked out cup," sat down, and made an inquiry as to how much Swinger had told me. Swinger told him, and the Bull took it from there. He said he really felt bad about the fellow who got hurt and by what he'd seen of him before the ambulance got there. He said it looked to him like the man was right at death's door and knocking. When he went down, it was at a point some 9,600 feet from the portal. It took a lot of time to bring up a litter from where it was stored in the powder magazine. Adding to the time involved was getting the injured man secured in it, and an even bigger problem was securing the litter on the man trip to bring him out. Things could not have been much worse when it came to being prepared for an emergency such as this.

There was no means of communication from inside the mine to the office outside. Worse yet was the fact that the mine office had no telephone system of any type. This was a serious problem, as there was no way of getting outside help to the mine. The Bull, Sweet Pea, Matt, and the others knew nothing of the accident until the man trip brought the victim out. When the men came out with the injured man, Sweet Pea made a frantic trip to the Peruvian Lodge in Alta to make the call requesting help at the mine. This was going to create many questions by various agencies.

Bull had more to say: "We are going to get our asses raked over the coals on this disaster and in grand fashion too. All the goddamned regulator kids will be up here with an army of clipboard-carrying flunkies to commence setting fire to the company's ass. There will be no valid excuses for how things were set up for just such an emergency like this one. I made plenty of noise about this kind of thing but the money boys controlled the sacks of gold and I may as well been jabbering to myself. I have always been against this show-and-tell bullshit. If I had my way there would never be a suit, a paper shuffler, a goddamn fruit observer, nor their like allowed underground. It is a sure thing that there will be a goddamn crash like today if they are allowed in the hole."

When that last was finished up, the Bull took a sip of coffee and looked over at me. I guess I must have looked a little taken back, worried about where this left me in the scheme of things around that project. The Bull set his cup down still looking hard at me and said, "Dick, you ain't in the ranks of those I just mentioned. Your situation around here is not changed in any way whatsoever. I've heard plenty from Dan, not to mention the Mormon sonofabitch. Just be careful, damn careful—if the big boys knew about you and what's going on they would shit their pants and then run me down the horseshit trail."

I was considerably relieved when I heard this and realized then what a risk the Bull had taken by going along with my free run of that mine. Even with all this hanging over his head, he never mentioned anything regarding my signing any kind of release of liability paper. Doing things like that now, there would be no doubt that someone would make that journey down the horseshit trail.

On almost all the explorations of the underground workings in the Little Cottonwood mining district, I went alone. This is a very risky undertaking made worse several times over when absolutely no one knew where I was going. Swinger made a point, many times, of telling me what I was doing was a very bad idea. I finally figured it out one time when I was in a bad situation. I had to sit quietly and try to calm a rising feeling of panic on that particular occasion, and I got the answer as to why I had not yet managed to gob myself. It was simple. There had been no more room in hell that day for another damn fool.

As hard as it had been, I kept my word to Dan concerning the two raises off the drain tunnel level. Either one would have taken me up to the 400 level of the old Col-Con. Keeping my word was no problem when it came to the cable raise. The other raise, the original, that went up into the 400, was another matter, however. Every time I was at the sill of that raise, I debated long and hard about ascending it. It was very hard not to make that climb. One night, the answer to that dilemma popped into my head. That answer was the inclined shaft, known as the 300, that collared at the main level of the old Col-Con. I had stood at that collar more than once and debated the descent of that incline.

It would have been a working Saturday at the drain tunnel when I headed for the Col-Con and the 300. I got up to the mine about 2:00 that Saturday afternoon. I figured Mack and Mark Jacobson would be there in the Howland, but they were not, which was not good. I had not stopped at the drain tunnel to tell Swinger where I was going, so no one knew exactly what I was up to or where. That was bad enough, but worse things were ahead, I would discover later. I had eaten my homemade sandwich on the drive up and did not bring any coffee with me.

The inclined shaft, the 300, went down on about a 40-degree angle, which is generally not too hard to negotiate if you watch your footing. The shaft itself was about 10 feet wide and near 8 feet, bottom to back, a typical production incline. It was in good solid structure, with a few stulls in strategic places. The manway ladder and the utility lines were on the right side. The ladder was wet, had missing sections, and definitely could not be trusted to hold any weight. There was another problem not apparent from the collar, and that was the ubiquitous red-orange mud. This wet muck was like grease.

In the case of the incline, there was no water running down, but everywhere the back dripped water, and the ribs were slick with it. With few exceptions, the bottom was wet with occasional spots being dry, but these areas were infrequent. Suspecting these conditions would worsen with depth, I should have given more serious thought about what I intended to do as I stood at the collar and looked down. I should have paid more attention to the warning buzzer in my head. Double-checking my gear to make sure everything was there, I started my descent of that old inclined shaft.

From the map I had of the mine, I knew the incline did not go down in a straight line to the 400 level. There was a 12-degree offset to the left 100 feet down from the collar, which was just visible with the three-cell flashlight. Things started to go bad about 50 feet down. The mud was starting to get more plentiful with depth, and it was wet and slippery. I was on the left side of the incline, and there was no timber of any kind, as the ground was solid rock. I had slipped a couple of times on the mud, and though I had not fallen, uneasiness was beginning to set in. At that point, I could see where the incline drifted left and see some stulls close to the rib that reached from bottom to back.

Had I stopped at that 50-foot mark, that would have been the first smart move. The next smart thing I should have done would have been to cross over to the right side of the incline. That the airlines and the big water line from the pump station on the 400 remained solidly anchored was almost a certainty. The ladder, heavily coated with the red-orange mud, would be more questionable than ever at this depth. That fact did not matter, because I would not have trusted the integrity of that ladder under any conditions. Instead of doing the second smart thing, I convinced myself that I could make it to the point where the incline made its slight turn left.

There was nothing at all to hold on to on the rib, and the bottom seemed to get more slippery with each downward step. I had slipped several more times but remained on my feet, and with each step regretted more and more having ever started down this nightmare. There were a number of stulls against the rib in this area, and thankfully, they were still solidly in place although covered with fungus. A few feet above the first of the stulls, I slipped and went down and could not stop the slide that followed.

I was close enough to grab the first stull in the line, but all I had on that wet slippery stull was my left hand. I could find no purchase with my boots on that mud-slick bottom. Knowing I could never hold with just one hand, I half rolled to my left, intending to get a hold on the stull with my right. My right hand slipped off it, but that half roll brought me closer to the rib, and my left foot jammed solidly into the next stull down, stopping my downward slide.

Sitting with my back against the rib and my left shoulder against a stull, I had some serious thinking to do. That was going to be a problem, as fear had me nearly paralyzed. I sat there for some time before I could think with any clarity. Finally, I got the flashlight out and looked down the incline. Then a feeling of intense panic settled on me. I was right on the bend of that offset, and I could see down on what would be 200 feet more of shaft. It was an incredible mess of mud and some fallen rock out of the back. The flashlight beam would not reach the bottom where the 400 level was located. Now what in hell was I going to do?

There was no way that I could climb back up where I'd come down, and if I tried and started to slide again, well, that would be it, I figured. The only possible route up lay on the far side of the incline in the form of the airlines and water pipe, which could be used as handholds to assist in the upward climb. Now, how in hell was I going to get across that mud slick of some nine-odd feet without losing my footing and ending up in a runaway plunge downward? At that point, panic really set its hooks in me, and I stayed frozen in my sitting position. For how long, I have no idea. To this day, I have no clear memory of how my crossing occurred. There is a blank space that will forever remain, because when clarity set in, I had already somehow scrambled across that incline and had firm handholds on the rusty mud-streaked air pipe.

That was the time that the only reasonable answer as to why I had not gobbed myself was simply no more room in hell that day for another damn fool.

I made it to the collar with the assistance of the airlines, avoiding what was left of the ladder. I had to sit for a while at the top before I headed for the outside, as I was so rattled and worn out that it took quite an effort to get up and move. The lamp was dim, the carbide used up, and I had to stop and recharge it when I got to the Howland Tunnel. When I got outside, I realized what a mess of red-orange mud I was. I was covered head to toe in the now drying muck. I had gloves in my bag but had never put them on, and that probably saved my life as gloves would have seriously interfered with my grip on stulls and airlines.

I took off my diggers and rinsed them off as much as possible in the ditch and cleaned up my hands as well as the water would allow, but they remained deeply stained. I had been in the mine just over four hours, but it had seemed like a week. I walked out to the old General Mess of Crap, loaded my gear, and headed for the Wasatch Drain Tunnel. All was quiet there. The night shift was in the mine, the day shift long gone down the canyon. I parked the old pile of junk, went inside, and climbed the stairs to the penthouse. Swinger was at the table, apparently just finishing his supper, and it took him only one look. "Jesus Christ and little Rizzi, kid, what the hell?"

Well, I told him the story, and when I had finished up, he told me there was coffee left and to get after it. I did just that.

"Goddamn it kid!" he started out. "I have told you time and again that one day you were going to get gobbed with this goddamned foolishness you keep on insisting on pulling off. Now if this didn't put some sense in your head I'll be damned if I know what will. You have got to quit doing this kind of shit, kid!"

I was still so shook up over that afternoon's bit of foolishness as Swinger finished with his little sermon that I swore to myself I would never do anything like that again. But of course, as is always the case, time dimmed the intensity of what I went through that afternoon, and I did something like that again many times, only ever surviving because there was never any room in hell on those days either.

33

Corky's Flight and Stolen Gold

SEPTEMBER IS A month of variety in the high country around the Wasatch Drain Tunnel and Alta. Snow can fall the first week of September but never stays on the ground except on the high peaks. Most years, and 1958 would be no exception, those early snowstorms would be followed by a series of warm comfortable days. There had been a light snowfall about three days into the month by the time I went up to the mine the first Saturday of September. The day was warm, sunny, and the snow gone.

Swinger liked to grow plants just for something different to do. He would use such things as peach pits, apricot pits, olive pits, avocado nuts, and anything else that struck his fancy. Each of these went into their separate containers that were simply empty tin cans filled with good black soil. It was amazing that most of them sprouted. Swinger seemed to have a green thumb. The orchard, as he called it, had been coming along well, and during the last two days, he had set them outside on a couple of benches against the sunny south side of the building.

I noticed that the lineup when I arrived up at the mine did not look too healthy for some reason, kind of droopy in appearance. I headed up to the penthouse to the usual enthusiastic greeting Corky put forth. Swinger was at the table and gave us a hard stare, which I decided was directed at Corky, not me. That is when Swinger outlined the great sin Corky had committed the day before.

"Did you happen to look at my orchard layout when you came in kid?"

I told him that it was not looking too good.

"Well, it was looking good before that little sonofabitch there, the fur-covered one, decided that the project needed irrigating. I came out the door just about the time Corky was finishing pissing on the whole damned orchard. It has had it for sure, and I guess I might as well put the whole layout over the dump."

That is just what he did a little later in the afternoon just before we headed for our hamburger steaks and curly French fries.

When I went up to the mine on the Saturday two weeks later, I got there about the same time as two other fellows in a pickup—almost as much of a junk pile as my General Mess of Crap. Almost. They got there first and went into the building, and they seemed to know where they were going. I was not far behind and started up the stairs to the penthouse when they were going through their hellos and howdys. Swinger apparently knew them, and they him. Swinger invited us all to take seats around the table, and we did. For some reason, Swinger never introduced the three of us, and a couple of hellos had to suffice.

The two were a little older than I was and had apparently been around the mining game, so the conversation followed along those lines. It took little time for the talkative one to get around to the subject of gold. I just kept quiet and listened while Swinger and the two talked. The talkative one asked Swinger if he had a sheet of paper, white being the best. Swinger said no but produced a paper plate that was white and told them that would have to do the trick. It did.

The talkative fellow produced a Prince Albert pipe tobacco can from his shirt pocket and dumped the contents on the paper plate. It looked interesting to me, and there was little doubt it was gold.

"What you think of that, Swinger?" the can dumper asked.

Swinger walked over to a little chest of drawers next to his bed and came back with a high-powered magnifying glass. He looked over the sample on the plate while stirring it around on occasion and nodding his head several times. Setting the glass aside, Swinger sat back on his chair and made his announcement concerning that which he had just finished looking at. "Well, kids, that is some pretty good gold you have there in that mix-up and it will run high."

That put a big smile on their faces. They sat back satisfied and comfortable in their chairs.

"Figured as much," the talkative one said. "The good part being there is a lot more from where that came from."

What Swinger said next turned their smiles into frowns and they straightened up, losing their comfortable slouched positions in their chairs. "Now, kids," Swinger started out, "if I were the two of you, I would load it all back in the can, all of it. Then when that is done, I would take a little walk down off the dump out there and go on down to the creek. When I got there, I would take what is in that can, shake it out slowly into that creek, then gob the can, and walk away." He leaned back more and gave them the eye. "Now I know that stuff was stolen out of the cleanups, either at the old Golden Gate mill in Mercur or from the mill in Manning. If you get caught with that you are going to go to college for a while, which you ain't gonna like."

When Swinger mentioned going to college he meant something entirely different from the everyday educational facility. *College* was what he called a jail or a prison. The two repacked the Prince Albert can, said that they had better get going, and left the penthouse. Neither Swinger nor I bothered to get up and go outside to see if the two actually did what Swinger had suggested. Swinger was up to heat up the coffee left in the coffeepot. It was still too early to head for town and our usual feed at the Center Drive In.

While he was doing that, he started talking again regarding the sample the two had just taken with them. "It was no trick to figure out where they got that stuff. I have had some of that stick to me at one time or another, but I knew where to unload it and how to stay out of college when I pulled it off."

There was at that time, in the canyon, a big dog that was a hybrid, probably malamute and wolf. That big fellow could be found anywhere at any time wandering the entire upper canyon areas. I had seen him up in Grizzly Gulch and Albion Basin as high as the pass that crossed over into Mineral Basin of American Fork Canyon. I'd seen him also in Collins Gulch and up in the high basin of Peruvian. He was a frequent visitor at the Wasatch Drain Tunnel.

He wore a collar, as I remember, and the story was that he called the Alta Lodge home. I have no idea who, up there, he owned. I put it that way because no one could ever own an animal like that. He owned him, her, or them, whichever the case may have been. Around the drain tunnel area, we called him Sam McGee. To this day, I do not know if that was his real name, but he seemed to pay attention to it when it suited him.

Sam McGee was the driving factor concerning an amazing stunt that Corky caused to take place one Saturday. Swinger figured prominently in making the whole incident what it was. There had been a snowstorm the day before, and there was snow on the ground, at least 10 inches close to the building. I was just coming into the yard when I see a sight that caused me to bring the old truck to a halt. I was not sure if what I was seeing was real at first. Corky shot out of the window in the upper floor—feet braced, ears pinned above his head—and thumped into the snow-covered ground outside the office door. When he touched down, he took off, as Swinger would have described it "like a mad God after a Lamanite." Corky headed for the building at the mine portal and disappeared inside. What the hell?

I parked the wreck and headed for the penthouse wondering just what I would find up there. The first thing I see is Swinger with his mop and bucket, working on the floor next to the table. The sliding windowpanes were at floor level up there, and one was open. I watched the operation for a minute and then asked, "What the hell is with Corky? I just watched him shoot out of that window like he came out of a cannon."

"Oh, the evil little bastard! The coffee's on, grab two cups and load 'em up while I finish taking up high bottom here. Then I will tell you the tale."

I took off my coat, filled two cups with coffee, and sat down at the table. Swinger finished his mopping, rinsed the mop, gave it a good squeeze in the bucket's wringer, and rolled the equipment off into a corner. That done, he sat down, took a good sip of coffee, and laid it all out.

"Well, kid, Sam McGee showed up for a visit and I noticed him out on the dump. Went downstairs and let him in, and us both came on up here. Now you know Sam ain't particularly friendly but not mean in any way. When Corky seen him coming up the stairs, he dove under one of the bunks and hugged the wall. Don't seem to much care for Sam, it would seem. Think he is scared shitless of him. Sam just lay down for a bit by the chair you're sitting on and took five. Well, more than five by quite a ways. He finally decided it was time to go, got up, and headed down the stairs. I let him out and came back up. So, here I sit, and Corky finally comes out from under the bunk and walks over to where Sam had been flopped."

At that point in the story Swinger takes a few good swallows of coffee and then goes silent for a few minutes.

"Then what?" I asked.

"Well, the little sonofabitch is sniffing around where Sam had been. Then, looking me straight in the eye, hikes his leg and commences pissing on the table leg. Must have pissed for two minutes straight, still staring me in the eye. That done it. I jumped up out of the chair, went over, and grabbed the little bastard by the collar. He was still pissing, would you believe it? So, I dragged the little sonofabitch on over and banged him out the window. I was gentle and I made sure the window was slid back before I helped him make the dive."

I could not even come up with my usual "Holy shit!" I just sat there and laughed, nearly running out of air. I was glad I had not had a mouth full of coffee. Corky did not get in any rush to come back from wherever he had holed up.

34
Finally

ALL TOO SOON, it seemed the year 1958 had nearly worn itself out. By November's end, the white stuff got seriously down to business. The old General Mess of Crap, somehow, kept right on going up that canyon. The tire chains that I figured were beyond use last winter, with the help of repair links and baling wire, were still taking the wreck and its driver up Little Cottonwood Canyon. Swinger was amazed that it was still operational. He made a statement more than once that went something like this: "Goddamn kid, you better watch out for it. That damn thing, it just ain't human, shoulda have died way back."

In the Wasatch Drain Tunnel about mid-December 1958, it had reached 4,500 feet from where the Cardiff drive began in 1955. At that 4,500-foot point, it was a little over 10,000 feet to the Wasatch Drain Tunnel's portal. I had been in the mine with Dan the last week of November. We had walked back about 50 feet from where the men were setting up to drill out the next round. Dan stopped at this point and said that he just knew they had drifted too far east to be below the Cardiff 1500 level. Dan looked at me and raised his arm, pointing upward on an angle and in a westward direction. He said, "If we were to put up some long holes on this angle, I think we would hit the 1500 in about 200 to 250 feet."

I went in with Dan's shift just a few days short of Christmas, and they had pulled back from the heading about 60 feet. They were starting a drift left, off the main tunnel. Dan had told the Bull he thought that they were going to miss the target. The Bull had paid attention and brought in the well-regarded engineer/geologist, Joseph J. Beeson, to run a survey. Apparently, Beeson had done that and said that they had to pull back from the heading and go west to get where they needed to be. This point would be 40 to 50 feet east and some 65 feet below the run of the 1500.

I do not know if that survey had taken place before Dan walked me back from the heading on the early December trip. When he had pointed out the direction in which he thought the 1500 was located, maybe that came from Beeson's survey. Then again, in the coming years, as I became well acquainted with several more old Alta miners, I came to know that what Dan had told me could well have been his idea alone. These old-timers seemed to have an unerring instinct of where things lay in that underground world. To this day, I have no solid evidence either way, but I highly favor the idea that Dan knew before Beeson had run the survey.

At this point, they put an inclined raise upward, and they drilled a number of long holes from the left rib on a horizontal plane. The first one hit the water-filled incline that connected to the 1500. Other holes followed rapidly, the number of which I no longer remember, all coming into the water-filled workings after passing through 30 feet of solid limestone.

It was a very wet business, and that water had a lot of pressure behind it. This type of work is not without a high risk of disaster, as the workings above the drain tunnel at that time held over 200 vertical feet of water. In those 200 vertical feet were four levels running off both sides of the Cardiff inclined shaft. Those workings had many feet of stoped ground in them, which added greatly to the volume of water.

Other than Dan, I doubt any of the other miners on the job were familiar with what had occurred August of 1920. When the raise going up to the 400 level of the Col-Con from the drain tunnel level was close to its objective, the calculations assumed that it would take three to four more rounds to hole through into the water-filled lower levels of the Col-Con. They were wrong.

On that day in 1920, at that suspected distance, that first round was drilled out, loaded, and fuse lengths cut to allow the crew to make the 6,000-foot walk to the portal with time to make it out safely. The chances are good that there was some trepidation on the part of the crew as they headed for the outside. The miners were correct in their silent assumptions, because as they neared the portal with several hundred feet to go, they heard the sound. They just made it outside when the tremendous flood burst out the tunnel. The tunnel run four feet deep with that raging torrent for hours before it subsided.

The knowledge of that incident by certain people involved in that Cardiff drive is one of the reasons for the long hole drilling. It was, of course, not the only reason. Controlling the release of the water from the flooded workings above the drain tunnel had a number of other benefits. Although the geologic structure of the area in the vicinity was solid, there was always a possibility of something going wrong, and that was always foremost in everybody's mind. If something would have caused a sudden uncontrolled breach and that water in the Cardiff had erupted all at once, there would have been no survivors in that mine, absolutely none.

The first working Saturday in January 1959 found me in the mine with Dan's shift. All but a couple of the crew were working in the hillside ore zone, and they were pulling a good amount of shipping-grade ore out of the area. I did not pay a lot of attention to what the two men were doing near where the drill holes had been put through. What I did pay attention to was what I'd seen when we got close to where the water was coming from those drill holes. The water blasting out of those drill holes looked like shiny steel bars. The amount of water flowing down that raise and the pressures involved were impressive.

The next question that needed an answer was at what rate the water was lowering in the Cardiff incline. There was only one way to gauge that, and that was by visual observation. Someone would have to make the journey starting from the portal of the Howland Tunnel. The observer would pass through the Columbus-Rexall workings to the D winze that lay 800 feet beyond the Jewel Stope. The winze went down on an angle of about 30 degrees for 200 feet. Descending the winze would bring the observer to the 800 south level of the Cardiff.

From there traversing the 800 to the main Cardiff incline shafts' collar would be a distance of 550 feet.

As the water level dropped, a descent along that incline would be required to observe where the water level was at the time. The Cardiff incline went down at about the same 30-degree angle as the D winze. As in the case of the D winze, there would be sections that had a good deposit of the slippery red-orange mud left by the retreating water. Old company maps, which were in possession of the new company, showed how the levels going down the incline lay. The major workings off the main shaft were the 1000 level, 1200 level, 1400 level, and the lowest, the 1500. With this knowledge, an observer could determine his position reasonably accurately.

To make this journey to check the water level in the Cardiff incline was not a quick and easy trip. When one stood at the collar of the incline on the 800 level, that individual had 6,900 feet of underground passage behind him. Some of that was not without problems, and the passage through Col-Rex's Death Valley could be stressful because of the conditions that existed there. The Bull assigned this chore to Sweet Pea, and Sweet Pea was not a miner. He had very little experience in the underground world. The Bull had never been in the Col-Rex. If he had, I do not think he would have assigned this task to the inexperienced Sweet Pea.

I would make a number of trips starting in early January 1959 and on through the end of February to check on the water levels in the Cardiff inclined shaft. I would share each of my findings with the Bull upon returning. On the first trip, I was unable to get down on the Cardiff 800 level. The water had dropped to the level of the 800, but in the drift, it looked like the water was still at least four feet deep. Back in the fall of 1957, when I first saw the D winze, the water level was about 30 feet below its collar. The decrease in the water level from where it had been in late 1957 compared to 1 January 1959 was substantial. When passage down the D winze and through the 800 level to the Cardiff incline became possible, what water was there presented no problem at all.

It was on the Saturday that I found the water at the 1200 level that I changed my usual routine. It was a working Saturday at the drain tunnel, so I headed up to the Col-Rex to make the walk to the Cardiff incline. The water level had been dropping surprisingly fast. I had made that trip enough times that I could make good time going in and out, although Death Valley always slowed me down more than any section of the Col-Rex. Looking back, I suppose I was getting a little complacent and should have known better, but I managed to get away with it for no good reason. On earlier trips through Death Valley, I had always carried a burning candle. On the last couple of trips, all I did was strike matches occasionally and observe their flare. Complacency.

When I came out the portal of the Howland Tunnel that January evening, I had passed through, roughly, 15,100 feet of underground workings. I got out of my diggers, including what was left of the bottoms; cleaned off my boots standing in the ditch; and washed off the coat in the stream. There was no point in cleaning up the tatters of the bibbed bottoms. The passage up and down the raise to the Cardiff was not the muddy mess the D winze was. Even with that, the diggers had enough holes in them that I gathered up some staining on my pants. The diggers had had it, and I knew all I could do with them was to gob them. I loaded up all my stuff and headed for the drain tunnel. There would be hot coffee there. That and the Swinging Door.

I arrived at the drain tunnel, went in the office door, and then went clumping up the stairs and made my grand entrance into John T.'s penthouse. He was sitting at the table with the feedbag on, as he liked to describe a meal.

"Figured you had abandoned me, kid, so I thought I better grub up so I didn't starve to death. I guess you don't get the privilege of buying me a hamburger steak and those curly fries today."

I thought to myself, *That will be the day. Me buying you anything.* I had yet to pay any part of our little supper sessions at the Center Drive In. Swinger just would not stand for it. Every time I protested, he just told me not to be such a greedy bastard.

Swinger had just shoved another forkful of something that smelled good but looked bad into his mouth. With that, he looked at me, finished chewing up the mouthful, swallowed, and then said, "Goddamn, kid! You take another dive in the baptism hole or what? You ain't none too shiny."

"Sprung some leaks in the old diggers," I replied.

"Looks to me like there ain't no goddamn diggers left, kid. I'd say you are out of rubber if I didn't know better. Soon as I get done feeding my ugly face, that will have to be taken care of. Now, just before that, what has to happen is this. I have a couple of spare pieces of liver that I incinerated for supper and I think that you ought to be puttin' them down as you look kinda' underfed about now."

Well, I felt underfed, all right. I had burned up a lot of energy on the go around up in the Col-Rex and Cardiff. I had never been a liver eater by choice, but I was ready for something to eat. I decided I had better give it a try. This guy had not killed me yet, and damn it was good. From that point on, I took a liking to liver and onions, and Swinger had the onions to put with liver that night too. As I got started on it, he said, "If you hadn't got it, I probably would have pushed off what was left on Corky but then again maybe not. Last time I did that didn't work out too good. The little bastard gobbled it down like he just inhaled it. Later when I hit the sack Corky hopped up on the bed like he does sometimes, then puked on my pillow. Maybe it was the onions. Hell, I don't know."

When I got the liver and onions, Corky, disgusted, wandered off and laid down under the bunks over at the west wall for a good sulk. That was the last time I saw Corky. The following week Slug, Swinger's son, came from Tooele and talked Swinger out of Corky, as they had started to miss him. Some deal, that business. They could not wait to unload Corky on Swinger; now they decided they missed him.

35

Farewell, General Mess of Crap

FEBRUARY 1959 WAS nearing its end, and some things were going to change. Among those items was the end of the romance of myself and the old General Mess of Crap. Along with that event, there would occur a shift in the order of my trips into the drain tunnel with Dan. With Robin Hood Johnson long gone the previous March, the Bull had hired an older fellow who was a mechanic of sorts and a general handyman. His name was Willy, and that was the only name by which I ever knew him. This was an odd thing, considering Swinger's penchant for assigning nicknames to most of the men working there. Swinger liked Willy and got along with him, but I never learned why he had not renamed Willy.

There were no changes when it came to Swinger, the Bull, and Dan Jacobson. We remained close friends. We were also partners in bullshit yarns, mixed with serious stuff when the occasion called for it. Comparisons made involving that relationship: Dan was the one least full of bullshit and quite different from Swinger and Bull Wondershek. I enjoyed my time spent with those men immensely. Swinger was the master of coming up with things that left you trying to get air, laughing so hard you forgot to breathe. The time he told the Bull the story of my big dive into Baptism Bend in the Col-Rex, we both thought the Bull was finished. He laughed so loud and long, he did run out of air. When he finally got air, he said, "Goddamn! You Mormon sonofabitch! You just about stopped my goddamn watch with that one. Jesus H. Christ!"

The way Swinger would put together some of the things he came up with would have one convinced he stayed awake nights thinking them up. This was not the case, as most things he came up with occurred on the spot. One observation he made one day that I will never forget occurred on a cold winter afternoon. We were standing out on the dump before we had enough of the cold wind coming up the canyon. It was blowing hard at the mine, but at higher elevations, it must have been two or three times as severe. We were looking up at Mount Superior.

From the summit of Superior, down and along the ridge, the snow, driven by fierce winds in horizontal clouds, then rose in ascending vertical columns. Just looking at that display chilled me almost to the bone, and then Swinger sent that chill bone-deep with one of his typical observations. "Goddamn kid, look at that show. How'd you like to be standing up there in that, dressed in a collar button and a conundrum?"

Only Swinging Door could have come up with a crack like that.

It would have been in the second or third week of March 1959 that dictated the parting of ways with the old General Mess of Crap and myself, but what put the events in motion began with my wife's car. For some reason, also not clearly recalled, I ended up taking the nearly new 1957 Ford Fairlane up to the mine on a Saturday. That probably occurred because my wife somehow was not working that Saturday. It would have probably been due to something she and her mother had going. The old GMC was getting somewhat untrustworthy due to new strange noises and a cracked cylinder head seeping water into the engine.

There were a good pair of snow tires on the rear of the car so that eliminated having to chain it up. It was a day of low-hanging clouds over the Wasatch Range, but it was not storming when I headed up the canyon to the drain tunnel. It was a working Saturday. That I clearly remember. It was just the usual coffee drinking and lie-telling that Swinger and I did when I did not go in the mine with Dan. By the time I got to the mine, it was starting to rain, something that was unusual at that time of year, as it generally was snow. The snow did show up about two hours later, and it came down hard. Just before the snow started, a fierce wind started coming up the canyon, and that always meant that it was going to get much colder.

When I left the mine, it was dark, and although the storm had laid down about five inches of snow at the time, I made it out to the highway without any trouble. Real trouble lay in wait down the canyon about two miles distant. I knew when I got on the highway that things were going to be touchy, as the road was unusually slippery. What had happened, I was to find out, was that the sudden drop in temperature preceding the snow had frozen the rain-wet road as the snow came in. There were about four to five inches of new snow on top of sections underlain with black ice. When reaching Tanners Flat coming down canyon, there was, and still is, a sharp bend in the road to the left just before reaching the entrance to the Tanners Flat Campground. This is where things went bad in grand fashion.

I suppose I was moving not more than 20 miles per hour when I started into that bend. I immediately knew I was in trouble because the car did not fully respond to what the steering wheel wanted it to do. The car went off the road in not quite a straight line and came to a sudden and jarring stop. I watched the right front fender area of the car fold inward and upward. The big granite boulder cropping out from the hillside never moved on impact, it just went ahead and customized the right front of the car. I sat there for a few minutes, not quite believing what had just happened. I did know, however, that I was in serious trouble because of this stunt.

After getting out of the car and looking things over, I knew that this was going to require a wrecker to get the thing back to Salt Lake. There was a drop off the shoulder of the road that, combined with the bumper, pushed in against the right front tire. The car would not be able to back out on its own. There was no traffic in the canyon; I had not seen any vehicles on that road going either way. That situation left but one choice on my part that was workable and that was a walk back up to the mine for a conversation with the Swinging Door. The only thing that helped in the least was the fact that it had quit snowing heavily.

I was warmly dressed and had on good sturdy boots, and the walk back up to the drain tunnel was no problem. However, my dread of what I knew I would have to face when I finally got home was another matter. That I underestimated by quite a large measure. When I reached the mine, I figured Swinger had not gone to bed, as he knew the chances that he would be rousted out to open the road when the night shift got ready to leave were good. It was a good assumption on my part, because after I clumped up the stairs and into the penthouse, there he sat.

"Well now, this ain't a-lookin' none too good, chum. Better be given me the rundown I guess."

That is what I did, starting with "I gobbed my goddamn kite at Tanners Flat and done it up good."

I gave him all the details, including what I figured it would take to get the car out of the canyon and the Salt Lake County Sheriff's office notified as required by law. Of course, there was no phone at the Wasatch Drain Tunnel operation, so that presented a small problem. To Swinger, it did not.

"We'll take my kite and run on up to the Peruvian and borrow the lend of their horn. One way or another, kid, we will get she done."

The storm had rendered the phone lines useless, we found out when we got up to the Peruvian Lodge. That put us down the canyon to the valley, and that was a slow operation due to the condition of the canyon highway. We ended up on 700 east and 90th south at a service station where Swinger bought most of his gasoline. The station was dark, closed up for the day, but as luck would have it, it had a phone booth.

I had a couple of quarters in my pocket and probably two one-dollar bills in my wallet, so I did not have to ask Swinger for phone money. I called dispatch at the Salt Lake County Sheriff's office, reported a no-injury accident in Little Cottonwood Canyon, and said it would require a wrecker. Then a thought occurred to me as I was talking to the dispatcher that might make things work a little smoother, and I asked, "Is there any chance that Keith Iba is on shift tonight because if I have any choice in the matter that is who I would prefer."

She told me to wait one while she checked. That is when the phone demanded more money or it would go silent. I fed another quarter, my last one, into the extortionist device seconds before the dispatcher came back on. Iba was on duty, and he was on his way to us.

Deputy Sheriff Keith Iba and I were good friends, so when he got to us it was the usual banter. Keith wanted to know what the hell I had done now, although he already knew that I had reported an accident. I told him immediately after I had introduced him to the Swinging Door. I rode up with Keith while Swinger followed, and then when we got to the bent-up Ford, Swinger went on up to the mine.

The Hintze family owned a body shop in Holladay at the time and a light-duty wrecker to haul damaged vehicles to their place of business. That is where the car ended up when towed out of the canyon. Keith took me home, and I would rather have gone anywhere but there at that particular time. It was after midnight when I came in through the door. The firing squad was ready and waiting. We were living in a basement apartment, having sold our trailer about six months before. It taxed the small apartment to the limits to contain the explosion that followed my entry.

The commencement of the diatribe started off with the fact that I had said when I left that I would be home no later than 6:00 that afternoon. There was no disputing that because it was true. Then another chapter commenced, having to do with how tired she was of my always being gone coupled with what I was doing. There was no arguing with any of that, as it was also true as could be. We had been married about three years at that time, and to this day, I cannot imagine why she put up with my antics. I knew in my mind that I had pushed this to the limit, and things were on real shaky ground now.

All this delivered in a loud, colorful, and forceful manner. Then when I told her what had happened in the canyon to the car, it got extremely loud. When she ran out of breath making loud piercing condemnations of me and the damage to the car, she went silent. That silence lasted for the next 24 hours. Before that period of silence descended on the establishment, one particular demand came forth.

The venerable General Mess of Crap had to go away, and forever would not be long enough. Tagged to the end of that demand was the noisy announcement that it was the old truck or her. Within two weeks, the General Mess of Crap went away, a couple of days after getting the Ford from Hintze's shop. A fellow named Abby looked it over, listened to it, pulled a $100 bill out of his pocket, and asked if that would get me to turn the wreck loose. It did.

At this point, we were back into a situation that was not going to work well. Once again, we had one vehicle between us, working at separate locations, and that brought forth, once again, the question of who got the car. This curtailed severely visits to the Wasatch Drain Tunnel due to the one-vehicle situation. I would generally drive the car, dropping off my wife at work and then picking her up when she got off. On Saturdays, she worked a full day, and I still worked until noon. If nothing went wrong, such as a heavy snowfall in Little Cottonwood Canyon, I could squeeze in about a two-hour visit with my friend Swinger. It took only a short time before it became obvious that getting rid of the old General Mess of Crap was not one of the best things.

I had received a $100 bill for the old wreck, but all that remained now was half that amount. I had owed my uncle Fred, who owned F. G. Ferre and Sons, $45 for various truck parts. It was more than past due because the accumulated bill was six months old. When I went down to his store and paid it off, Uncle Fred said he was never worried about it, as he knew I would eventually pay it. I do not recall what I had done with the $5, but I had $50 still available. What the hell would $50 buy that was not 10 times worse than the old General Mess of Crap? At work I kept grumbling about the one-car problem until Cris, my boss, got tired of listening to me go on and on about my rotten luck, et cetera, et cetera. Cris had the answer in the form of a 1948 Hudson two-door coupe.

Cris had acquired the Hudson a few months before I went to work at Lambert's and had paid $35 for the car. The original flathead, six-cylinder engine powered the car at the time. That engine was in very poor operating condition. When I went to work in the shop for Cris, him and Ross Montgomery, a shop employee, had cured the engine problem. Cris had purchased a used Studebaker V8 engine from the "Palestine Swede," who was in reality one Glen Hanson of Hanson auto wrecking. Cris had given Hanson the enormous sum of $25 for the thing. Ross was a master when it came to making engine swaps such as that Hudson/Studebaker changeover.

Cris told me he would sell the Hudson to me for $150 and the promise to quit grumbling and growling about my one-car situation. That sounded real good, but I told him all I had was $50. We worked out a deal that was good for me but not so much for him. In 1957, I had joined the Utah National Guard as a member of the 653rd Field Artillery Observation Battalion. Every quarter, I received a check for the time spent in the unit. It paid little, as I had no rank yet, just a specialist 4. Out of that quarterly check, Cris would receive $50, half of what I was drawing at that time. Why he went for it, I do not know, but he did. My wife and I now owned a 1948 Hudson powered by Studebaker. It would turn out to be a remarkably good car. The best road car we ever owned.

36

Bad News, among Other Things

BY THE FIRST week of April 1959, things were back on a reasonably solid basis on the home front. A modified schedule of things came into play relating to the Wasatch Drain Tunnel, the Col-Rex/Cardiff explorations, and the time spent with my old friend Swinger. All this would become less extensive than previously to keep things working satisfactorily on the home front. The first trip I made up the canyon with the Hudson was on a nonworking Saturday about two weeks into the month of April. I received some bad news from Swinger as soon as I walked up into the penthouse. Swinger told me the Bull had taken sick at the first of the month and had ended up in the hospital. Our old friend Albert Joseph Wondershek did not survive the hospital stay. The Bull called it deep enough after six days in the Veterans Hospital in Salt Lake at the age of 65. Pneumonia and lung cancer accomplished the trick and took him across the line.

Near the end of April, I went into the mine with Dan's shift. By that time, the water in the Cardiff lower workings had drained almost completely, leaving the drill holes seeping very little water. They were getting ready to open up an eight-by-eight-foot drift into the 1500 level, and the suits were anxiously waiting for that to take place. The big-money boys, Dan explained, had all kinds of rosy dreams regarding what they expected would be uncovered by the connection. Dan told me all about this when we were standing next to those weeping long holes. Dan was of the opinion that the suits were going to get a surprise and it would not be a pleasant one, saying that what he was looking at did not look to him like there was much possibility of the bonanza they were expecting.

From the end of April and through the month of May 1959, I made a number of trips into the Col-Rex workings. There no longer remained any reason to go down the Cardiff incline to check drainage, because the lower workings were now free of water. I made some walks into the west drift of the Col-Rex, also known as the Toledo Crosscut (see map 1, before the introduction) by the old-timers, to see what existed in that area. At a point immediately after entering the drift, a raise on a moderate incline went upward from the drift level. The ladder looked to be in good condition, wet as usual, and all that told me it should be an easy climb. All progress upward came to a sudden end about 10 feet up the ladder. It was the common plague in that mine that did the job. The flame of the candle snuffed out suddenly and completely—no oxygen, classic bad air.

The air quality throughout the Toledo Crosscut would vary due, the old-timers would tell me, to changes in atmospheric pressure. I always carried a burning candle every foot of travel I made through that crosscut as soon as I left the Col-Rex's main run. There would be times that the candle flame suddenly snuffed and other occasions the candle would burn brightly in the same location. About 150 feet in after leaving the Col-Rex's main run, the drift had followed a mineralized fissure, and this section was timbered and lagged for 175 feet.

Making that turn after a short walk of about 50 feet, the sill of a raise came into sight. At the tunnel level, things appeared to be in very good shape. There was muck against the gate timbers, but no sign of them giving way under the load. When I reached the raise, I was hoping that it would be accessible. Standing at the foot of the ladder, I directed the beam of my three-cell flashlight upward. As usual, everything was extremely wet, with drops of water coming down like a light rain. What put an end to the idea of going up was what the flashlight revealed in the raise near the end of the beam's reach. There appeared to be hanging lagging partially blocking the manway.

It would be many years later that I was told the story of that raise and why it was put up. The maps in my possession stated that the raise went up 400 feet, but there was no illustration or written documentation of what lay at the top of the raise or any indication of levels below the top. Over 50 years would pass before I knew what that raise accessed. Dan Jacobson was the man who gave me the information concerning what was there. The workings were extensive, he said, and they paid well, as most of the ore was direct ship.* Dan had been all through the area when it was working. I never tried going up that ladder and did not see any of it for myself. Along with the loose lagging and timbers, it was almost a surety that the air would be bad.

The portal elevation of the Frederick was 8,542 feet above sea level, the Howland/Col-Rex at 8,540 feet. A gently increasing upward inclination in driving the tunnels facilitated drainage and bringing loaded cars out. This method was a standard in all tunnel driving in the mining business. The Col-Rex Tunnel rose on a steeper incline than the Frederick rise and accounted for the 35-foot difference where they connected in the Col-Rex/Toledo west drift. The collar elevation of the raise coming up from the Frederick is 8,640 feet.

Explorations such as these and occasional trips into the drain tunnel with Dan's shift were what I did on the Saturdays the Wasatch Drain Tunnel worked. The trips into the drain tunnel always brought some not-too-gentle reminders from my wife, because those trips always got me home later than she thought was reasonable, putting a few bumps in the surface of the home front. On the nonworking Saturdays when I went up to the mine to visit Swinger and make our hamburger steak and curly French fries run, I made it home at what she considered a reasonable time. Alterations of that, on occasions, occurred when we would go to Tooele to see how things were going with Swinger's family.

Making a trip out to Tooele was to most folks a simple thing to do. Do it enough and it just becomes routine. Swinger being Swinger could sometimes make that trip anything but the usual

* Commonly designates ore of sufficient value that it does not require concentration at the mine. This grade of ore goes directly to the smelter from the mine.

everyday jaunt. I met Swinger's mother and stepfather on the first trip we made together to Tooele. Both of them were most interesting to talk with, and over the period of three or four months, I would meet most of the family, all of them very friendly. The first trips, maybe two if I remember correctly, Swinger took us out in his Ford Ranch Wagon. After that we started going out in my Hudson, and Swinger really liked that old car. He said it beat the hell out of his Ford for comfort, and not only that, he could sit back and tell me lies while I was, as he put it, flying the kite.

Comfort and lie-telling were only part of the reason I talked him into going out in the Hudson. Swinger never got in a hurry, and driving under the speed limit was almost a religion to him. It was on one of those under-speed days that I decided that we ought to look at an alternative. The slow driving did not bother me, so that was not the prime reason to suggest a change. A unique Swinging Door episode and the poking along is what prompted the change.

We had finished our usual meal at the Center Drive In and he decided a Tooele run was on the docket. The masterpiece took place on Redwood Road, which in those days was just a two-lane road. Swinger was driving along at his usual 10 miles below the speed limit. The traffic was moderately heavy going both directions. A woman was driving the first car behind us. That person could not see any humor whatsoever in Swinger's poking along and started crowding his rear bumper. Swinger did not care and, after noticing what she was doing, slowed another five or so miles per hour. A red light came up, Swinger stopped for it, and the woman—now "Boo-Coo," as Swinger described her—pulled alongside the Ford on my side.

It was a tight area, and she was well off the shoulder, almost too far. My window was down, and she commenced getting excessively noisy. Had a good voice. There was little chance to miss much of her rant, and she finally ran out of breath. She was just building up to get started again when Swinger leaned over me getting close to the window. Swinger, to his mind, asked her a simple question: "What's the matter kid, late for your shift in the whorehouse?"

I could not quit laughing for the next half mile and all Swinger could say was "Bet that was her problem, chum. What you think?"

Another memorable Tooele run took place that I title "the shaver incident." On a nonworking Saturday I arrived at the mine somewhere around 1:30, and after we had a cup of coffee, Swinger announced that a trip to Tooele was required. The reason was a shaver problem; it had quit doing its job. He said what we needed to do was load up and head west with the merchandise. We would do Tooele first then stop for our hamburger steak and curly fries on the way back. He said the shaver deal would not take long. We headed out to the Hudson and set off on the Tooele run.

On the way, Swinger gave me the run down on the shaver business. He had dropped the shaver, he admitted, and it did not operate too good after the drop. He said it would buzz for a minute, grab a whisker, and piss him off. After a couple of tries, he decided that a bath in gasoline would clear up the problem. It was anybody's guess what kind of logic determined that was the answer. It occurred to him, he said, that it would not do to "fire it up" after the "douche job." It could, he reasoned, go off like drilling into a miss. *Good thinking,* I thought to myself. It was time she went into the muck pile, he added.

When we arrived in Tooele Swinger directed me to a small shop on a side street running west off Main Street. It was here that he had purchased the shaver, and he knew the owner. Most all the old merchants in Tooele knew Swinger, and he knew them. We walked into the little shop, the owner immediately told Swinger how good it was to see him and asked what he could do for him. Swinger explained that the shaver he bought from him had "shot craps," and he wanted him to look at it, as it had tried to kill him. The fellow took this all in stride, as he knew Swinger and wanted to keep him happy. Swinger told him to plug it in and try it. I thought to myself, *Oh shit!*

The fellow held it in his left hand, I held my breath, and Swinger's face remained without any expression as the fellow plugged the cord into a wall socket. There was a sort of strangled buzz, and the shaver started to smoke. The man immediately dropped it and yanked the plug out of the socket. The shaver hit the floor with a thud, immediately followed by Swinger saying, "Jesus Christ, now look at what you've gone and done, you goddamn Greek." The fellow was indeed Greek. "You have ruined my shaver."

The fellow knew Swinger well enough to know what was going on, and Swinger knew that he had figured it out too. The shopkeeper told him that it was a sure thing that the shaver was defective. Even though he had sold it to him two years ago, he would cut him a good deal on a new one. Swinger could have the new one for the shopkeeper's cost. Out came the new shaver, and Swinger then laid an extra five-dollar bill on the counter and asked him if the price really had been the cost of the shaver. The fellow told him he had lied a bit, and he had drilled him a little. Swinger left the extra five, and both of them laughed like hell. With that, we were on our way back and on to the Center Drive In.

37

Wino, and Other Changes

SWINGER HAD AN old friend that lived in Sandy and would on occasion visit with Swinger at the mine. I thought that he had probably been a miner at one time but never learned much about him and did not have the opportunity to meet him. I did find out that he worked for the Sandy City Animal Control. The reason that I became aware of the fellow's existence, who he was to Swinger, and what he did for Sandy City occurred one Saturday afternoon somewhere near the end of June 1959. The reason had a name. Swinger introduced him as Wino, who was a Labrador/Weimaraner mix of very impressive proportions.

Swinger told me that his friend had shown up after the night shift had gone in the mine. Apparently, Swinger had just finished his supper and, as he put it, was in the middle of "douching the pearls" when his friend walked up the stairs and into the penthouse. The fellow had apparently met Corky at one time and made an inquiry concerning his whereabouts. Swinger told him the tale. They came up with the idea between the two of them that it would be a grand idea to bring a new dog on the job. As Swinger tells the tale it went like this: "We headed on down to the pooch lockup to spring one of the inmates of the joint. The place was closed up tight and damned if my chum had not lost his key, or so he said. We had to swipe the dog and it turned into quite a project. We tried to rope one first and haul him over the fence. That went sour. The first dog chewed the shit out of my pal and that made him a candidate for the gas chamber for sure. The next one we hooked up did not chew anybody, but he was so goddamn big that it near ruined the both of us. But we got him sprung."

Upon introduction to Wino, I was impressed first by his size and second by his gentle demeanor. When he stood on his hind legs, he could put both front legs over your shoulders and look you straight in the eyes. He was bigger than the legendary wanderer of the Alta high country, Sam McGee. The biggest difference between Wino and Sam McGee was Wino did not radiate the high degree of danger and no-nonsense that Sam did. Swinger had good things to say about Wino, and it was apparent they liked each other.

"Goddamn, kid, he's a pippin but he is a big eater. Hell, I can lay out two of those big cans of food and they are gone so fast you ain't sure you really laid them out. Then the big bastard looks at you like he's starving to death and wondering when it's going to be time for the real dinner."

When we would go down to the valley, we usually left the mine about 3:00, and that gave ample time to have a good dinner and go back up and tell lies before I headed for home. This worked out well, as I always made it home before I caught hell for being gone for too long of a time. One Saturday, Swinger decided that it would be a grand idea to take Wino along, as he said he was very good about going on rides and would stay put while we had our usual feed. That meant that Swinger was going to be the pilot and we would take his ranch wagon on this run. With the back seat laid down flat, it gave that big dog plenty of room to lounge around.

When we had finished our usual supper, Wino was just lying in the back as contented as he could be but was ready to come out when Swinger opened the back. Swinger grabbed hold of his collar just for safety's sake, and Wino was happy to lift his leg and hose down the rear wheel and tire. That accomplished, Wino jumped back up into his place in the wagon, and it was apparent that all was well with the big dog. With Wino loaded, we headed for the mine.

Swinger was, as usual, in no big hurry to get up the canyon. There was no traffic of any consequence going up or coming down Little Cottonwood Canyon. Midway up the canyon, the Tanners Flat Campground appears on the right side of the highway. Just a little above this, on the left side, is where the big granite boulder had done the custom bodywork on my almost new Ford Fairlane a few months prior. About midway between these two points, Wino sprung his big surprise. That surprise came in the form of a horrendous, odoriferous fart of epic proportions.

Swinger suddenly jerked the wagon sharply right, off onto the road's shoulder. In the middle of that move, he bellowed out, "JESUS KEEH—RIST!"

I was already almost out of my door when he jammed the transmission shift lever into the park position and bailed out through his half-opened door. The wagon was still kind of rocking forward and backward when we crash-landed outside. I was busy taking gulps of air in and exhaling rapidly, trying to rid my nose and upper throat of the biting sting of Wino's masterpiece. We both finally got somewhat cleared out and stood on each side of the wagon, looking at each other across the top. I managed to croak out, "GODDAMN!"

To which Swinger replied, "That big rotten sonofabitch near gassed us both to death, chum. Shit, kid, I bet I'll have to burn this whoopee to get unloaded of that goddamn stink."

We opened every window in that wagon, including the swing up window above the tailgate. Swinger even dropped that down to its level position, muttering something about how he wished the kite were a convertible with a lift-up lid. All through this business, Wino just lay contentedly, most likely wondering what the hell the big problem was with the two idiots. I posed the question about chances that the big dog would bail out the back going on up. Swinger replied that it was unlikely, as the monster knew that more fart fuel was available up home at the mine.

Prior to my introduction to Wino and his ability to conduct his version of chemical warfare, I had not been up to the mine for three weeks. That period had taken up most of June, starting the first week of the month. I had a military obligation to fulfill, and two full weeks and an extra three days at Camp Williams, Utah, was part of that. It was my third annual camp as a member of the old 653rd Field Artillery Observation Battalion of the Utah National Guard. At its start, I had no idea that it would be my last camp with that outfit. Things were about to change in a big way, and I would never have believed I would do what I ended up doing. The battalion executive officer, Major Jones, cornered me on one of the last days of that training period and had a proposition to put forth.

The Department of the Army had authorized a very small number of National Guard Units across the United States to organize Special Forces units. They were very selective, as the Special Forces were an elite group, also known as the Green Berets. Major Jones was one of the few in the Utah National Guard tasked with putting together the new units in the state of Utah. These units would accept volunteers only. When the regular army Special Forces came into being, an individual had to be a three-time volunteer to join. First: voluntarily joining the army. Second: volunteering for airborne training to become a qualified parachutist. Third: volunteering for Special Forces.

The good major spread it on thick. In the beginning of my artillery career, I was a clerk in battalion headquarters, which put me in close proximity to Major Jones, the battalion executive officer. The battalion sergeant major, the highest-ranking NCO, was located in this area also. Because of this, we came to know each other well. I have to suppose I must have made a favorable impression in high places. That impression was good enough that it resulted in my assignment as the battalion commander's driver. That assignment gave me privileges that few enlisted men enjoyed. Major Jones made it sound like my coming into that Special Forces unit was critical, which of course, it was not. He added a little incentive to the offer, that being in the form of a promotion in rank. Should I decide to join the outfit, he said, I could kiss my rank of specialist 4 goodbye. I would get my E-5 rating, which was the three stripes of a buck sergeant. Being young and stupid, I volunteered.

It would have been early September when I heard about Slick's new undertaking about to take place up at the Col-Rex. Swinger and I had been sitting out on the edge of the dump, plinking at small stones in the high bank across the creek. We did a lot of that. Me with my Colt Buntline Scout and Swinger with his nine-shot

Iver Johnson revolver. We were sitting there thinking about maybe reloading for another round of shooting when Swinger told me what Hansen was up to.

Hansen, along with a couple of men that had a financial interest in the operation, decided to drive an adit* portal in west of and about 150 feet in elevation above the Howland portal location. According to their calculation, 300 feet of adit would reach the Olympic Stope. It would eliminate the constant problems with areas of very questionable timber soundness and the infamous section of "floating track" that was a constant headache and the inspiration for profane sermons.

Swinger and I were well aware of what existed in that section of the mine, and it had apparently become more of a problem than when we were there. Swinger added to that and said that if a state mine inspector was to look over that project, he would shut it down until brought up to acceptable standards. Knowing the potential of this, Hansen and his backers decided it would be cheaper to drive an adit than to do the work that such an inspection would demand. Swinger was of the opinion that, from what he had seen, there was no chance that Slick and his backers could ever come out ahead on it.

Swinger moved away from the antics up the canyon and said some other things that did not sound too good to me. He said that now that the Bull had taken up residence in hell, things were not the same around the mine. Matt was trying to do his own job *and* fill in for the Bull, something he did not have the experience to accomplish. Added to that, Dan had told Swinger that big changes were ahead because the bonanza expected in the 1500 level did not exist. It never did. The big-money boys were very disappointed with the outcome and the heavy expenses involved getting to this point, all for nothing.

During a trip into the mine with Dan, just after the money boys had their look at the bonanza that was not there, he told me

* Horizontal tunnel driven from the surface into an existing mine. Usually done to reach a specific target. An example would be to intersect a shaft or stope.

what he thought would take place in the very near future. Dan said it had turned out as he expected it would. The stories concerning what was in the lower levels had been dressed up to the point that anyone with any familiarity with the Cottonwood mining districts would have discounted 90 percent of the tales told. This bunch did not do that and either did not know or ignored the reasons that the original backers of the extensive Wasatch Drain Tunnel extension venture quit halfway through the drive for the Cardiff.

Because he was a veteran of many years in the district, both groups questioned Dan extensively as to what he knew about the lower levels of the Cardiff. Dan had told them truthfully that he had never worked in the lower levels of the mine and could not say whether the alleged ore was fact or shined-up bullshit. There were, however, indications on the drain tunnel level that would be worth exploring. That would take more money than the recently added current Denver crowd backers were willing to put into exploration.

The ore in the hillside zone was fast approaching exhaustion due to extraction only. There had been no development work undertaken to try to locate more ore. Dan said he was positive minable ore bodies were in that area, but it would require a lot of money to locate them. The Denver crowd wanted no part of this, and there would be no further funding by them for any exploration work. In the area that encompassed the drain tunnel's opening of the 1500 level, Dan showed me several places he believed were good choices for further exploration.

The inescapable fact remained, in his opinion, that the days of a large company venture along the lines of exploration and the production of ore found was at its end. This was exactly what happened, just like Dan said, but it was to take place after 1960. By that time, I no longer had free access to the drain tunnel. I did in fact see some of it, but it was on a more or less clandestine basis. I'd come the long way around, using the Cardiff Mine for access into the drain tunnel.

By mid-August, Slick and his crew, one of whom was Tokyo Joe, had cut a road to the location where the adit would portal in. When I made my first visit up there, they had drilled and blasted two drift rounds, putting the adit in about 15 feet. They were in good solid limestone structure, so no timberwork was necessary. They mucked out both rounds by hand, and they laid rails up to the working face.

I do not know how or when they unloaded that load, and as it was getting late and to keep myself out of trouble on the home front, I told Swinger I had better head for home before curfew came around and I got in deep. We had to pass up our usual run for a hamburger steak and curly fries for that time, but we would do it the next available Saturday. Because of Wino's great and terrible fart episode, he found himself confined to the penthouse when we went down to the Center Drive In.

38
How Not to Do Things

IT WOULD HAVE been probably some three weeks after the adit visit that a nearly disastrous, but somewhat hilarious, event occurred at the drain tunnel. This masterpiece was another over-the-dump event that, unfortunately, I was not on the ground to participate in one way or another.

Heading directly from work just after noontime, I arrived in Little Cottonwood Canyon. I decided to stop at the drain tunnel just to say hello to Swinger and tell him I intended to go to Slick's new enterprise.

When I neared the buildings coming down the road, I encountered a scene that was far from the usual. Just west of the first building and right on the edge of the dump in that area sat the Banana Wagon, the old FWD dump truck. Back from it, about 30 feet or so, sat the International dozer, Swinger's favorite toy. There were several piles of chains near the machine, and Swinger, Willy, and Matt Martinson were standing together watching me come in.

Naturally, I was curious as to what was going on, and Swinger was more than ready to lay it all out. He unloaded a big spit of Cope, took his cap off, then put it back on and gave forth as only the Swinging Door could: "Christ kid, that goddamn burr head put the Banana Wagon over the dump, and she has been hell to get back up because most of the muck was still in her. Now the burr head knew damn well the brakes weren't worth a shit on that old kite. Sometimes the pedal will go all the way down and you have to pump the hell out of the pedal to stop the crate. Who knows what the hell that damn burr head was dreaming about this time?"

It was obvious beyond a doubt that Swinger was unhappy with Almond Joy's stunt, as he only called him the burr head when he was mad at him. The Banana Wagon had gone over the dump back end first right down into the creek. Luckily for Gus it had gone straight, so it did not roll over. Gus went down with it, kinda like a sea captain goes down with his ship.

"Matt and Willy climbed down the dump while I went after the International and some chains. The burr head's hands had death grips on the steering wheel, frozen in place, and he was staring back up the dump. Matt said his eyes looked like two pie plates in a coal pile, they were so big, and he either would not or could not say a word. Willy said they couldn't open the heavy door because of the angle and it smelled really bad in the cab. So, we had to suck the Banana Wagon back up with the seized-up burr head still in it.

"When we got her up and the rear wheel blocked with a stick of timber, it was time to get the burr head out. Willy finally shook his hands loose from the steering wheel and said that they would need a shovel to pry his ass loose from the seat. Well, it smelled near as bad as Wino's big unload at Tanners that night, but not quite. He was sort of wobbly when he hit the ground and he headed straight for the dry. You remember how Slick done that funny lookin' walk when he headed for the shithouse up at the Col-Rex that day the car went over the dump? That's about what the burr head looked like headed for the dry. Hell, he didn't say nothin'. Wasn't much to say, I guess, and you can bet he is busy scraping his leg about now."

Apparently, the brakes on the Banana Wagon had been very unreliable for some time. Willy tried to fix them on a couple of occasions, Swinger said, but needed parts, and they were hard to find for that old FWD.

Willy had more problems than the brakeless Banana Wagon, I found out, and that problem came in the form of Wino. Wino loved everybody but he had a special treat for Willy. If Wino were anywhere in sight, Willy always made his way from the dry to his little shop in the portal building walking backward. This posed a risk of its own, but that risk was minimal compared to what prompted Willy to adopt this form of travel. Swinger explained it like this when he gave me the story: "That big sonofabitch Wino decided to give Willy some special attention for some reason. It took only a few treatments before Willy got real cautious and took up walking backwards. Willy for some reason always kept a big bag of tools with him and they left with him when he took off out of the dry for his hole up yonder. Willy would swing this bag over his shoulder to make his march. If Wino was out and saw Willy walking towards the portal, he took off after him like a mad God after a Lamanite. Willy can't hear much of anything, so he couldn't tell that big bastard was coming in behind him. Goddamn! Wino would hit him like a runaway truck and down Willy would go flat on his front, tools scattered all over the dump, and that big mutt standing close looking pleased as hell."

Things held steady as to the order of things involving the new adit Hansen and his associates were driving for the Olympic Stope area, and they were making good headway on the project. Willy was still walking backward from the dry to his shop in the portal building. Swinger said that Wino was putting away food as if he was starving to death. It was making a big hole in his grocery budget. Swinger also added to this that with all the groceries the big bastard put away, the potency of his farts were on the same run.

September of 1959 started what I termed a downhill run. Charlie Steen's Grand Deposit Company took over the drain tunnel operation and the Cardiff Mining and Milling Company signs went away forever. Steen's company brought in the needed money to do some serious exploration work. This made possible the development of new ore and some of it looked good, as good as any that came out of the hillside ground. Almost immediately after Grand Deposit took over, the mine went to a day-shift-only operation. They still worked alternating five- and six-day weeks, and the new management had the good sense to hold on to Dan Jacobson.

With that change, my privileged access to the drain tunnel ended. I probably could have gone in with Dan's shift on a Saturday but decided that I would not even ask. Swinger said that things were starting to look spooky as far as his job at the mine went, and he said it might be time to pull the pin. No one had said anything to him concerning any change in what he was doing, but he knew how things ended up eventually in the mining game.

All this was change enough, but then on the early evening of Wednesday, 2 September 1959 a disaster of monumental proportions took place. This event bothers me to this day and the fact that it delighted certain individuals in Alta intensifies my eternal disgust and black hatred for a certain class of people in the Alta area nowadays. By the time men and firefighting equipment arrived in Alta from the closest valley location, all the buildings, snowsheds, and big ore bins of the Col-Rex were just glowing embers. The entire complex had burned to the ground. Nothing survived but ashes, heat twisted rails, and other unidentifiable iron and steel objects. Gone forever were structures that had survived major conflagrations, the first in 1914 and another in 1947. Luckily, Mack and Mark Jacobson were not at work underground in the mine at the time. At this time of the year, the flow of air was being pulled into the mine from the outside, and that spelled the end of them if they'd been working. As it was, they lost all their personal belongings that were in the shack where Swinger had been living when we first met. The fire consumed the transformer station that was in close proximity to the portal also. Electrical service was never restored, and the mine ended forever.

The Jacobson brothers, earlier, had taken their truck and headed up to the Flagstaff Mine to "borrow" some heavy timber that was up there. Mack and Mark loaded their truck with all it could carry and started down and back to the Col-Rex. They were halfway down the road approaching the mine when they noticed the billowing smoke. They did not attempt to get any closer than about 100 feet and all they could do was sit there, cuss, and watch the old Col-Rex's final curtain call.

The timber the two brothers were bringing down from the Flagstaff were originally part of a tramway loading station high up in

Grizzly Gulch. The Michigan-Utah Mining Company built the structure originally, and it had fallen into disrepair, unused for many years. The major supporting timbers were 12 by 12 inches and were still solid and usable.

Old Francis Jolley decided this timber was just what he needed for holding the ground he was working in the Flagstaff Mine. Jolley had moved many of those timbers up to the Flagstaff. He used very few, if any of them, in the mine. His advanced age forced him to give up on his project sooner than he anticipated. Francis Jolley was about 75 years old when he hauled the timber up to the Flagstaff's dump using his old Model A Ford pickup.

On two occasions, our paths crossed up in Grizzly Gulch when he was hauling or loading the timbers, a sight never forgotten. Another time I met him coming up the steep road below the Flagstaff dump. He had just crossed the dumps of the Vallejo and South Star mines over which the road passed. The old Model A was laboring hard as it made the final climb up to the Flagstaff. I walked behind the truck on up to the dump, and it was easy to keep up with it. If Jolley had stopped when he'd seen me, and he knew better than that, it would have been impossible for the old truck to get moving again on the steep grade. I just stood there when he came to a stop and stared at the spectacle.

When the old Model A came to its wheezing halt, Francis Jolley squeezed his way out of the driver side window, a tight fit. He had no choice but to exit the truck's cab using the window as no other way out existed. The timbers he was carrying were as long as the old Model A. There were two of those 12-by-12s, one tied down on each side, resting on the front and rear fenders. Jolley acted like it was just a normal thing, nothing out of the ordinary, and just part of a normal day on the mountain for him. I helped him untie the timbers and helped stack them on the growing pile. That timber was heavy, and he had managed that alone until that one day I helped him.

On one of the two times I met Jolley on the road in Grizzly Gulch he had already loaded his timbers and left the site of the old tramway loading station. I run into him at the Alta Consolidated just above where the road passes between the numbers one and two dumps. It was the same layout as before with a 12-by-12 tied down across the fenders on each side of the truck. He did not climb out the window to talk, he just sat while we talked, and I asked a few questions.

The one that he furnished the most interesting answer to was when I asked what the hell he would do if the old crate decided to run away on that steep downgrade. Those old trucks were not known for having good brakes, as they were mechanical, not hydraulic. There would be no such thing as a rapid bailout, being as he had to go out the window. Jolley kind of chuckled and said, "Hell, if this old crate decides to take a quick run down into the bottom that is not a problem for me. I would most likely get gobbed in the wind up and that isn't a bad way to go out. I would rather that be the ticket out or, better yet, have the whole of Flagstaff hill come in on me in the hole. Would beat the hell out of making the run out of a goddamn hospital bed."

Then down the steep Grizzly Road went Francis Jolley and his rattling, backfiring, timber-laden old Model A truck.

39

Getting Close

WHITNEY "SLICK" HANSEN and his crew, which had a habit of varying greatly due to turnover, kept up a six-day workweek on the Olympic adit. Tokyo Joe was always there with Slick and at least one other man. Swinger would go up and work every Saturday after the Wasatch Drain Tunnel went to a five-day workweek. That gave me an opportunity to get a little more hands-on experience. Up until the end of October 1959, I had a chance to do some more drilling with a jack leg drill. I was too slow at that, so they would let me put in a couple of holes and then take over the machine. Tokyo Joe and Swinger put those holes in as if they were puncturing cheese instead of solid rock. Slick was much faster on the "leg" than I was but could not come close to Tokyo and Swinger when "making hole."

When I was working with Swinger back in the beginning in the old Col-Rex, we never had a missed hole, but we had three or four at the Olympic adit when I was up there. There was a lot more powder used in that project because it required more blast holes drilled for a drift round. If Swinger was doing the loading, which always seemed to be the case when I was there, he always asked me to give him a hand on it. I just simply handed him the sticks of dynamite out of the box, and he split the sticks and tamped them in the drill holes. He had the primers made up before the holes were loaded, always far removed from the boxes of dynamite. When everything was ready, the face of the drift appeared to be covered with dangling fuses that the miners called rattails.

Swinger would stand there, studying the loaded holes for a minute or two just to make sure that fuse lengths were right so the round would fire in the correct sequence. When he was satisfied, he commenced spitting the fuses, starting with the burn hole and working outward. It still gave me a bit of discomfort to be standing there when it looked like the entire face of the drift was smoking or spitting sparks. Swinger told me he had seen inexperienced men take off "like a mad God after a Lamanite" down the drift before the round was half spit. Well, I never did, but I cannot say that in the beginning I had not been tempted to run like hell. When Swinger knew everything was burning as it should, we turned and walked away.

The drift was not in so far at the time that we could not walk all the way out to sunshine, sit down, and wait for the thumps to begin. Everyone that was on the job made his own count of those thumps. It would be apparent if there was a miss on one of the holes, and if there were, "aw shit" would be the mildest of utterances that came forth from the participants. There were a number of ways to take care of a missed hole; among them was to reprime the hole and shoot it again or clean the loaded hole out using compressed air and reload the hole. The fix I recall on most of them was Swinger cleaning out the hole with compressed air.

In most cases, a missed hole that was in the lowest part of the round, near the bottom, rarely ended up buried in the muck pile. The last holes to fire were the lifters, and their angle and location lifted the muck up and back. That is if they all fired. At best, it was not easy on the nerves and not being cautious could end in disaster. Something could always go wrong, and as Swinger liked to say, "If she should go bad you could find yourself airmailed to hell in the blink of an eye."

When the time came to muck out the pile left by the blasting operation, either Tokyo Joe or Swinger, if it was a Saturday, operated the Eimco mucking machine. I never had a chance to try it, and I wish I had had the opportunity. Slick could operate it but usually left it to Tokyo Joe, Swinger, or another experienced operator. The closest connection I ever had with the mucker was the job of keeping the flexible air hose clear of the wheels of the machine as it moved back and forth. If the man doing that job did not move fast enough, the wheel of the mucker passed over it and cut the hose. When that happened, a wildly whipping hose and a blizzard of flying rock made a dangerous situation for anyone in close proximity. Luckily, I managed to avoid pulling that stunt when I was tending the hose.

There were two cars up on that project, and they were enough to get the job done while I was involved. There was no trammer on that project, only workers. Usually two men trammed the cars, loaded or empty. A loaded car weighed on average about a ton, and to push them outside was not extremely hard work, because like any tunnel or drift in that country, it went in on a gentle ascending grade.

It was during this time that I made the acquaintance of two of Slick's sons. The younger of the two, Norman, was still in high school and was doing general flunky work around the project to earn a few dollars. Norman's biggest desire was to earn enough money to buy a high-fidelity record player, also known as a hi-fi outfit. Modern stereophonic equipment was not around at the time, and high fidelity was the thing to have.

Swinging Door, being Swinging Door, did the usual nicknaming and dubbed him Hi-Fi. That nickname stuck to Norman like glue. To this day, when I happen to run into Norman, I still have to remind him of that moniker. The older son, Gaylon, was close to graduating from Westminster College with a degree in Geology. Gaylon and I became close friends and were to remain so for nearly 50 years. That association ended only because of Gaylon passing on at age 75.

It would have been sometime in the last weeks of September that my minimal involvement in the adit ended. It was not my idea. The breakaway from that little enterprise had to do with my friend Swinger. Due to bad luck on Swinger's part, he got hurt on the job. What occurred was something that could have happened to anyone. It was Saturday, and I was up at the adit but was not in the drift when it took place. They had just fired the shot, which went just fine, which is always good news. Gaylon and I were hooking cars and getting ready to go back into the adit. That was when Swinger came limping outside. He was favoring his right leg and doing a little cussing as he came up to us.

The round having fired and the heading having ventilated itself enough such that Swinger walked in with a scaling bar while Slick and Tokyo busied themselves with who knows what outside. Gaylon and I were not paying any attention to what they were doing.

The first thing, once a man could go back in the drift after a shot, was the chore of barring down any loose rock that might exist in the back and on the ribs. This type of work, known as "scaling 'er down," always preceded the mucking operation. Big enough and heavy enough, a rock fall out of the back could kill a man. Any loose "hangers" on the ribs came down as part of the job, all in the interest of safety.

Upon limping out after, Swinger leaned on the bar and gave us the story. There were a couple of "hangers" in the back, and he was off to the side near the rib when he was breaking the last one loose. That is when, as he explained it, "The goddamned Tommyknocker tipped one off the rib." Was not exactly a rock, more like a slab, he said, and it took him down as it hit his leg. He said he got loose from it with the bar, lucky that it had not broken the leg.

On Sunday, Swinger went down to the valley, called Matt Martinson, and told him he was headed for Tooele because he had a bad leg. Matt told him to get it taken care of and he would call Gus to go on up and set up housekeeping at the Wasatch Drain Tunnel until Swinger could get back.

I was only two weeks away from taking a so-called vacation for a stay in a delightful resort in Georgia known as Fort Benning. There I would enjoy the hell of basic airborne training to become, hopefully, a U.S. Army qualified paratrooper. It did not amount to a pleasant outing. Faced with that, I headed for Tooele the next Saturday to see Swinger, who was still in the Tooele Valley Hospital. The slab off the rib that knocked Swinger down had broken a number of blood vessels. His lower leg was a colorful mass of purple and yellow streaks, quite an ugly mess.

Swinger was more than ready to get out of the place and said he did not know if he still had a job with that outfit or not. He also mentioned that even if he did, he figured it was just about ending up there for him anyhow. He added to that by saying it did not make a big pile of rat shit, as it was just about deep enough. I told Swinger what I was headed for and that I would not be back until 1 December, but I would hunt him up either at the mine or here in Tooele.

I was back home for December, as I had told Swinger I would be, and with a bit of a problem to deal with. Usually when I start reminiscing about my time in the military, I start with the remark "When I was young and stupid" and go from there. Unexpectedly, myself and the proud but well beat up group I was in at Benning arrived in Salt Lake City early Thanksgiving morning, 1959. Our group training at Fort Benning, because of not a small effort by Major J. E. Jones, had the last two weeks of scheduled training jammed into six days. It was tough!

Two days prior to our departure from Fort Benning, every man's family received a phone call advising them of the status from Major Jones. He must have spent a lot of time on the telephone, but that is how he operated. Everyone concerned here at home knew we would be in Salt Lake early Thanksgiving morning. When I got off the aircraft, I was wearing my Class A uniform, which was ill fitting due to the fact that I was wearing a plaster cast under it. The cast, courtesy of Martin Army Hospital in Fort Benning, went in place the day before. That occurred after the doctors had put my dislocated left shoulder back in place on my last jump. But that didn't matter; the silver wings of a qualified U.S. Army parachutist were now part of my uniform.

The management at Lambert's said they would be very happy to have me back because the shop had been busier than normal, but the doctor at the Veterans Hospital told me I couldn't go back to work until the end of January. I was still drawing army pay until I could go back to my civilian job and was making better money drawing grade E-5 pay than I would be making when I went back to Lambert's, so that was fine with me. It was somewhere in the first two weeks of January 1960 before I got back up to the Wasatch Drain Tunnel to visit my friend Swinger. I was still wearing a sling to support the injured shoulder, and even with that, it was no trick to drive the Hudson up the canyon. She was a good ride.

40

Shutting Down

THE DAY WAS a cold one. As I recall, it was the second Saturday of January 1960, and I had just arrived at the Wasatch Drain Tunnel. It had been almost three months since Swinger and I had last talked, back when he was still an inmate of the Tooele Valley Hospital. There was no danger we would run out of things to talk about this day. The questions began before we got up to the penthouse, as he met me just inside the door, noticed the sling my arm was occupying at the time, and said, "Jesus Christ and little Rizzi kid. What the hell?"

With that out of the way, we headed upstairs. With cups full of good strong Swinging Door coffee, we got right to it. The first thing I noticed right off was the fact that the big monstrous hulk, the architect of noxious gas, was missing. There was no Wino in residence. Swinger gave me the run down on that business right away.

He had loaded Wino and took him along when he and his swollen colorful leg headed for Tooele to have it looked at. As Swinger put it, the "bastards" banged him right into a ward at the hospital. Of course, the people at the hospital decided that the big Weimaraner/Labrador would not be a good fit for the establishment, so Wino ended up boarding with his son, the one he called Dunc, and his family. Swinger had two grandkids belonging to Dunc and his wife, and I do not know if I ever knew their real names. Swinger called them Steamboat and Kokomo, and they fell in love with the big dog. When Swinger got ready to head back to Alta, there existed no way they were going to turn loose of Wino.

As to Wino, now living the good life in Tooele, Swinger said it was likely for the best. Both Matt Martinson and Dan Jacobson had told Swinger that there were going to be changes up there and some jobs would disappear. Matt said Swinger could likely hang on, as what he did still needed doing on the outside. Almond Joy was going to leave soon, as he had finally completed his schooling to become a barber. He wanted to set himself up in a little shop somewhere and go into business. Dan would have no worries, though, because if that mine went to the long-term lease now under consideration, Dan, with his knowledge of the ground, would be indispensable to the new company.

The word was, as far as known at the time, that the operation would eventually pass into the possession of Joseph J. Beeson under the name Beeson Exploration. Joseph J. Beeson, the renowned geologist, known well and highly respected, had made his mark in that country. He was the man who had finally located the faulted ore body of the Emma Mine. This ore body, when cut off by a fault, had baffled many experts as to where it went. It had also caused an international incident, a congressional investigation, and many hearings. Much has been written about this business in many volumes, so there is no need to recount it here. Called "Old Joe" by some, he would partner with his wife, Desdemona S. Beeson. Desdemona held a degree in mining engineering, and her history in the mining game was colorful to say the least.

On that January day in 1960, the only mine in the entire Cottonwood mining districts working was the Wasatch Drain Tunnel. The Jacobson brothers, Mack and Mark, would normally have been working in the Col-Rex, but the fire the previous September had made that an impossibility. With all the surface buildings now in ashes, there was no way to operate during the winter months. Swinger could not tell me what the brothers were doing to make a living.

We had been talking for about three hours when the subject came up of hamburger steaks and curly French fries. There was no dispute when the idea of a run to the Center Drive In came up. On the way down the canyon, a brief disagreement cropped up when I told Swinger I was buying this one. I had a little pocket money that had accumulated during the preceding three months, and it was way past time I picked up the feed bill. He did some complaining and grumbling, called me a "greedy bastard," but gave it up after a few minutes.

It was near the center of January when I went back to work at Lambert's. Everything fell back into the usual routine that had existed before I went to Benning. We were working the same old five and a half days a week as when I left. My wife still had to work Saturdays, and so I would, like in the past, head for Alta on Saturday afternoons. I did not stay too late up there, and that made things on the home front much smoother than when I was underground half the night with Dan.

During the winter months and up until the late spring, I never set foot underground, and I was missing it. The deep snows of winter completely buried the portal of the Howland, and Slick's Olympic adit, shut down, had to wait for the snow to go off. Money was getting tighter now that I was back at Lambert's due to the low wage I received. It was a source of embarrassment to me that my wife was making almost twice as much money as I was. We had moved out of the trailer we had been living in and sold it and had set up housekeeping in a basement apartment. It was nice to be out of that cramped little trailer and have some room.

I always enjoyed my time with Swinger, and we continued the bullshit sessions and, on occasion, rat hunting in some of the older abandoned buildings in Alta. Runs to the Center Drive In took place nearly every Saturday. If we happened not to do that, we did some creative messing around. The windows of the penthouse on the north side faced a blank face of quartzite that was solid, with little fissuring in it. The wall was about six feet distant from the building and would soon become useful. The weather was cold and snowy during the first three months of the year, and playing around outside was not too pleasant most times, so Swinger cooked up a neat idea.

He laid it all out one Saturday afternoon just before we went down the hill for our usual dining episode. He explained it somewhat along these lines: "Now, you know kid, we can't let our marksmanship go all to hell before rat season comes along. This business of sitting out on the dump edge banging away at rocks across the creek always results in a frozen ass, which ain't good for the 'rhoids. What we will do is buy us a bunch of targets somewhere, slide the window to the side like I did when I banged Corky out, and hang up targets there where the window ain't."

That is what we did and set it all up the next Saturday to do some short-range target shooting from across the room. We never put a round through any of the windows above or to the side and never put any into the floor either. It was a successful setup. Kind of noisy but a lot of fun, and we could sit in a chair to do it. The quartzite wall on the north side of the building made a perfect backstop for .22-caliber bullets.

Hansen and his crew got started on the Olympic adit again about the last of May 1960. They were forced to do some snow shoveling on the road leading to it because of shady spots where the snow had not melted. The rest of the hill outside of those shady spots was snow-free by that time, because the hillside was on the south facing side of the canyon. Slick and company pulled the wagon compressor that they had taken down to the valley back up the same week. The Eimco mucker had been stored in the drift during the down time. The Jacobson brothers already had their wagon compressor at the Howland/Col-Rex. The snow had gone off earlier at the Howland/Col-Rex portal area due to it being at a slightly lower elevation.

It was not until the end of June 1960 that I was able to get back up to Alta. This was due to my being obligated to attend the annual two-week summer camp with the Utah National Guard. Swinger said things were fast approaching the deep-enough stage for him at the mine. Matt Martinson had been, as Swinger put it, sent down the horseshit trail. Almond Joy had pulled out to get his barbershop going. Willy and his tools had left the place for good also.

Due to all the rearranging, that left Swinger the only outside man at the mine. The soon-to-depart outfit had hired a new fellow as a general office flunky to handle the mine paperwork. The people now in charge really wanted Swinger to stay on the job so there would be somebody on the property on the weekends. Overall, it was not a bad deal according to Swinger, because he could take one day during the week off. Another thing that he neglected to say out loud, and we both knew it, was the fact that this was the only place he could call home at that time. We had spent a lot of time catching up, and the time had arrived to head for the Center Drive In.

The following Saturday when I got to the drain tunnel, it was decided that a trip up the canyon was in order. The time had come to find out the latest involving Hansen's enterprise. Swinger had not been up since the work resumed in May, so anything could have taken place, including a Slick-patented disaster. Tokyo Joe was not up there that day, as he was off somewhere with his dump truck doing some hauling. Slick did not know whom he was doing the work for but said he would be done in a couple more days.

Hansen had two men up there with him that I never had seen before. Swinger called them by name, so he was familiar with them from somewhere. The two men and Slick had one thing in common, which was a downcast look on their faces. Hansen said that the last round had opened up nasty-looking ground and he asked Swinger to look at what had opened up. He knew Swinger could give him the best assessment of the present situation. Swinger said he would be glad to look it over.

Not having any gear, we borrowed two hard-boiled hats and the carbide lamps from the two who were working for Hansen. My hat did not fit good at all; must have been set up for a pinhead, I decided, and Swinger's fell into the same category, but they would do the job. It did not take long to go in for our look and for Swinger to do a little poking around with a scaling bar. He spit a couple of times and kind of mumbled to himself and we backed up about 15 feet. He propped the bar against the rib and said to me, "Well, I would say these kids are on the edge of some serious trouble. They have opened up a fault zone filled with gouge* between the two

* Abbreviation for a *fault gouge*, this represents the movement between two sides of a fault, which results in a grinding action or a natural milling process. This action is also known as brecciation. The width and depth of this brecciation/gouge varies a great deal, sometimes measured in inches, other times many feet.

sides. I would guess that it is going to be extensive from the look of the material. It is going to take a lot of timber and it will have to be lagged tight. The kids are going to have to get this caught up tight before they can keep going with the drift. Somebody is going to get gobbed if they play this wrong. Slick ain't gonna like what I have got to tell him."

Slick did indeed not like what Swinger told him, but he was afraid from the start that it was just as Swinger outlined it. By late summer, he and his backers and associates walked away from the project. They pulled the rail out of the adit and hauled all equipment down from Alta. Not only did they give up on the adit run but it ended all work in the Col-Rex also. Whitney C. "Slick" Hansen had finished his run in Alta. The Jacobson brothers were the only ones left in the Howland/Col-Rex area.

When Slick and the boys quit the country, I was no longer going up to Alta on a regular basis. I found out about the shut down when Slick's son, Gaylon Hansen, called me and gave me the information. About two weeks before Hansen pulled out, Swinger had called it deep enough and left the Wasatch Drain Tunnel for the last time too. He headed for Tooele to establish a place there to settle down for a while.

Thus, in September 1960, a unique period of my life ended. It was a time not possible to repeat and with a breed of men that would never again exist after they were gone.

41
Life and Death

THE CLOSING OF the period the foregoing stories cover is now 64 years in the past. It is doubtful that any of the participants remain among the living with the exception of the writer. The main characters are all in the ranks of the deceased, and those that were on the periphery were relatively unknown except for an occasional name, most of which were nicknames. There was no effort made to search out any of these individuals. There were those, however, who will live in my memories until the final blackness descends. Maybe beyond it, for all I know.

John T. Campbell, better known as Swinger, stands a head above all others. Swinger was the man who taught me the basics of being a miner. And he introduced me to most of the characters I came to know in Alta during the five-year span covered by these stories. When he finally called it deep enough and left Alta forever, it was far from the end of our association. That went on for another 11 years before he passed on. John T. Campbell died in the LDS Hospital here in Salt Lake 7 May 1971. He was born 24 September 1902 in Silver City, Utah.

Whitney Charles Hansen was the first man I met of the many I came to know in what I term the drain tunnel days. He carried the name of Slick because somewhere down the trail Swinger bestowed that moniker on him. Prior to the drain tunnel days, he had spent some years in the mining business. He was president of Eldorado Mining Company and Whitco Development. It seems he operated on thin margins and struggled holding together most of his ventures. Whitney also had a monumental problem with alcohol.

That problem was part of what would turn out to be his final windup, as Swinger would have termed it.

Nevada State Highway 93, some miles south of Wells, Nevada, late on Monday night, 1 October 1962. A pickup truck with two occupants traveling too fast drifted off onto the right shoulder. The driver attempted to adjust but overcorrected. That overcorrection caused the truck to cross the highway, go off the opposite shoulder, and roll two times. The rolling truck crushed one man, killing him, and the other was thrown clear. The fatality was Whitney Hansen. John T. Swinger Campbell was critically injured and spent close to a month in the hospital in Elko, Nevada. Whitney had a small exploration project going high on Wiregrass Mountain south of Mesquite, Nevada, at the time, and the two had been in Salt Lake to pick up supplies and take a short break. A detour to Wells, Nevada, was in order for the return trip. The reason, even though it would add over 100 miles to the journey, was the Hacienda Ranch. Here, they intended to take on a tank full of old busthead and get their bell ropes pulled.

The day I met the "Bull," Albert Wondershek, it was apparent that this was a man you stayed on the right side of. Over the years, I talked with many old miners who had worked under him, and all agreed it was not good to get on his bad side. Some called him a rough old cob, and he was. Al was a hard man but fair. If he liked you all was good; if not, find somewhere else to be. I had free run around the drain tunnel job, on the surface or underground, and Al was good with that—otherwise, even with the pull Swinger and Dan Jacobson had, I would never have had such a privilege. Lung cancer and pneumonia put him in the ground in the end. He died in the Veterans Hospital here in Salt Lake 13 April 1959.

Swinger introduced me to Dan Jacobson, who he called a real miner. A title like that out of Swinger was a rare thing. Dan and I became fast friends from our first handshake. He was born in Alta, Utah, 28 August 1919. Dan was getting blisters in the mining game from the time he was 10 years old. He attended school, but any free time, including summer vacations, he worked in some facet of mining. Because he could, he spent a lot of time showing and telling me things involving the Wasatch Drain Tunnel and the other properties that surrounded it. I learned a lot from Dan and valued his friendship. After everything mining shut down forever in the Alta area, we lost contact for a number of years. Our paths would cross occasionally in the canyon, but it was rare. In 2004, we reconnected and got together many times at his home. That resulted in a large notebook that contains copious notes concerning Alta's mines and the men involved with them. Dan called it deep enough 28 August 2013.

Dan's younger brothers Mack and Mark, like Dan, grew up in the mining game. Mack once said to me, "Mom had just finished changing our last diaper when the old man put us on the hill." The two brothers had much to do with my finally locating the Jewel Stope in the Columbus-Rexall. Both of them issued strong warnings about the hazardous conditions I would encounter. Mack I knew the better of the two, but I remember going to Mark's home with Gaylon Hansen one time, and Mark produced an old Flagstaff Company map of the mine that I hope someone still has in their possession. A detailed map, it measured six feet by four feet, as best I remember. That map would be a museum piece now. Mark died at the young age of 49 in 1980. Mack lived until he had 67 years of back trail behind him. It was deep enough for him in December of 1995.

Gus Almon, known as Almond Joy, as far as I know, may have been the only Black miner to work in the district. Now wrong I may very well be, but my friends in the game could not recall another man of Gus's lineage. What Gus ended up doing after the mine shut down, I have no idea. I would like to think that he got his little one-chair barbershop in operation, as was his dream.

The other men I was in contact with to varying degrees over the years, but most disappeared completely. I do know Matt Martinson passed on about three years back. Alimony Bill I liked, as far as I knew him, and met an unfortunate end. Tokyo Joe, whose real name could have been Smith, is in the category of the vanished. Robin

Hood Johnson most likely ended his tour on earth doing a little farming and operating a Sinclair gas station in Kanorado, Kansas. Vernon Barr, known as Sweet Pea, left the drain tunnel operation under circumstances never adequately explained, and if he were still alive, it would come as a surprise.

I suppose I should put down a few things regarding the individual who put together such a bullshit yarn about what would prove to be some of his favorite days. This person, me, has lived too long, and my kind of days are long in the past. All that is left are memories, and that is what led me to put some of those to paper. In truth, I wrote this stuff for me, so I could go back in time, and for no other reason.

My obsessive interest in mining goes so far back in the past that there is no clear recall of when it began. But for a point of beginning, I will say that the mining bug had bitten deeply when I was eight years old. If I spotted a hole in a hill or in the side of a mountain, it pulled me toward it like an iron filing to a magnet. My first foray into a mine had but one purpose, and that was to scare the hell out of me. That was the prime reason; the secondary was to shut down my constant begging to go underground.

With the concluding of the Second World War, the rationing of gasoline ended. That made it possible to go on a family ride in the car. Because money was always in short supply in my family, those rides were of limited length. Big and Little Cottonwood Canyons were the usual destination on a Sunday afternoon. We would often end up in Brighton, and if there were a few extra coins available, Dad bought us all a bottle of soda pop at the little store up there.

The narrow two-lane road in Big Cottonwood still passed beneath the trestle that carried the snowshed and rails of the Maxfield Mine over to the big waste rock dump south of the highway. That layout fascinated me to no end, and I always kept it in sight as long as possible. I had no idea of what it was all about in those days. West of the Stairs Power House, about a half mile, somewhere in the narrows, I managed to locate a tunnel at the base of a rocky outcrop close to and level with the road. Every time we went up that canyon, I begged my dad to let me go into that black hole.

He got tired of the constant begging and decided it was time to cure his noisy son's fixation. So one Sunday afternoon, he pulled off the road, produced a flashlight, and said, "Let us go." Mom was well aware of what he intended to do, and my little sister could not have cared less. It was a short tunnel, and when we reached its end, the flashlight, somehow, went out. Dad said something along the lines of "Uh-oh" and then asked how I liked this business now. It did not work well for my old pappy; the cure was a failed endeavor. I told him I loved it and wanted to sit there for a while. That was the start of it all.

As time marched on from that episode, I spent all the time possible in anything to do with mining-related activities. How I managed over the years to cram so much time into that type of activity and learn so much has no answer. Many people will say that such a thing was not possible. Think what you want. I, by God, did it, but at times, the cost was steep. I was never able to be involved in the mining industry to make a living. I tried several different lines of work, a couple of which were nothing but disasters.

In the end, I became involved with trucks and trucking. I cannot say that I loved the business but for the most part did not hate it either. I put 40 years in that line of work. I did a stint as a line driver for a while, was involved in three major truck repair shops, and became part owner of one of them. My time in one organization involved operating heavy truck wreckers, a job I really liked. For some reason, in all three shops, I ended up as supervisor. My main specialties were engine repair and rebuilding. Anything to do with the gear trains on trucks such as transmissions and drive axles, I knew from top to bottom.

Also crammed into this long span of time was my military obligation. From 1956 until 1964, I got my feet slightly wet in that business too. I started into it because it was required by law, and I had to. The situation was such back then that reserve time alone could cover your obligation. Otherwise, I had no real desire to be involved in the military in any way. That changed with the organization of and my joining the Special Forces unit that looked so intriguing. And I was glad I did. If my home situation had not been what it was, I would have gone regular army in a heartbeat and made a career of it. As it was, I put in some extra years not required by law. Why? It is the same old story: being young and stupid. Now I am just old.

GLOSSARY

adit: Horizontal tunnel driven from the surface into an existing mine. Usually done to reach a specific target. An example would be to intersect a shaft or stope.

back: The top or roof on the inside of a tunnel mine. In the earliest days of mining in England, the miners considered the mines to be snakes due to the way they wove through the earth. Back, like rib and belly (the floor of a mine tunnel), referred to the part of the snake. Eventually, these terms found their way to the United States via Cousin Jacks.

bohunk: A denigrating term for an immigrant, typically a laborer, from central or southeastern Europe.

breaking picks: A slang term for two or more individuals that have reached their end of association with one another, usually under unfavorable or hostile circumstances.

cap, or cap timber: The horizontal timber at the top of a timber set (see photo insert).

carbide, or calcium carbide: Known simply as "carbide" to miners. When exposed to water, it produces acetylene gas that is extremely flammable and explosive.

carbide lamp: For many years, these lamps were the primary source of light in mines. Acetylene gas powered the flame (see calcium carbide), intensified by a reflector surrounding the burner orifice. Carbide filled the screw-on cup on the lower part of the lamp. Water added to a separate compartment, above the carbide, controlled by a drip lever, allowed a measured amount of water to reach the carbide and determine the amount of light.

catching up, caught up: A miner's term for that which needs serious attention.

collar: The point at which a shaft intersects the surface or where a raise intersects an upper level.

come in, or came in: Describes a collapse of any kind, especially a cave-in. Example: *The timber gave way, and half the stope came in. Three men were caught under it and got gobbed.*

country rock: Any rock that is in the surrounding mountain but not holding ore or value.

Cousin Jack: The nickname bestowed on the immigrant Cornish miner. Cousin Jenny designated the immigrant women from Cornwall. It is usually considered a compliment, not a slight.

crib set: A box-like structure made up of heavy timbers laid at right angles to one another. Used to support the back (roof) in large excavated areas such as stopes. The timbers used in construction are usually eight feet in length and eight inches square. Filling these structures with waste rock is common practice. This increases the load-bearing capacity of the crib set (see photo insert).

crosscut: A level tunnel/drift driven across a mineral vein.

direct ship: Commonly designates ore of sufficient value that it does not require concentration at the mine. This grade of ore goes directly to the smelter from the mine.

ditch: The ditch carries the water encountered in a mining operation. Ditches require ongoing maintenance, as the mine rails and other low-mounted utilities must be as water-free as possible. Clearing them is not a sought-after job in a mine.

doghouse: The common name given to an area where the miners take their lunch breaks. It is off the main run of the mine and walled off, with a door for access. A long table with attached benches runs down the center. Most doghouses have a heat source and electrical lighting. The doghouses are relatively comfortable, and depending on the mine, some are plusher than others.

drift: Often-used term to describe a tunnel, typically used when following an ore vein. Example: *They were driving a drift following a tight mineralized fissure.*

drift round: A drift round is the explosive charge placed at the working end of the drift.

dry, or the dry: The staging area near a mine entrance for miners to prep for or derig after working a shift.

dump: The waste rock brought out of underground workings. It is a slang term, short for *waste rock dump*. It is often confused by the layperson with *tailing*, which is waste rock that has been processed for ore.

ells: Slang for elbow or 90-degree angle.

fissure: A narrow break or crack in the rock. Many fissures will carry mineralization that may have exploration drifts driven on them. Assay values determine if this occurs or does not.

floating track: A section of track that will not stay in place. This generally occurs in mines that produce large amounts of water. Spikes hold the tracks of the rail system securely to wooden ties (sleepers) keeping them in position and at the proper gauge. If the ties deteriorate due to water saturation, the spikes will loosen, shift easily, and pull out completely at times. The "floating track" is the result and makes derailments a certainty. Poor ditch maintenance is the usual cause of this problem.

galena: Sulfide of lead, a type of ore.

gauge: The inside distance between the rail track heads determines the gauge of the railroad system. Example: *The typical gauge of a Cottonwoods district rail system is 18 inches.*

gob: Technically an obscure and seldom-used term describing waste rock, in most cases in coal mining. It also means to do oneself harm or to die. For miners, it can describe so many things as to require a full chapter to itemize them. It is the most versatile word in their vocabulary and to truly appreciate this term, it has to be experienced.

gouge: Abbreviation for a *fault gouge*, this represents the movement between two sides of a fault, which results in a grinding action or a natural milling process. This action is also known as brecciation. The width and depth of this brecciation/gouge varies a great deal, sometimes measured in inches, other times many feet.

grade: The slope of a tunnel. These always trend upward from the tunnel entrance to facilitate drainage. Example: *The Columbus-Rexall Tunnel's angle upward is 1.89 percent.*

grizzly: A grizzly is a dump hole for waste rock.

hardrock, hard rock: Hardrock, used as one word by miners, is a term to indicate a fellow miner. Hard rock, when separated, is used to denote the hardness of the rock encountered in mining operations.

heading: The end of the drift, crosscut, or tunnel, generally where the miners work. The term *working face* means the same thing and is often used in place of *heading*.

Irish buggy: The Cornish miner supposedly is responsible for giving this name to the wheelbarrow. They did this simply to aggravate "they bleddy paddy," or Irishman. It became a well-used designation throughout the mining industry.

jumbo: A machine used in underground mining to drill blasting holes. The machines use multiple drills that are in most cases controlled by one operator. In medium-sized tunneling jobs, they have from one to three drills. Miners identify them as one, two, or three machine jumbos. The earliest type of jumbo required an operator for each drill.

kite: Another name for an automobile or a pickup truck. It is commonly used by a mining individual to create confusion in the mind of the listener.

lagging: Rough, unplaned planking used in the construction of timber supports, most often 2 by 10 inches or 2 by 12 inches. Lagging put in place above the cap timbers and between the ribs (walls) and posts of timber sets prevents small rocks and other loose material from falling into the tunnel. It is also used as bridging (see photo insert).

leg: An alternate name for a post. A leg and a post are the same thing (see photo insert).

level: The elevation of the workings below the shaft or mine entrance—that is, *700 level* is 700 feet below the collar of the shaft.

man trip: A rail car that transports the miners in and out of a mine. They come in varieties, some enclosed and having individual seats for each man. In some mines, the man trip is simply a flatbed car. The flatbed has a bench running down its center, front to back. The men straddle this bench, one behind the other, usually facing forward.

man way: Man way refers to a mining lane of traffic in an adit or raise reserved for the passage of miners. In adits, there may be one or two lanes for rails with a man way adjacent for the miners to climb or descend safely and so as to not impede the flow of ore or muck traffic.

miss: To drill into a miss is to drill into a previously placed dynamite charge that failed to detonate. It is one of the most dangerous events in a mine, because a charge set off by a miner's drill will almost surely kill that individual and any others working the face of a mine.

muck: The waste rock broken up by blasting that has very little or no value as ore.

muck cars: A seldom-used term describing the transport cars used to transport muck or ore from the underground workings to the outside.

on the grass: A slang term describing the surface plant and processing area of a mine on the outside of the tunnel. It actually has nothing to do with grass. The workers outside the underground workings were said to be "on the grass."

ore bin: A structure that holds ore until the accumulation is sufficient to transfer to a truck or railroad car for transport to a smelter or other type of refining facility. Sizes vary greatly depending on the ore-producing capacity of the mine.

portal: The entrance of a tunnel or adit into the side of a hill or a mountain.

portal set: The timber structure at the entrance of a tunnel or adit into the side of a hill or a mountain.

post: The vertical timbers of a timber set that support the cap (see photo insert).

railhead: The part of a rail that the wheels of the cars run on. The T rail consists of the base, the web, and the head.

raise: A vertical or inclined passageway driven between levels. The average raise rises upward on about an 80-degree angle.
rib: A slang term for the side or wall of a tunnel. See "back" for origin.
scaling bar: A bar, usually varying in length from four feet to eight feet. These bars have a chisel point at one end and a straight point of various designs at the opposite end. The primary use of this tool is to remove loose rock from the back and ribs after blasting, but it can also serve as a pry bar or lever. The scaling bar is a most versatile tool.
sprag: A miner's name for a horizontal brace, usually running from the post of a timber set to stabilize or render immovable various objects such as floating rails. Like other terms in the miner's vocabulary, sprag can cover nonrelated items. Such an example would be in order to keep a loaded car from overrunning the mule on a downgrade, the skinner (mule driver) would sprag the last pair of wheels on the last car (see photo insert).
stick of timber: Miners' slang for any type or dimension of timber or lumber.
stop chain: A length of chain wrapped tightly around both rails at the end of their run. It is a simple and effective way to prevent any runaway ore cars from leaving the tracks.
stope: A cavernous area opened up by the extraction of an ore body.
strike: Ore discovery.
stull: A single support timber. It can be mill-cut timber like a post or simply a tree trunk cut to length, as was the practice in early mining days. In the jargon of miners, such things as canes and crutches are also called stulls (see photo insert).
switch: A device that allows a train to change from one set of tracks to another. There are many different configurations.
tail track: A length of trackage used for the temporary or long-term parking of idle cars not in use at the time. The maximum number of cars used in the operation determines the tail track length.
trammer: Also known as a motor, it is the locomotive used to pull

the train of cars into and out of the underground workings. Batteries most often power them.

tugger: A winch operated by compressed air. The method of mounting depends on the location and usually utilizes heavy timber as the base.

winze: A shaft put down on an angle that starts underground. It is used to follow a lead to see if it will open up into a minable ore deposit. In many cases, it will be used to intersect another level of the mine or in some cases, by mutual agreement, another mine's workings.

working face: The end of the drift, crosscut, or tunnel, generally where the miners work. The term *heading* means the same thing and is often used in place of *working face*.

wye: A triangular arrangement of three rail lines with a switch at each corner connecting to each incoming line. This allows the reversal of the direction of travel of a trammer or a full train. The tail of the wye is usually where a siding, also called a tail track, is located.

ACKNOWLEDGMENTS

MANY INDIVIDUALS CONTRIBUTED in one way or another to the creation of this memoir. There are a number whom, unfortunately, I never learned the true names of, only nicknames. The men that I can name have now traveled on for the most part some time ago. The following named individuals were miners in the true sense of the title. Never to be forgotten are John T. Campbell, a.k.a. Swinger; Dan A. Jacobson; Mack and Mark Jacobson; Albert J. Wondershek, a.k.a. the Bull; Whitney C. Hansen, a.k.a. Slick; Gaylon W. Hansen; Harry Thorkildsen; Frank Yanchar; John Malmborg; Frank Reedy; and Francis Jolley. Others shall remain anonymous.

A special thanks to a friend who was a master of research and an excellent writer. Quietly and by example, Charles L. Keller gave me the inspiration to put this story together. I wrote this memoir so I could relive old times and lose myself in the past, with no intention or desire to see it published. To this point, special thanks goes to Dan Schilling, who convinced me that the work should become a published book. The editing of a chaotic mess and the handling of the complicated path to a publisher and publication would never have occurred without him.

—DICK FLUEHE

Thanks, Dick, for laying this history down and doing such a damn fine job or it'd be lost to the sands of time, and that would be criminal. And from one airborne soldier to another, also for your friendship, you lying old bastard. I'd like to thank Keith Hansen, not only for introducing me to Dick but for your friendship, the adventures we've had in Alta's mines, and building the Peruvian Tunnel into a first-class museum of the canyon we all love so dearly. Much appreciation to Jed Rogers from the University of Utah Press, who responded so positively when I dropped an unsolicited manuscript proposal into his inbox, and to Jessica Booth for the wonderful map adaptations. Finally, and always, my wife, Julie, who lets me run wild and unsupervised across, underneath, and sometimes above the slopes of Little Cottonwood.

—Dan Schilling

ABOUT THE AUTHORS

Comes now a short dusting over of the history of this worn-out old fart. I was born 2 July 1938 in the LDS Hospital here in Salt Lake City to Helmuth and Frances Fluehe. My father was born in Germany in 1912, my mother in Salt Lake City in 1912. I was raised here in Salt Lake City, had one sister, Nancy, and a brother, Paul, both younger than me. Nancy is no longer living, leaving Paul as the surviving sibling. The early times, up until I was 10 years old, were tough. We never went hungry but came close to it many times, and what we lived on was far from fancy. My education, such as it was, took place in various elementary schools scattered around the valley. I did reasonably well with this part of the process, but my high school years were a disaster. Somehow, I ended up with a diploma. On 10 September 1956 I married Janet Lewis. We were 18 years old (barely) at the time. That enterprise lasted until 12 October 2022 when Janet went end of watch. We had two daughters, Lisa and Denise, and a son, Scott. Denise went end of watch in 2010. I was over the years involved in several kinds of work to make a living. I got my feet slightly damp in the military but spent the bulk of my working years involved with the heavy truck industry. That is about it in a small thimble, the bare bones. I could expand on that considerably, but I see no use in doing so.

Tap 'er light, Dick

Dan Schilling is a *New York Times* best-selling author and 30-year military special operations veteran. He and his wife, Julie, call Alta home. Visit him at DanSchilling.com.